CHURCH, STATE, *AND THE* AMERICAN

R. PIERCE BEAVER

Two and a Half Centuries of Partnership in Missions
Between Protestant Churches
and Government

CONCORDIA PUBLISHING HOUSE

و§

INDIANS

SAINT LOUIS, MISSOURI و§

Concordia Publishing House, St. Louis, Missouri
Concordia Publishing House Ltd., London, E. C. 1
© 1966 by Concordia Publishing House
Library of Congress Catalog Card No. 66-27692

MANUFACTURED IN THE UNITED STATES OF AMERICA

Table of Contents

Church, State, and the American Indians

Preface

⌇§ A high "wall of separation" between church and state has been erected by judicial decisions of recent years, especially by those of the Supreme Court of the United States. Protestant churches and churchmen generally accepted the legal judgments and added bricks to the wall from their side until the recent decision of the Supreme Court on prayers in schools. Most of the larger and older denominations have supported the court by issuing official pronouncements or by the personal statements of their leaders. Vast numbers of Protestants, however, have recently expressed strong dissent because of the issue of prayers.

Separation today is something far different from what it was to the founding fathers and the ministers and laymen of the churches at the time of the framing of the Constitution. The judgments of the Supreme Court in the Everson, McCollum, and School Prayers cases may be what the Constitution — a living agency in our public life — means in terms of the present moment in the separation of church and state in our pluralistic, multireligious society. American religious agencies, including the churches, may accept this view; but churchmen should not assume that this has always been the stand of the denominations. The views and practices of our forefathers were quite different in many respects, and in spirit. Moreover, many of our denominations even today are inconsistent and do not let their right hand know what their left hand is doing. Churches which vigorously oppose the application of public tax funds for the support of private religious schools in the United States frequently accept grants and subsidies for mission schools abroad. This contradiction of the official position is usually overlooked or forgotten. Indeed, there are blind spots in the historical memory of churchmen. They are apt to regard events and attitudes and formulae of the Reformation period as living realities today and yet in many matters conveniently to forget what does not accord with contemporary ideas about church-state relations.

There were two and a half centuries, from the beginning of the missionary work of the Mayhews and John Eliot about 1641 to about 1890, when there was a partnership between church and state in the maintenance of the Protestant mission to the American Indians. That long period was preceded by a century of British exploration and colonization, the avowed intention of which was first and foremost the evangelization of heathen peoples. State support of the Indian missions was the logical consequence of that profession of purpose.

Baylor University invited the writer to give the J. M. Dawson Lectures on "Church and State" in March 1962. The subject of the lectures was "Church, State, and the Indians: Protestant Missions in Relation to Government." There were five lectures in the series: (1) "The Inheritance from the Colonial Period," (2) "Indian Missions in the New Nation," (3) "The Churches and Indian Removal," (4) "Partnership with Government Under President Grant," (5) "Missionary Efforts to Shape Government Policy." Both the gracious hospitality of Baylor University and the keen interest of the faculty and audience were greatly appreciated. The second, third, and fourth lectures were subsequently published in *A Journal of Church and State* in Vol. IV, No. 1 (May 1962), No. 2 (November 1962), and Vol. V, No. 1 (May 1963) respectively.

Ever since the lectures were given and published in the journal, repeated requests have come to the author for publication of the whole series of five lectures in book form with documentation added. The writer was reluctant to publish them in this form, for he intended to investigate and write up other aspects of this story and then publish it in a volume of 400—500 pages. The pressure of other studies has not permitted this. However, he has now yielded to entreaties and offers this account of the partnership between church and state in its essentials from the beginning to its dissolution. Every part of this story could be told in greater detail, but that would obscure the forest by drawing too much attention to the individual trees. It would be interesting to treat the developments with respect to the Dakotas and to give special attention to the far Northwest, but this would add little except details to the essential development. The relationship of churches and government in the Indian mission during the last 70 years is another topic that might be discussed. This includes the subject of the contract schools. There are still vestiges of the old partnership, but the partnership was dissolved by 1890, and so the book may properly end there. At any rate it seems best to publish the book in this size and with this scope and hope that it will stimulate other historians to investigate aspects of the partnership not covered here in detail.

General Grant's "Peace Policy" has recently been attracting the attention of scholars. Two doctoral dissertations have appeared since Chapters 4 and 5 were written, but they have added nothing essentially new. A third dissertation is being written by a student under the guidance of this author. It will make a genuine and valuable contribution to the literature.

The five chapters here are not the five Dawson Lectures, with the exception of Chapter 2, "Indian Missions in the New Nation." This chapter is the lecture as given and printed in *A Journal of Church and State* but enlarged and with the documentation added in footnotes. It is used here with the permission of the editor, and that permission is gratefully acknowledged. The other four chapters are much fuller treatments of the material covered by each lecture. The "Note on the Attitude of the Churches in Later Years" is the concluding portion of the lecture and article published in the journal, Vol. V, No. 1 (May 1963), pp. 89—94, and is used here with permission.

The reader will note that this book is not the history of the American Indian mission but only of one aspect of it. It does not treat, except incidentally, the motivation, aims, and goals of the work among the Indians. Consequently there is no discussion of the attitudes of the missionaries and their supporters toward Indian culture and of the continuous drive of the missions to "civilize the Indian," a matter in which the missionaries saw eye to eye with government officials. The writer from time to time contributes articles on such subjects to historical or missionary journals. This book deals with but one chapter, an important one, in the glorious and often terrible story of the mission to the Indians. Every promising beginning was brought to a sad end by the injustice of the white citizens to their red brethren. R. P. B.

CHAPTER 1

The Inheritance
from the Colonial Period

‍ᕤ When the American colonies became independent of England and embarked upon a new national life, Protestant churches
had already been engaged continuously for a century and a half
in missions to the Indians. Ideas and attitudes about the proper
relations of such missionary endeavor to government were quite
naturally carried over from the colonial era.

BRITISH EXPLORATION AND MISSIONS

An early association of Protestant missions with government
is to be found in the avowed evangelistic intention of British exploration and colonization in the 16th century. Some repetition
of that theme continued in the 17th and 18th centuries. The
literature of the navigators, trading companies, and the colonial
charters gives the impression that among Englishmen missionary
zeal was fully as strong a motive to empire building as among
the Spaniards. The lack of interest on the part of the Crown,
however, and the general disinclination to implement the avowed
purpose in action make the professed zeal for missions appear as
a possible camouflage for less noble motives.

It is not surprising that historians have made contradictory
estimates of this supposed missionary motivation. Thus James
A. Williamson states: "The religious motive . . . was that of

converting the heathen to Christianity. It appears in most of the discussions of colonization, but since in actual fact it appealed to but a limited number of minds no great stress need be laid upon it." [1] Louis B. Wright, on the other hand, seeks to show that religion was of tremendous consequence and that zeal for evangelization, though mixed with material interests, was genuine. He argues that the clergy were successfully enlisted in promoting colonization.[2] Sir Charles Lucas asserts that the main outcome of Henry VIII's church policy "was that religion became to Englishmen a most powerful motive of empire." This religious motive, however, he considered to be largely a negative desire to checkmate the Roman Catholic powers; but nevertheless "conversion was one of the standard motives in the mouths of English advocates of empire in the sixteenth century." [3] The conversion of the heathen appears repeatedly as the high purpose of exploration and colonization to about 1660. Thereafter it declined but was not lost.

The English seafarers not only believed in God but were certain that He was on their side. Whether on a slave-trading expedition, on a piratical raid against the Spanish ships and settlements, or searching for new lands and the Northwest Passage, the navigators sailed in agreement with Sir John Hawkins' celebrated orders to his men: "Serve God daily, love one another, preserve your victuals, beware of fire, and keep good company." [4] The historian Sir Walter Raleigh, descendant of the Elizabethan colonizer, concluded that Captain John Davis of Sandridge was unique among the explorers in actually believing that it was England's highest mission to propagate Christianity among the heathen.[5] Davis maintained in his book *The Seaman's Secrets* that navigation was indeed a divine science because it made missions possible. It provided England with the opportunity and means of diffusing Protestant Christianity to the ends of the earth and of driving Roman Catholicism back into Spain and Portugal.[6] England's material success, he declared in another book, would be in proportion to its missionary effort. Both God and nation would be glorified by such pious endeavor.[7]

Whether they were in earnest or not, from the time of Frobisher's voyage of 1576 onward the narrators of voyages linked their efforts to the extension of the kingdom of God. Frobisher's companion, Captain George Best, recounting that voyage, wrote about an expedition among icebergs and Eskimos: "[By this voyage there has been] Christ's name spred; the Gospell preached; infidels like to be converted to Christianitie, in places where before the name of God had not once been hearde of." [8]

Sir Humphrey Gilbert made the first actual effort to combine missions and colonization. He recruited Roman Catholics and Puritans along with middle-of-the-road Anglicans in his expedition of 1583, which aimed at founding a permanent settlement in North America. Both of the two extreme parties hoped to establish a refuge for their fellow believers, while Gilbert aimed at evangelizing the natives according to the Anglican pattern.[9]

Richard Hakluyt, however, was the great apostle of imperialism in the name of God and for the sake of the propagation of the faith.[10] This clergyman and brilliant geographer was the editor of *Principall Navigations*. These volumes were likely to be found alongside the Bible in every literate home. Under Hakluyt's tutelage influential men of affairs, merchants, and clergymen were indoctrinated with the creed that colonization would spread the Gospel among the heathen aborigines of America, thwart and counterbalance Spanish power and the Roman Catholic religion, and relieve England of the pressures caused by overpopulation and pauperism. This was England's moment of destiny.[11] As a member of several of the new trading companies this canon of Westminster Abbey and rector of a parish saw to it that the missionary obedience was acknowledged by them. It was he, quite probably, who was responsible for the insertion of the missionary clauses into some of the charters.

Francis Bacon went along with Hakluyt's objectives in colonization, but warned that the propagation of religion should never be made the pretext for the extermination of the natives.[12]

COLONIZATION AND EVANGELIZATION

The Rev. Richard Hakluyt was closely associated with Sir Walter Raleigh and had some influence on him. Raleigh, though something of a freethinker, at least publicly and expediently acknowledged the missionary obligation inherent in colonization. If the document entitled *Of the Voyage to Guiana* is correctly ascribed to him, he puts tremendous weight on the opportunity to convert "infinite nombers of soules" and to stop the mouths of Roman Catholic Spaniards.[13] He also, in a deed made to Sir Thomas Smith, Hakluyt, and others, when assigning trading rights in all the lands covered by his patent, provided the sum of £100 for planting Christianity in those barbarous and heathen countries.[14] However, no special instructions about missionary work appear to have been given to the settlers at the short-lived settlement of Roanoke. Yet Thomas Hariot, the mathematician, did there teach the Bible to some Indians and prayed with those who asked it in time of illness. Moreover, at Roanoke, Manteo was the first Indian convert baptized by Protestant rites.[15]

The missionary purpose of colonization was made explicit in the first Virginia charter of 1606. The King, in the preamble, graciously accepts and approves the desires of the adventurers to give glory to God "in propagating the Christian religion to such people, as yet live in darkness and miserable ignorance of the true knowledge and worship of God, and may in time bring the infidels and savages, living in those parts, to human civility, and to a settled and quiet government."[16] The "Instructions" for the government of the colony included the requirement that the authorities "with all diligence, care, and respect, doe provide, that the true word, and service of God and Christian faith be preached, planted, and used, not only within every one of the said several colonies, and plantations, but alsoe as much as they may amongst the savage people which doe or shall adjoine them, border upon them, according to the doctrine, rights, and religion now professed and established within our realme of England." [17] This provision enjoined missions upon both the state officers and ministers of religion, but it forbade such work to dissenters.

The second charter of Virginia of 1609 makes the missionary declaration the climax of the document. It seeks also to guard new converts from subversion by Roman Catholic agents. Solicitude for the spiritual welfare of the possible converts is made a convenient cloak for London's concern about Roman influence among the colonists. The passage reads:

> And lastly, because the principal effect, which we can desire or expect from this action, is the conversion and reduction of the people in those parts unto the true worship of God and Christian religion, in which respect we would be loath that any person should be permitted to pass, that we suspected to effect the superstitions of the church of Rome: we do hereby declare that [all must take the oath of supremacy]. [18]

The Governors and Counsellors of the Virginia Plantation, in reply to various charges, printed at the end of 1609 *A True and Sincere Declaration*. This tract states:

> The *Principal* and *Maine Endes* (out of which are easily derived to any meane understanding infinitlesse, and yet great ones) were first to preach and baptize into the *Christian Religion,* and by the propagation of the *Gospell,* to recover out of the arms of the *Divell,* a number of poor and miserable soules, wrapt up unto death, in almost *invincible ignorance;* to endeavour the fulfilling, and accomplishment of the number of the elect, which shall be gathered from out all corners of the earth; and to add our myte to the Treasury of Heaven, that as we pray for the coming of the Kingdome of Glory, so to expresse in our actions,

the same desire, if God have pleased to use so weak instruments, to the ripening and consummation thereof.[19]

A circular letter of the Virginia Council in the next year, 1610, opened with the assertion that "the eyes of all Europe are looking upon our endevors to spread the Gospell among the heathen people of Virginia." [20]

The official documents were supplemented by tracts which had a much wider circulation and were intended to win popular support for the colony. These were sermons by eminent divines and published by the Virginia Company. The most important of them were the sermons which were preached at the annual meetings of the company between 1609 and 1624. The first of the series was preached by William Symonds of St. Saviour's, Southwark. It set the tone for those to follow. This sermon was violently anti-Roman but, based on God's command to Abraham in Genesis 12:1-3, it moves on to a climactic charge to Englishmen to glorify God's name by propagating the Gospel abroad.[21] Another sermon, by Robert Gray, printed almost simultaneously with Symonds' discourse, voiced much more the sentiment of the actual settlers in Virginia than that of the promoters at home. This tract, entitled "A Good Speed to Virginia," admonished the settlers to do what they should ever after consider to be their divine right, namely, to "caste out the Canaanites." [22] God gave them this Virginia; let them take it. Yet it is better to convert the heathen than to put them to the sword, if the land can then be taken peacefully. The aborigines will be compensated for the loss of their land and liberty by receiving the Gospel and civilization.

William Crashaw's sermon of 1610 is probably the "classic" among the tracts. It directs that the inhabitants not be killed but converted. They then will become a blessing to the English. Profits will flow into the pockets of both company shareholders and the colonists if they put first the carrying out of God's plan for the colony. The principal aim of the colony is the conversion of the heathen, the second the creation of a Protestant bulwark against the Papists.[23]

Despite such clear assignment and acceptance of missionary responsibility in the case of the Virginia Company, and the haranguing of preachers notwithstanding, neither magistrates nor settlers showed much sympathy for the cause. Robert Beverley, the first historian of Virginia, makes no mention of efforts to convert the Indians. He does offer the opinion that if many colonists had followed the good example of John Rolfe and Pocahontas, most of the Indians would have been converted through such intermarriage.[24] Unlike the overwhelming majority of his fellow settlers, Beverley had a very high regard for the character and virtue of the Indians. In view of Rolfe's marriage, it is interesting to note that Symonds in his 1609 sermon had threatened the wrath of God upon any Englishman who might take an Indian maid as wife. Some prodding continued to come from England. Sir Edwyn Sandys was responsible for the establishment of a college at Henrico "for the training and bringing up of Infidels' children to the true knowledge of God and the understanding of righteousness." He secured from King James the authorization for the bishops of the Church of England to take a subscription collection for this purpose.[25] After George Thorpe arrived in Virginia in 1620 to take charge of the college lands as well as to acquire his own plantation, he expressed the conviction that "all the past ill success was owing to the not seeking of God's glory in converting the Natives, which are peaceable and wanted but meanes." [26] The Indians, no longer peaceable, killed Thorpe in 1622. After the massacre of that year the Virginia colonists had not the slightest interest in the conversion of the Indians, but desired only to exterminate them.

The Massachusetts and Connecticut charters of the same period are similar to the Virginia charters in giving high priority to missions, but the developments in those colonies are quite different. Missions were actually undertaken, and the unbroken continuity of all American missions issues from them. Because of this fact however, before proceeding to an examination of the situation in New England, the developments in New York, Pennsylvania, and Georgia may be noted.

The first missionary effort of any magnitude in the colony of New York was politically inspired and undertaken at the request of the state. Previously Dutch Reformed pastors at Albany and Schenectady had taught some Indians and made certain translations into Iroquois dialects. The Dutch West Indies Company had shown none of the interest in missions which animated the Dutch East Indies Company and which resulted in the planting of great churches in Ceylon, Malaya, Indonesia, and Formosa.

The colonial administrators in New York feared the adherence of the Iroquois nations to the French in Canada. They suspected that this end was actually being advanced by the work of the Jesuit missionaries. As early as 1687, when the Five Nations were recognized as British subjects, Governor Dongan had told the tribes that English missionaries would replace the French Jesuits, but none had been sent.[27] When the Earl of Bellomont became governor, he urged action upon the Lords of Trade and Plantation in London, asking specifically for two missionaries.[28] Robert Livingston, the secretary of Indian Affairs at Albany, simultaneously wrote the officers in London about the same matter.[29] Having decided that "such Ministers . . . may be of very good Use and Service as well for the Propagation of the Reformed Religion as for Improving the Interest of England," the Lords of Trade and Plantation laid the proposal before the archbishop of Canterbury and the bishop of London, who had jurisdiction in ecclesiastical affairs in the colonies.[30]

Bellomont died, but his successor, Lord Cornbury, repeated the request for missionaries. The Lords of Trade and Plantation thereupon petitioned the Queen, and the very next day, April 3, 1703, an order-in-council was promulgated. It referred the matter to Archbishop Tenison for effective action. The motive for the mission as set forth here is purely political. The order in part reads:

> . . . lest the Intrigues of the French of Canada, & the Influence of their Priests who frequently converse & sometimes inhabit with these Indians should debauch them from her Maty's Allegiance, their Lordships are humbly of opinion that besides the usual method of engaging the said Indians by Presents, another means to prevent the Influence of the French Missionaries upon them & thereby more effectively to secure their Fidelity, would be that two Protestant Ministers be appointed with a competent Allowance to dwell amongst them in order to instruct them in the true Religion and confirm them in their Duty to her Maty; It is ordered by her Maty in Council that it be as it here is referred to his Grace the Lord Archbishop of Canterbury, to take such care therein as may most effectually answer this service.[31]

The archbishop referred the problem to the newly chartered Society for the Propagation of the Gospel in Foreign Parts, with whose officers he had already conferred. Robert Livingston attended a meeting of the society and gave information that might assist their decision.

Before the year was ended the S. P. G. had appointed two clergymen as missionaries, but only one, the Rev. Thoroughgood Moore, actually sailed.[32] The secretary of the society informed the Lords of Trade that these two missionaries had been appointed at a salary of £20 with some additional allowances. He enquired "what assistance they may expect in an affair that does at least as much concerne the State as the Church."[33] He said that four more missionaries were needed for this work. The Lords of Trade replied that the Queen would allow each missionary £20 for passage money, and that the men would be commended to Lord Cornbury, the Governor.[34]

Moore took up residence at Albany in November 1704 and began a mission to the Mohawks. He became discouraged, how-

ever, and left within a year. He served white churches in New
Jersey for a short period, and was lost at sea while returning to
England. The mission then languished until four Iroquois warriors, posing as mighty potentates in the New World, visited England and stimulated new interest. They presented Queen Anne
with an address, which included this word of welcome to such
missionaries as might be sent to them: "Since we were in Covenant with our Great Queen's Children, we have had some
knowledge of the Saviour of the World, and have often been
importuned by the French by Priests and Presents, but ever
esteemed them as men of Falsehood, but if our Great Queen
wou'd send some to Instruct us, they shou'd find a most hearty
Welcome." [35] Despite the interest stimulated by these visitors,
it was not until 1712 that William Andrews went to Albany to
renew the mission to the Mohawks. His salary was cut off in
1719. The mission had a very precarious existence until the
appointment of Henry Barclay in 1737.[36] He was the son of
the missionary to the settlers at Albany.

Despite the discontinuity of the mission, the governors of
the colony had evidently been interested and gave some help.
Lord Cornbury had provided a government-paid interpreter to
serve the missionary. Thomas Barclay, by doubling as missionary
to the whites as well as to the Indians, was given an Indian youth
to train as a teacher. Governor Hunter had built "forts" as resi-
dences for the missionaries and chapels for their worship. Queen
Anne gave altar furnishings and a Bible.

The Society for the Propagation of the Gospel was, however, extremely niggardly with the mission. It invested little in
either men or facilities. Its directors were far more interested in
efforts to win over dissenters to the Church of England and in
working with the much more stationary and tractable Negro
slaves. The annual sermons preached before the S. P. G. for
a short time stressed the Indian mission and the indebtedness of
the English settlers to the aborigines, which could be discharged

in this manner. But after a few years they manifested far more concern for the slaves, the Anglican colonists in need of pastoral care, and the dissenters who might be won over. Henry Barclay was in despair, and although he was supposed to receive a salary of £50, he wrote to John Sergeant, the missionary at Stockbridge, Mass., that he was given only £20 a year.[37] Sergeant thereupon recommended him to the Boston Board of the Society for the Propagation of the Gospel in New England for additional support.

The New England sons of the Puritans resented the sending of Anglican missionaries among them. Barclay's report to Sergeant gave them all the more cause to complain that if the S. P. G. were really a missionary society it would devote more care to the Mohawk Mission and initiate other work among the Indians. It was not proper missionary activity to send their emissaries to towns "where the Gospel has been faithfully preached since they were first planted, and where those of the persuasion of the Church of England are so numerous and wealthy that they are well able to give their Ministers an honourable support, without the help of the Society at home." [38] The friends of missions in Massachusetts thoroughly approved of the Mohawk Mission, both its spiritual purpose and its political intent, because Christian Mohawks would provide a bulwark of defense for New England against the French.[39]

Henry Barclay reported in 1743 that only a few of the Mohawks remained unbaptized. John Stuart, the missionary at the time of the Revolution, described them as "a Christian nation, living a life of settled agriculture and trade." [40] It was Sir William Johnson, the Superintendent of Indian Affairs for New York, who was more influential than the missionaries in solidly cementing the bond between the Mohawks, the British Crown, and the Church of England.[41] What Johnson began was completed by the paramount chief of the Nation, Joseph Brant or Thayendanegea.[42] Bishop (later Archbishop) Secker in a famous sermon of 1740—41 had said of the Indian mission work: "Nor

should it be forgotten, that every single *Indian,* whom we make
a Christian, we make a Friend and Ally at the same time; both
against the remaining Heathen, and a much more dangerous
Neighbor, from whose Instigations almost all that we have suffered by them is allowed to have come." [43] The Anglican Christian faith was one of the most powerful resources used by Sir
William in turning the Iroquois against the French and a potent
means of both Johnson and Brant in keeping the Mohawks
loyal to Great Britain.

Sir William for some time sent Mohawk youths to the
school at Stockbridge, Mass., and especially to Eleazar Wheelock's
school at Lebanon, Conn., which was later moved to Hanover,
N. H., in connection with the founding of Dartmouth College.[44]
Sir William had also assisted the missionary efforts of Dr. Wheelock and Samuel Kirkland for some years. However, the New
Englanders and especially Wheelock irritated both the superintendent and Brant. The alienation eventually became complete.
The break was hastened by Sir William's ever closer association
with the Society for the Propagation of the Gospel. He was
clearly convinced that the predominance of the Church of England in colonial society was essential to the security and welfare
of the colony and the Empire. However, unlike all other advocates of missions to the Indians, Sir William did not equate British
civilization with the Gospel. He did not consider "civilization"
of any kind to be prerequisite to evangelization. The Indians
could remain thoroughly Indian and still be Christians. He would
follow the example of the French Roman Catholic missionaries
in disturbing as little as possible the hunting culture of the Iroquois. Consequently Sir William utterly abhored the villages of
"Praying Indians" in New England, which he considered to be
the inevitable product of Puritan missions. It was his opinion
that such Indians as were "brought up under the care of Dissent-
ing Ministers became a gloomy race & lose their abilities for
hunting." [45]

The Society for the Propagation of the Gospel made Sir William Johnson its chief counselor in Indian affairs from 1749 onward, and in 1766 elected him a member of the society.[46] Although always professing to accept his advice, the society seldom acted on it. This man represented the Crown to the Iroquois as did no other officer of the colony. Because of his efforts, especially the Mohawks more or less consciously identified loyalty to England with adherence to the Church of England. Chief Joseph Brant's influence doubled the effect of Johnson's efforts. Brant was a staunch Anglican, and his people respected, trusted, and followed him. The scanty missionary assistance given Johnson and Brant by the S. P. G. supplemented their work and nurtured the movement. When finally a full-time, long-term missionary, John Stuart, came into the service of the society, he was able to build up the Mohawk nation in Christian life through faithful pastoral care. No missionary can really be credited with the winning of the Mohawks. It was the work of Sir William and Brant. Had the former been given adequate missionary assistance, quite likely the other Iroquois nations might also have been won to the Church of England.

From 1749 until his death in 1774 the Superintendent of Indian Affairs was indefatigable in pressing the claims of the Indian mission upon both the colonial authorities in New York and London and upon the S. P. G. Sir William repeatedly asked for missionaries. He pressed for an educational system which would offer an alternative to the New England schools, and which above all would train Indian youths in their own home country. The French and Indian War drew again from the directors of the S. P. G. and the colonial officers profession of high regard for the political consequences of missions. Yet it was not until long after the end of the war, indeed not until 1767, that the society finally gave approval to Sir William's scheme of education. It voted also additional missionary priests and catechists. Yet the only item of the resolution which was carried out was the commissioning of the Rev. John Stuart. When Sir William died in 1774, he was still striving for the establishment of his educational program. He aided Stuart in every possible way. He repaired the chapel at Fort Hunter and erected a new one at Canajoharie. Sir William and his son-in-law, Daniel Claus, prepared a new edition of the Mohawk Prayer Book. Sir William was planning to pay for the printing of new literature when he died. Claus later re-edited the prayer book. Brant added to it his own translation of the Gospel of Mark, and he personally saw to the printing of the book in London. Loyal to England, the Mohawks moved to Ontario after the revolution.

The Mohawk Mission in the colony of New York was thus called into being through the recommendation of a governor and promoted and sustained by the Superintendent of Indian Affairs. But another mission in the colony was destroyed through the joint persecution of officers of state and the frontier populace. This was the Moravian Mission at Shekomeko in Dutchess County and at Wechquadnach or Indian Pond on the New York-Connecticut border.[47] This mission was begun by Christian Heinrich Rauch in 1740. A branch station was opened at Scaticook on the Housatonic River just above the falls in the north end of the town of New Milford. Prosperous villages of Christian Indians, making rapid progress in "civilization" and in piety according to the Herrnhut pattern, developed at those places. Their presence infuriated the settlers who wanted the Indians eliminated. These persons took out their spite on the missionaries and persecuted them unmercifully. The missionaries at Scaticook were arrested and jailed on the charge of being Papists plotting with the Indians to join the French. When the charges could not be proved, the Moravians were released but prohibited from residing and teaching in Connecticut. On the New York side of the border one magistrate after another hailed the missionaries before him for examination. The officers, knowing that the Moravians were pacifists, summoned them to do militia duty.[48] They were repeatedly ordered to take oaths when it was known that this was against their conscience. Finally the Legislature of the colony enacted a law which required all suspected persons to take an oath of allegiance. It specifically forbade Moravians and others to preach unless a special license was granted them.[49] Consequently a sheriff on Dec. 15, 1744, served notice that all services and instruction were prohibited. Shortly thereafter legal persecution forced the abandonment of the very promising mission.[50]

When Parliament recognized the Unitas Fratrum as an ancient episcopal church, the Moravians were protected against further legal persecution.[51] However, this did not safeguard them against the hostility of the white settlers to their work with the Indians. The law gave them no immunity against aggression. Christian Indians had followed the missionaries from Wedquadnach, Scaticook, and Shekomeko to Pennsylvania, where a mission among the Delaware Indians had been begun. One after another the Christian Indian towns were broken up by violence and irresistible pressure. They moved by stages across Pennsylvania into eastern Ohio. The colony of Pennsylvania, despite all its vaunted friendship to Indians and hospitality to all religious groups, did not stand by the Moravian converts with any show of authority and strength. The missionaries and their people could scarcely be suspected of being agents of the French after the Indian allies of France in Canada raided Gnadenhütten on Nov. 24, 1755, and killed 11 inhabitants. The remainder were taken temporarily to Bethlehem, and then to Nain and Wechquetank. However, renewal of hostilities in 1763 led to new attacks on the missions. The Christian Indians were herded together by the colonial authorities at Nazareth. Then "for their protection" they were taken to Philadelphia. A mob, bent on killing them all, gathered. Officials interned the Christians on an island in the Delaware River. They sought to get rid of the problem by shipping them to New York. The officers at New York, however, refused to permit them to land and sent them back to Philadelphia. The mob again threatened, but this time some influential men came forward and faced down the mob. But few of the Indians were saved because disease did to them what the mob had wanted to do.[52]

Missionary motivation in colonialism is generally considered to have passed by the time of the Restoration in 1660. It reappears, however, to a slight degree in the cases of Pennsylvania and Georgia. At least some verbal acknowledgment of it is made in the instance of the former. When William Penn presented to King Charles II his petition for a grant of land in America, he declared that one object of the colony was to be the conversion of the poor Indians to Christ's kingdom "by just and lenient measures." [53] The charter which the King granted in answer to the request to "transport an ample colonie unto a certain Countrey" was issued on the grounds that William Penn was motivated by "a considerable desire to enlarge our English Empire, and promote such useful comodities as may be of benefitt to us and our Dominions, as alsoe to reduce the Savage Natives by gentle and just manners to the love of civill Society and Christian Religion." [54] The Friends hold that Penn's peace policy was an effort to carry out this indirect evangelistic method and that it worked.[55]

Neither the colonial government of Pennsylvania nor any of the Friends' meetings, however, undertook direct missionary work. Numerous individual Friends, including John Woolman and George Fox himself, preached to and taught Indians. R. W. Kelsey states that down to the beginning of corporate missionary efforts in 1795 preaching was considered to be entirely a "personal concern." It was therefore sporadic. Kelsey adds: "But the *practice* of the Christian virtues in dealing with the Indians was a very passion among Friends." [56] The land policy of the Quakers to purchase the land at a fair price was regarded as the very heart of this policy.[57] But the Quaker "fair price," like the New England Puritan "fair price," looks very different from the perspective of the present and from the viewpoint of the Indians than it did to the settlers in the 17th century. Other aspects of this practice were the prohibition of the sale of intoxicating liquors to Indians, the employment of mixed juries in trials of Indians, and the prohibition of Friends owning Indian slaves.[58] The great missionary enterprise in Pennsylvania would not be Quaker but Moravian. The Moravians got no help from the state.

General Oglethorpe's colony of Georgia was launched with several aims in view. It was intended as a charity for the relief of paupers and prisoners. It was to provide a refuge from religious persecutions on the continent of Europe. It was also to be a military bulwark against Roman Catholic Spain. There is at this last point a reversion to the early 16th- and 17th-century ideal of colonization.[59] Although nothing was stated in the patent about missions, the chief trustee, General Oglethorpe, personally had something of a missionary motivation. When Thomas Rundle, prebendary of Durham, preached a sermon at Saint George's, Hanover Square, London, in 1734 "to recommend the Charity for establishing the New Colony of Georgia," he urged as the final aim of the enterprise the extension of the kingdom of God, and he seems to reflect Oglethorpe's mind. Rundle asserted that the trustees of the Charity "hope to make the light of this settlement shine before their neighbors that they may glorify their Father which is in heaven. The force and eloquence of this silent argument for Christianity will convert those who cannot so well feel the force of other reasonings; tho' no other will be omitted, as opportunities to enlighten their minds, and friendly meetings shall offer." [60]

The Georgia trustees in the autumn of 1734 made a grant of 500 acres to Count Zinzendorf to be the base of a Moravian mission to the Indians. The first Moravian company sailed in February 1735 and a second in 1736. General Oglethorpe aided them further by taking a collection for them, and he made them a loan. A mission to the Creeks was well under way in 1737

when a threatened invasion by the Spaniards in Florida resulted
in the calling of all settlers to arms. The pacifist Moravian Brethren insisted that the compact made by the trustees with Zinzendorf
exempted them from military service. However, public sentiment was aroused against them, and the trustees took the position
that "to allow the Brethren when they were not citizens, to send
missionaries to the Indians, would be construed to mean that the
English had no one to preach the Gospel." [61] The Moravians
thereupon removed to Pennsylvania.

General Oglethorpe apparently put much hope in his col-
onists converting the Indians by the power of their Christian
example. He besought the bishop of Sodor and Man, Thomas
Wilson, to prepare a manual for the guidance of the settlers in
Christian example and in more active witness to the Indians.
The bishop then wrote the book entitled *The Knowledge and
Practice of Christianity Made Easy to the Meanest Capacities, or
An Essay towards an Instruction for the Indians.*[62] Wilson denounced the bad example of settlers living a life which turned
the heathen against Christianity. Most remarkable for the time,
he asserts that there is an evangelistic function inherent in church
membership. Each Christian should work for the coming of the
kingdom of God as well as pray for it in reciting the Lord's
Prayer. The settlers of Georgia have a God-given obligation as
well as an opportunity to convert the heathen Indians and Negro
slaves. They can do it by example of life, by conversation, and
by direct instruction. The book is intended to assist them in
this work.

THE NEW ENGLAND MISSIONS

Two centuries later, when New England was the powerhouse
of a rapidly expanding foreign missionary enterprise, the participants in that movement looked back to the early period of settlement as the golden age of missionary zeal, just as they idealized
it in most other respects. They urged their contemporaries to

take inspiration from the devotion of their forefathers. They challenged them to match it. For example, Joseph Tracy, an early historian of missions, wrote in 1839:

> The first settlement of New England was a missionary enterprise. . . . They . . . came . . . for the sake . . . above all, of extending the Redeemer's kingdom in lands where Christ had not been named. . . . From 1646 to 1675, New England did more in proportion to her ability for the conversion of the heathen than she has done from 1810 to 1839. The spirit of missions was as general then as now, contributions were as liberal in proportion to their means, and missionaries exposed themselves as readily to equal hardships and dangers.[63]

The total devotion to mission on the part of the whole populace of New England as presented by Tracy is much overdrawn. New England differed, however, from the other colonial regions in North America in spontaneously raising up a strong minority which actually implemented the missionary profession of the charters. It is, on the other hand, quite true that most of the settlers were more interested in extending the kingdom of God by the displacement or extermination of the Indians than by their conversion. John Higginson's description of the transformation of the heathen wilderness into a veritable Garden of Eden, given in his "Attestation" to Cotton Mather's book *Magnalia Christi Americana,* reads:

> The Lord was pleased to grant such a gracious *presence* of his with them, and such a *blessing* upon their undertakings, that within a few years a *wilderness* was subdued before them, and so many *Colonies* planted, *Townes* erected, and *Churches* settled, wherein the true and living God in Christ Jesus is worshipped and served, in a place where time out of mind, had been nothing before but *Heathenism, Idolatry,* and *Devil-worship;* and the Lord has added so many of the blessings of *Heaven* and *Earth,*

for the comfortable subsistence of his people on these *ends
of the earth.*[64]

This transformation and the spread of the kingdom of God came
despite the Indians. It was thought that God intervened directly
to open the land to the Puritans. Their grandchildren gave
thanks that "God sent a mortal Sickness among the Indians who
inhabit near the Sea-Shore, in this part of the Country, which
destroyed multitudes of them, and made room for our Fathers." [65]
That great advocate of missions, Cotton Mather, designated the
struggles with the Indians as "the wars of the Lord." Yet there
was good ground for Foxcroft's assertion at the centennial of the
First Church of Boston that the founding fathers "hoped to be
the blessed Instruments of spreading the Gospel of Christ among
the heathen Nationes." [66] There were many who took seriously
the pious sentiments of the charters and had enough motivation
to put them into practice.

The charters had put the usual pious intentions about evangelism on the lips of the King of England. The Plymouth charter states:

> In contemplation and serious consideration whereof, we
> have thought it fit, according to our Kingly Duty, so much
> as in us lieth, to second and follow God's sacred will, ren-
> dering reverent thanks to his Divine Majesty for his gra-
> cious favour in laying open and revealing the same [i. e.,
> this relatively unoccupied land] unto us before any other
> Christian Prince or State; and by which means, without
> offence, and as we trust to his glory, we may with boldness
> go on to the settling of so hopeful a work, which tendeth
> to the reducing and conversion of such savages as remain
> wandering in desolation and distress, to civil society and
> the Christian religion.[67]

The Massachusetts charter of 1629 grants to the governor
and freemen of the colony powers to make laws and regulations
"for the directing, ruling, and disposing of all other Matters and

Thinges, whereby our said People, Inhabitants there, may be soe religiously, peaceably, and civilly governed, as their good life and orderlie Convercacon, mae wynn and incite the Natives of the Countery, to the Knowledge and Obedience of the only true God and Sauior of Mankinde, and the Christian Fayth, which in our Royall Intencon, and the Adventurers free Profession is the principall Ende of this Plantacion." [68] The seal of the colony bore out this assertion about the principal end of the plantation by having as its design the figure of an Indian crying out, "Come over and help us." [69] Connecticut and New Haven were founded on the strength of patents, and when the former received a charter from King Charles II, it repeated the exact words of the Massacusetts charter, but strengthened them by adding *only:* "evangelization is the onlye and principal end of this Plantacon." [70]

Connecticut, unlike Massachusetts, never did much to make good the profession of its charter. There was on the negative side an effort by the state to compel the Indians to keep the Sabbath. When the Commissioners of the United Colonies assigned a reservation to the tiny remnant of the Pequots on the Pawcatuck and Mystic rivers, the first of the laws imposed was: "They shall not blaspheme the name of God, the Creator of Heaven and Earth, nor profane the Sabbath Day." [71] The Court of Election at Hartford on May 9, 1667, followed this example by ordaining that any Indian who worked or played on the Sabbath be fined five shillings or sit in stocks for one hour.[72] If the offender paid the fine, half of it was to go to the public treasury and the other half to the informer who caused the arrest. More positively, in 1642 the General Court decreed:

> Judging it necessary that some meanes should be used to convey the light and knowledge of God and of his Worde to the Indians and Natives among us [the ministers with the help of a certain Thomas Stanton, evidently an interpreter], shall be desired, twise at least in every yeare, to go amongst the neighboring Indians and indeavor to make

known to them the Councells of the Lord, and thereby to draw and stir them up to direct and order all their wayes and conversations according to the rule of his Worde.[73]

Referring to this law some eight years later, the court admitted that little had been done "through want of an able interpreter."

Action was then taken to improve the situation. "Desirous of promoting a work wherein the glory of God & the everlasting welfare of these poore, lost, naked sonnes of Adam is so deeply concerned," the legislators in 1652 ordered Thomas Mynor (or Minor) of Pequot to send his son John forthwith to Hartford for training as an interpreter to such missionary ministers as the court might designate and as a future missionary himself.[74] The court would provide his maintenance and schooling. This action was supplemented by a decision of the Commissioners of the United Colonies about a week later. They assigned this John Minor to serve as interpreter to the Rev. Messrs. Stone and Newton and any others designated by the court. Furthermore, Minor was to be instructed and fitted by Mr. Stone "to be a meete instrument to carry on ye work of propagating ye Gospell to ye Indians." Consequently they asked that the magistrates of Connecticut see to John's maintenance at Mr. Stone's home or some other suitable place, and they would order that "due allowance bee made for his dyet and education out of the corporation stock," that is, out of the locally held or invested resources of the New England Company.[75]

However, the General Court never put pressure on the ministers, and only a very few were personally interested enough to undertake evangelistic work. Stone and Newton labored at Hartford, Windsor, and Farmington, while James Fitch of Norwich tried to convert the Mohegan chief Uncas and his family.[76] John Eliot was rebuffed by the Podunk Indians at a council in Hartford because the English had taken their lands and were trying to make servants of them. Benjamin Trumbull considered the greatest impact to have been made on the Quinibaug tribe near

Plainfield, where as a result of conversions in the revival of 1745 a church-state was formed.[77] James Noyce of Stonington had numerous Indian members in his church, and some of them, moved by a revival experience in 1743, went to the area around Waverly, R. I., and converted many Indians there. The minister who made the greatest progress with the native language was Abraham Pierson of Branford, near New Haven, and the Commissioners of the United Colonies commended him to the New England Company for support.[78] Samson Occum gathered up the remnants of these earlier efforts and moved the Christian Indians to New York at a later date. Wheelock's school and mission, described later in this chapter, were to be the principal efforts made in Connecticut, and Wheelock was unable to get much assistance from the state.[79]

The ink was scarcely dry on the Massachusetts charter when Matthew Craddock, Governor of the plantation company, wrote to John Endicott, Governor of the colony, reminding him not to be "unmindful of the mayne end of our plantacon by indevoringe to bring ye Indians to the knowledge of the gospell." He was, with that end in view, to keep a watchful eye over the settlers so that they behave justly and courteously toward the natives and gain their affection for the English and their religion.[80] In the first general letter from the company to the colony, dated April 17, 1629, it was announced that ample provision was being made for ministers. Since the company professes that the propagation of the Gospel is "above all to be our mayne ayme," it is intended that these ministers not only shepherd the English settlers but also reduce the Indians to obedience to the Gospel of Christ.[81] However, the initial demands of settlement took all the time and attention of magistrates and people for the first decade or more. Plymouth Colony, so it is often said, enacted a law in 1636 providing for the preaching of the Gospel to the natives, but it does not appear to have been implemented.[82]

Except for granting the towns power in 1637 to restrain

the Indians from profaning the Sabbath,[83] the General Court of Massachusetts does not appear to have dealt with the issue of Christianizing the aborigines until 1644. By that time some individuals were privately preparing themselves for the Indian mission. Henceforth the activity of these men, supplemented by the interest of the greater part of the ministers and a considerable minority of the populace, would keep the court attentive to the matter. Cotton Mather's report that all the good men of the country were glad of John Eliot's work and that the ministers supported him indicates the contrast between Massachusetts and all the other colonies.[84]

The success of the Massachusetts enterprise is to a considerable extent to be explained by the genuineness and simplicity of the motivation.[85] The political motivation so evident elsewhere was here in the early stages a very minor factor. The political consequences of French missions were a far greater cause of fear in the 18th century than in the 17th. The Mathers, the missionaries, and their friends did not so much want to destroy Roman Catholic missions as to emulate, rival, and surpass them. Cotton Mather made a great attempt to demonstrate that in proportion to their numbers and strength the New England Puritans far surpassed the achievements of mighty Rome.[86] It is noteworthy, too, that in New England, except in the case of Eleazar Wheelock a century later, there was little reference to expediency and military security, so often advanced in England, New York, and to an extent in Georgia. There was no complicating sense of moral indebtedness to the Indians. They had not been cheated. The land was mostly open and unoccupied. The Puritans had paid the Indians their own price for every square inch of it. Moreover, the Indians lost their land but got salvation. All indebtedness was on the part of the Indians. The evangelization of the Indians brought no gain to the settlers. It was disinterested service done to the glory of God. So this could be counted as "one of New England's peculiar glories." The mission was God's work, not that of men — "the work of the Lord amongst the Indians for the forwarding of publishing of the glad tydings of peace." [87]

The Massachusetts General Court at first attempted on Nov. 13, 1644, to put responsibility upon the county courts, ordering them to take measures to civilize and bring to the knowledge and the worship of God the Indians who resided in the several shires.[88] Meanwhile the House of Deputies had in June ordered all Indian subjects to attend instruction on the Lord's Day.[89] Then a year later, when nothing had as yet been done and being mindful of its duty, the General Court appealed to the ministers. It requested them to consider the matter and to make a report at the next session of the court, giving their advice as to the best means of discharging this responsibility.[90] The following year, on Nov. 4, 1646, that august body took both negative and positive action. It decreed the death penalty for any Indian who might blaspheme God or the Christian religion, and it prohibited the Indians from "pawpawing" or performing worship to false gods.[91] A companion law required the ministers at the Court of Election each year to select two of their number, along with any volunteers, to instruct the Indians. An interpreter would be provided, and the court would present gifts to all Indians willing to receive such instruction.[92] Apparently unknown to the court, the Mayhews were, however, already evangelizing the natives in their own domains of Martha's Vineyard and Nantucket, and John Eliot had made his first approach to the Indians at Newton. Yet Eliot's interest was surely known, because earlier this very same day the General Court had ordered the Surveyor General along with a committee of the court to confer with Messrs. Eliot, Allen, and Shepherd and select parcels of land "for encouraging the Indians to live in an orderly way among us" and to pay for the land out of the treasury.[93]

The mission of the Mayhew family on Martha's Vineyard, Nantucket, and the Elizabeth Islands is the outstanding example of a church-state mission. It also is the outstanding example in America of the implementation of the Calvinist doctrine of the responsibility of Christian magistrates for the conversion of pagan subjects. However, the motivation of the Mayhews was much more warm and vital than that. Thomas Mayhew had come to Massachusetts in 1631 as factor of Matthew Craddock.[94] Ten years later, in 1641, he purchased from both counterclaimants, the Sterling and the Gorges interests, the group of 16 islands. There he set himself up as governor, proprietor, and lord of the manor of Tisbury. Mayhew honored Indian land claims and insisted on buying title from the natives before any parcel of land was resold to Englishmen. The first settlement was made in 1642 at Great Harbor, or Edgartown, on Martha's Vineyard under the direction of the younger Thomas Mayhew.

Thomas, Jr., had studied theology, and when the settlers gathered a church, he was elected minister. Almost at once this young man, who knew the language, began working with the Indians. Thus began a family mission that was carried on by five successive generations until there was no longer need of a special mission to the natives. It is a unique story of devotion.

Blessed with the gift of patience, the younger Thomas began with a personal, individual approach to the Indians rather than with mass meetings and preaching. He invited a young man, Hiacoomes, who showed special interest, to come to his home for conversation and study every Sunday night. He was baptized in 1643, became Mayhew's assistant, and was eventually ordained. Public services were begun in 1646. The pawpaws opposed the new religion, but resistence crumbled in 1648, and then accessions came speedily. In 1652 the converts drew up a covenant for a Christian community but a church was not fully organized until 1670 because the Mayhews wanted to be absolutely certain about the quality of the converts. Thomas, Jr., was lost at sea en route to England in 1657. Then his father, who had already assisted, took over the mission work. Much of the strength of the Christian community was due to the fact that the elder Mayhew honored the Indian social structure. His converts did not have imposed upon them the artificial government imposed upon the Indians of the mainland, but their towns grew naturally under the authority of their own sachems. Converts and eventually churches multiplied. Nantucket was evangelized from Martha's Vineyard, and also some of the mainland. The New England Company gave a small amount of aid beginning in 1651.[95] The Mayhew mission, being in a remote and out-of-the-way place, did not receive the publicity of John Eliot's mission.

John Eliot, the minister at Roxbury, had long been concerned about the remnants of tribes in his neighborhood.[96] He learned the Massachusetts language by employing a young Indian, Cookenoe, to live in his home and teach him. He felt sufficiently prepared to begin public preaching in the early autumn of 1646, and he had made some translations. Encouraged by a first attempt at Dorchester Mills in September, he held his first formal service at the residence of the sachem Waaban at Nonatum, or Newton, on Oct. 28. Thereafter a service was held every two weeks. Beginning with the third service conversions occurred. Soon the Roxbury pastor was preaching regularly at half a dozen points. His English congregation became enthusiastic about the Indian work and called an assistant so that their pastor might have time for evangelism. Neighboring pastors also often relieved Eliot of pastoral duties. The following May the General Court made its first contribution to Eliot's program, granting £10 from a fund given by Lady Mary Armine.[97] Eliot enlisted friends in the venture — Thatcher, Rawlinson, Daniel Gookin in Massachusetts; Richard Bourne, Treat, Tupper, and John Cotton in Plymouth; and soon there was a flourishing mission.

This pioneer missionary and his colleagues believed that the Christian Indians must be segregated from their pagan brethren on the one hand, and protected from the influence of bad Englishmen on the other. Protective laws might accomplish something, but not all. At Eliot's request the House of Deputies made provision that Indians might buy wine only from William Philips in Boston.[98] To Eliot the best means to the desired end appeared to be the establishment of towns of "Praying Indians." There under the eyes of ministers, teachers, and native evangelists the converts could be isolated from contamination by evil pagan influences and the bad example of many settlers, and there be nurtured in Christian knowledge and trained in the ways of English civilization. The first of these towns was gathered at Nonatum but moved to Natick in 1651. The General Court ordered that a township of 6,000 acres be laid out at Natick in 1652,[99] and five years later confirmed the Indians' priority over the claim of some Englishmen.[100] John Eliot's petition for three more towns was granted, and they were ordered to be laid out in 1657. Others were authorized at state expense as requested.[101] By 1674 there were 14 towns of Praying Indians with a population of 4,000, of whom 1,800 were in the Mayhew villages.

A Biblical plan of government, based on Exodus 18:21, was devised by John Eliot for these Indian towns. The population was divided into tens, fifties, and hundreds under tithing men and rulers. The people made a covenant with the Lord to be governed in all things by the Word of God. However, the General Court was not satisfied with Eliot's scheme. They wanted the ultimate authority and control over the Indians to rest with the state. Therefore in 1658 the Court appointed Indian Commissioners over the towns.[102] Eliot wrote a book advocating the application of his system of government to England and all British Dominions. That got him into some trouble. The church and school, built at state expense, were the chief institutions of the towns.

The Massachusetts missionaries were very slow to organize churches. They delayed long so that all criticism about the quality of the converts' profession and practice could be disarmed. Councils of ministers and representatives of churches were called, and examination after examination was held. The first church was then gathered at Natick in 1660. Others soon followed. The Christian life of these congregations and towns was nurtured by preaching, teaching, catechizing, Bible reading, and devotional literature. The schools aimed at making the Indians literate through ordinary primary instruction both in the vernacular and English. They taught agricultural and domestic crafts so that the inhabitants could supply their own needs and support themselves by sales and services to the English.

It is to the high credit of the Massachusetts missionaries that they never doubted the essential humanity and the native intelligence of the Indians, in contrast to most American settlers. They possessed immortal souls to be saved; they had powers of reason which could make them understand and accept the Gospel; and they had the ability to provide their own teachers and pastors if proper education were provided. It was recognized that English missionaries could never fully meet the need. Very early a seminary was established for the training of native teachers and evangelists. Even in a time of decline, about 1700, there were 37 Indian preachers of the Gospel compared with 7 or 8 English ministers in the mission. A few select Indians were sent to study in the Grammar School at Boston and the Indian College at Harvard College in Cambridge. Eliot produced the literature for the schools as well as the churches, and his publication record is astounding. His greatest achievement was the Massachusetts Bible, the first Bible printed in America.

State support continued in Massachusetts, but on a rather small scale. It is impossible to estimate what funds were given locally and voluntarily by individuals and churches. The missionaries were indefatigable in collecting what they could, and friends of the work, like Cotton Mather and his relatives, were active. That there were considerable local contributions is indicated by the fact that the New England Company could never induce Eliot to give an accounting of them.[103] He apparently feared that the company would cut the grants if he made an accounting of all funds. There was never enough local support, however, to carry the expense of the mission, and reliance had to be placed on interested friends in England.

The first and oldest still existing missionary society was founded in England in 1649 specifically to support the New England work. Communication between Boston and London was so full and frequent that Eliot had no more than begun preaching to the Indians when the news was spreading through England. Eleven report letters and descriptive pamphlets, the "Eliot Tracts," as they are called, were published from 1643 to 1671.[104] The first of these, "New England First Fruits," antedated the beginning of the mission. It declared that the time was ripe and asked for help in evangelization. Coincident with the publication of this earliest tract, Parliament adopted on Jan. 31, 1643, a resolution permitting the agents of the New England Colonies, Hugh Peters and Thomas Weld, "to collect the free contribution of all well-affected people, in all the parishes of London, Westminster, and the borough of Southwarke, and parishes adjacent, on the next two Lord's Days: for the transporting of divers poor children droven out of Ireland and others."[105] The collection was a success.[106] In addition to about £830 for this purpose, the agents collected during the next two years about £330 for miscellaneous causes, including £20 per year from Lady Mary Armine for Indian evangelization.

This Parliamentary approval of a collection for New England was the precedent for another appeal to Parliament in 1648. The House of Commons agreed upon consideration of a charity for promoting piety and learning in New England.[107] Shepard's tract "The Clear Sunshine of the Gospel Breaking Forth upon the Indians of New England" has been published only a few days earlier. Included with Shepard's report was a statement endorsing the mission work to which prominent Independent and Presbyterian ministers subscribed. They called upon Parliament to aid the agents of Divine Providence. The drafting of an ordinance was referred to the Committee on Foreign Plantations, which reported back to the House.[108] There were various delays until after Pride's Purge and the reorganization of Parliament. Winslow, then agent of the United Colonies, published a fourth tract early in June 1649. A few days later the proposed act got its long-delayed reading. It was referred to a special committee, brought back, and finally amended on the floor of the House of Commons. The amendment was drastic. It changed the act from authorizing a charity for education and evangelization to authorization of a pure missionary society. The words specifying Harvard College and other schools were deleted, and the passage substituted: which "shall best and principally conduce to the preaching and propagating of the Gospel of Jesus Christ amongst the natives, and also for maintaining schools and nurseries of learning, for the better educating of the children of the natives." [109] Parliament then formally passed July 27, 1649, an act establishing a Corporation for Promoting and Propagating the Gospel of Jesus Christ in New England.[110] The corporation was to be designated as The President and Society for Propagation of the Gospel in New England.

Since the legislation enacted by the Long Parliament was all cancelled at the Restoration in 1660, the society automatically became defunct and lost its property. However, through the efforts of the Honourable Robert Boyle and other influential men in London an order of King Charles II in Council was obtained on April 1, 1661, granting a new charter and confirming the ownership of the property.[111] The name was altered to The Company for Propagation of the Gospel in New England and the Parts Adjacent in America. Boyle was named governor of the company. Among the members were noblemen, London aldermen, and very substantial citizens, both Anglicans and dissenters.

The New England Company, to use the common designation, took up a collection, invested the funds, and added some

substantial legacies from time to time. Out of the annual revenue
from the investments supplies and funds were sent to the missionaries in America. An attempt was made to secure a local
financial income by sending out stock for sale, but it was not
successful. Meager grants for salaries and allowances were made
to missionaries, schoolteachers, and Indian evangelists. Costs of
publications were met. The largest single project was the printing of the Eliot Indian Bible.[112] The company sent over for that
task a printer, Marmaduke Johnson, to collaborate with the local
printer, Samuel Green. The company seemed more ready to bear
publication costs than to allow more than a pittance to the missionaries.

The company officers in London urgently needed local agents
to manage its business with the missionaries and to make recommendation concerning persons to be employed and projects to
be aided. The Commissioners of the United Colonies of Massachusetts, Plymouth, and Connecticut were asked to serve as a local
board of references and action. They agreed. Officers of state
thus became the actual field directors of the mission. Government directly participated in mission. Moreover, there were no
special sessions for mission business. Such matters were handled
in the ordinary routine of their state affairs, as is evident from the
remnants of their records preserved in the archives of Connecticut.[113] The General Court of Massachusetts got the impression
that the commissioners spent so much of their time on mission
matters that insufficient time was left for official state affairs.
Therefore the court requested the commissioners in 1658 to make
a "proportionable allowance" for mission business.[114] The Governor of Massachusetts was chairman of the commissioners.

When the last meeting of the Commissioners of the United
Colony was held in 1684, it was necessary to find a new solution
to the problem. The company asked five of the commissioners
to constitute a new board, called the Commissioners for Indian
Affairs, or Commissioners for Propagation of the Gospel.[115] To

them others were added and replacements were necessarily made from time to time. Increase Mather wrote the company in 1697 that only two besides himself were able to attend meetings because the others had died or were incapacitated. He nominated his son Cotton, son-in-law Nehemiah Walter, who was successor to John Eliot at Roxbury, Judge Samuel Sewell, and two others.[116] Cotton Mather became one of the most active and conscientious members.

King Philip's War of 1675—1676 inflicted a staggering blow on the Indian mission. Harassed by pagan Indians and white men, the towns of the Praying Indians were broken up. Their inhabitants were killed, dispersed, or interned.[117] Nevertheless the mission survived and even recovered to a considerable degree. But henceforth the Indians east of the Connecticut River were a dying race. Cotton Mather continued to promote the good cause, but by his death in 1728 the mission had sunk to an extremely low point. However, a new chapter in Indian evangelization was about to open west of the Connecticut River. Solomon Stoddard, called "the Pope of the Connecticut Valley," at Northampton in 1723 raised the question "whether God is not angry with the country for doing so little towards the conversion of the Indians." He called on the people to fulfill the profession which their fathers had made in the charter of Massachusetts.[118] The Society in Scotland for Propagating Christian Knowledge turned its attention to America in 1730. A new partnership of church, state, and a British society then came into being, with the Indians of the Housatonic Valley in western Massachusetts and the Six Nations, or Iroquois, as its chief objects. The increasing threat of French power in Canada as well as more purely missionary motivation turned the attention of both the Scots and the Massachusetts men to the Iroquois.

The society which now entered the field was composed of Presbyterians, and it could easily make common cause with the Calvinist Congregationalists of New England and the Presbyterian and Reformed people of the Middle Colonies. The Society in Scotland for Propagating Christian Knowledge was chartered by Queen Anne in 1709. Its headquarters were and still are in Edinburgh. After some years of successful activity in the Scottish Highlands it received a large bequest from Dr. Daniel Williams to be used to send three missionaries to "infidels." Therefore it turned to the Indians in America.[119] The society then commissioned Governor Belcher of Massachusetts and "other gentlemen of character and influence" to form a Boston board of field managers for its affairs. Ten years later a second such "New York Board," or "New Jersey Board," as it was also known, was set up. Ebenezer Pemberton, pastor of the Presbyterian Church in New York, was chairman, and members were drawn from New York and neighboring towns in New Jersey. The missionaries employed by this Middle Colonies board were all New Englanders, including Azariah Horton on Long Island, David Brainerd, and John Brainerd. The Brainerd mission was highly influential in the inspiration it later imparted to missionary developments, but it had no enduring results, and no church-state relations were involved in it.

There was considerable overlapping in membership between the Boston Boards of the New England Company and the Society in Scotland for Propagating Christian Knowledge. Governor Belcher and the Reverend Benjamin Colman seem to be examples. Consequently it is extremely difficult often to tell which society is supporting whom. Contemporaries were confused as to the identity of the two, and persons of later generations have tended to confuse these two societies with the better-known Anglican Society for Promoting Christian Knowledge and the Society for Propagation of the Gospel in Foreign Parts. Actually, as the century progressed, it was often the case that both societies partially supported the same individuals and projects. The Stockbridge Mission was such a case.

The new phase of Indian evangelism began when the

S. S. P. C. K. in Edinburgh assigned to its commissioners in Boston the sum of £56 as the annual income of the Williams bequest and requested that it be applied to the support of three missionaries on the western and northern borders as either a direct or indirect approach to the Iroquois.[119] Governor Belcher took the matter to the General Court of Massachusetts. It gave approval and added additional support from its own treasury for a period of five years.[120] Three volunteers were accepted: Stephen Parker, Ebenezer Hinsdel, and Joseph Seccombe. Their joint ordination service was a noteworthy affair. Benjamin Colman was moderator. Joseph Sewall preached the sermon. Thomas Prince extended the right hand of fellowship, and 10 ministers laid on hands in ordination. The instructions of the Scottish Society were read, laying down principles much the same as those which guided the earlier missions, except that the missionaries were not required to establish segregated towns. They were to preach, catechize, and teach. School instruction was to include writing and arithmetic, understanding of the English language, and how to pray and conduct oneself as a Christian. Whenever the missionaries judged converts to be ready, they were to admit them to Baptism and the Lord's Supper.[121] The young missionaries thereupon went off to various frontier forts and trading posts: Seccombe to Fort George, Hinsdel to Fort Dummer, and Parker to Fort Richmond. However, within three years they gave up their work. The Indians were said to be too much under French influence.[122]

The next venture was directed toward the peoples of Mohegan stock in the Housatonic Valley in the Berkshire Mountains of western Massachusetts. The so-called River Indians, or Muhekunnucks, lived all along the Housatonic River in Connecticut and Massachusetts and west of the border in the colony of New York. Influential ministers in the Connecticut Valley wrote to the commissioners in Boston asking about prospects for a mission to these Indians. They included the Rev. Samuel Hopkins of Springfield, Col. John Stoddard of Northampton, son of "the Pope," the Rev. Stephen Williams of Springfield, and a Rev. Mr. Williams of Hatfield. The Boston people asked these same men then to go to the Housatonic Valley and confer with the Indians. Governor Belcher sought to make contact for them by inviting two sachems to make the journey to Springfield and there receive military commissions. This would allow the Springfield parsons to meet and converse with them. Captain Konkapot declared himself eager to have a missionary come to reside with his people. Then two ministers, Williams of Springfield and Bull of Westfield, went to the Housatonic, where Konkapot assembled the people for a council with them. At the end of four days they made an agreement to receive a minister. Mr. Williams traveled to Boston and personally reported to the Governor, not to the commissioners. The Governor then discussed the matter with the commissioners, who decided on Aug. 16, 1734, to support such a mission. They deputized the Rev. Messrs. Bull and Williams to secure a missionary.[123]

Fortunately it was already known to this committee of two that there was at Yale College a tutor, John Sergeant, who was eager to undertake missionary service. He was given the call, and he accepted it. Governor Belcher made the ordination a great affair of state, making it the high point of a week-long treaty-making council with the Indians at Deerfield. The Governor, many members of his council, members of the House of Representatives, prominent gentlemen, and military officers were present. The moderator, Mr. Williams of Hatfield, gravely informed the Governor that the right man had been found and inquired whether the ordination should proceed. The Governor assented. The Housatonic Indians were tremendously impressed with the honor being shown the man who was to be their missionary, because through him they were being honored. They sat in a body separate from the other Indians. After the charge had been given to the ordinand, the moderator asked the Indians whether they would receive Sergeant. They stood solemnly in token of assent.[124]

John Sergeant was preaching in the vernacular within three years. The mission prospered. When the young missionary died at the age of 39 in July 1749, the town numbered 20 houses in English style with 218 inhabitants. He had baptized 182 persons, of whom 129 were then living in the village and of whom 42 were full communicants. A day school was begun immediately in 1734, and within a year it had 40 pupils. The General Court of Massachusetts in 1736 purchased from the Muhekunnocks a tract of land along the Housatonic River and then granted a township of six square miles to the Christian Indians. It was named Stockbridge. Quite soon the Christian Indians came to be generally recognized as a separate "Stockbridge Nation." The missionary unfortunately held to the old idea of the desirability of the example of godly Englishmen whom the Indians might emulate. He therefore asked the state for an allowance of land for four carefully selected English families. This later proved to be a curse and a source of great trouble to Jonathan Edwards, when he was the missionary. Sergeant continued the day school under an assistant who was schoolmaster, adding a boarding school. The youths in the latter were under two masters, one teaching academic subjects and the other instructing in practical agriculture and crafts. The schoolboys cultivated 200 acres of farmland. Iroquois youths as well as Muhekunnocks came to the school. The colonial officers were interested in the mission, but apart from providing the land and some buildings they apparently invested little money in it. Support was provided principally by the New England Company and the Society in Scotland for the Propagation of Christian Knowledge.[125] A number of students in the boarding school were maintained at the expense of the Rev. Isaac Hollis, who also endowed the Hollis Professorship at Harvard College. Sergeant was succeeded by Jonathan Edwards and eventually by his son John, Jr.

The next project of the Scottish Society was a thrust far into New York into the land of the Six Nations.[126] Eli Spencer opened a station at Onohoquaga on the Susquehanna River in 1747. Gideon Hawley, who had been Edwards' schoolmaster at Stockbridge, served there from 1753 to 1756. Eleazar Wheelock sent Joseph Wooley there in 1764, but he died the following year. The Boston commissioners then forestalled Wheelock's attempt to establish a school there by sending out their own man, Moseley.

Connecticut at long last had gained a more prominent place in the mission through the work of Eleazar Wheelock at Lebanon.[127] Wheelock's scheme of missions was to teach Indian lads in his boarding school, to train along with them white missionaries who would learn the language from them, and then to send both white and Indian evangelists among the tribes. Great reliance was to be placed on Indian evangelists since they could live cheaply among their people. Wheelock had earlier tutored Samson Occum and some others. In 1874 he established his seminary, named More's Charity School. This was removed to Hanover, N. H., in 1770, when he founded Dartmouth College. John Brainerd sent the first students, and some Mohegans were added to them. Samuel Kirkland, son of a friend and an admirer of Wheelock, was the first white student, entering in 1760. Then Wheelock got the idea that if he educated Iroquois youths he might get the support of the society in Edinburgh. Through the assistance of Sir William Johnson a first contingent of three, including Joseph Brant, was sent him. Thereupon the government of Massachusetts allowed him a grant from the fund established by Sir Peter Warren for the education of Iroquois youths. Samson Occum and the Rev. Nathaniel Whitaker raised funds in England and Scotland, but to Wheelock's disgust the society in Scotland held and invested the money raised there and allowed him only the annual income. The General Assembly of New Hampshire made a grant. The Legislature of Connecticut authorized a collection in 1763 and again in 1766. Wheelock failed to get a charter from Connecticut. At its peak his school had 22 students, 8 teachers, 3 missionaries, and 2 interpreters. Hanover was just as poor a location for such a school as Lebanon had been. The Indian school speedily declined while Dartmouth College grew.

Wheelock sent Samuel Kirkland to the College of New Jersey at Princeton for two years of study. Then in 1764 he sent him on a mission to the Iroquois in central New York, largely with the intention of recruiting students for the school. Wheelock for a short time had a fairly large number of missionaries in the country of the Six Nations, but while his basic strategy was sound, his tactics were bad, and he never had sufficient resources to back up his missionaries. Most important, he made an enemy of Sir William Johnson, New York's Superintendent of Indian Affairs. His support was necessary to any successful mission in the area. Kirkland had no success among the Senecas, and so in 1766 he was sent to the Oneidas. Kirkland spent the rest of this life with this tribe. Practically abandoned by Wheelock, Kirkland appealed to the commissioners of the New England Company and in 1770 was taken into their employment. Just before the American Revolution the society in Scotland also agreed to share his support. By that time Kirkland had such influence with the Oneidas that he was able to retain their friendship for the Americans and keep them from joining the Mohawks and others in alliance with the British. This final venture on the part of New England had no support from the colonies, but Kirkland was soon to enter into official relationship to the Continental Congress and the American Army.[128]

NOTES

Chapter 1

1. *A Short History of British Expansion,* 2d ed. (New York: Macmillan, 1931), pp. 157—58.

2. Louis B. Wright, *Religion and Empire: The Alliance between Piety and Commerce in English Expansion, 1538—1625* (Chapel Hill: Univ. of North Carolina Press, 1943).

3. Charles Lucas, *Religion, Colonizing, and Trade, the Driving Forces of the Old Empire* (London: S. P. C. K., 1930), pp. 6, 8.

4. Clements R. Markham, ed. *The Hawkins Voyages During the Reign of Henry VIII, Queen Elizabeth, and James I,* Hakluyt Society Publications, LVII (London: Hakluyt Society, 1878), 9.

5. *The English Voyages of the Sixteenth Century* (Glasgow: MacLehose, 1906), p. 48.

6. Albert H. Markham, ed. *The Voyages and Work of John Davis, the Navigator,* Hakluyt Soc. Pub., LIX (London: Hakluyt Society, 1880, also 1910), p. 236.

7. Ibid., p. 228.

8. Richard Collison, ed. *The Three Voyages of Martin Frobisher in Search of a Passage to Cathaia and India by the North-West, A. D. 1576 to 1578,* Hakluyt Soc. Pub., XXXVIII (London: published for the Hakluyt Society, 1868), p. 20.

9. Wright, pp. 23—25.

10. Ibid., Ch. iii, pp. 33 ff.

11. For Hakluyt's writings, see: E. G. R. Taylor, ed. *The Original Writings and Correspondence of the Two Richard Hakluyts,* Hakluyt Soc. Pub., 2d Ser., LXXVI—VII (London: Hakluyt Society, 1935); for his life: George B. Parks, *Richard Hakluyt and the English Voyages,* ed. James A. Williamson (New York: American Geographical Society, 1928).

12. *The Works of Francis Bacon,* comp. and ed. James Spedding et al, 7 vols. (London: Longmans, 1857—59), VI, 457—60; James Spedding, *The Letters and Life of Francis Bacon,* 7 vols. (London: Longmans, Green, 1868—90), VII, 21—22, 49—52; Lucas, p. 21.

13. Wright, pp. 28—29.

14. Lucas, p. 9.

15. William M. Manross, *A History of the American Episcopal Church* (New York: Morehouse-Gorham, 1959), p. 4.

16. Alexander Brown, comp. and ed. *The Genesis of the United States; . . . a Series of Historical Manuscripts.* 2 vols. (Boston: Houghton Mifflin, 1897), I, 53.

17. Ibid., pp. 67—68; also p. 74.

18. Ibid., p. 236.

19. Ibid., p. 337.

20. Ibid., p. 463.

21. William Symonds, *Virginia. A Sermon Preached at White-Chapel, 25 April 1609,* reprinted in Alexander Brown, *The Genesis of the United States,* I, 283—91; see especially 290—91.

22. Wright, pp. 92—94.

23. Wright, pp. 99-102, full review of the sermon.

24. Robert Beverly, *The History and Present State of Virginia,* ed. Louis B. Wright (Chapel Hill: Univ. of North Carolina Press, 1947), p. 38.

25. *The Records of the Virginia Company of London,* ed. Susan M. Kingsbury (Washington: Gov. Printing Office, 1906—35), I, 220—21, 314; Wright, p. 108.

26. Alexander Brown, ed. *Genesis of the United States,* II, 1031.

27. John W. Lydekker, *The Faithful Mohawks* (New York: Macmillan, 1938), p. 4.

28. *Documents Relating to the Colonial History of the State of New York,* 15 vols. (Albany: Weed, Parsons, 1853—87), IV, 717; Lydekker, p. 9.

29. Lydekker, p. 11.

30. *Documents . . .* See note 28. Letter to the Archbishop of Canterbury is quoted in full in Lydekker, p. 9.

31. Ibid., IV, 1035.

32. Lydekker, pp. 12—13; Frank J. Klingberg, *Anglican Humanitarianism in Colonial New York* (Philadelphia: Church Historical Society, 1940), p. 52.

33. *Documents Relating to the Colonial History of the State of New York,* IV, 1077.

34. Ibid., p. 1078.

35. Lydekker, p. 28.

36. For fairly detailed accounts of the mission, see Lydekker, *The Faithful Mohawks;* Klingberg, *Anglican Humanitarianism in Colonial New York;* and the official S. P. G. history by H. P. Thompson, *Into All Lands: The History of the S. P. G. F. P. 1701—1950* (London: S. P. C. K., 1951), pp. 76—84.

37. Samuel Hopkins, *Historical Memoirs Relating to the Housatunnuk Indians* (Boston: S. Kneeland, 1753), p. 78.

38. Ibid., pp. 79—81.

39. Ibid., p. 80: "Both charity and policy do certainly call for the most vigorous endeavours to propagate the Gospel among the Mohawks." Cotton Mather had commended the earlier Dutch Dominie Dellius on his efforts.

40. Stuart sometimes contrasted the devoutness of the Mohawks with the nominal faith and practice of the white Anglicans in his reports.

For example, see the letter printed in Lydekker, p. 135. *A Memoir of the Rev. John Stuart, D.D., the Last Missionary to the Mohawks* is to be found in *Documentary History of the State of New York,* ed. Edmund B. O'Callaghan (Albany: 1849—51), IV, 505—20.

41. For documents relating to Sir William Johnson and religious matters, see Edmund B. O'Callaghan, ed. *Documentary History of the State of New York,* section entitled "Papers Relating Principally to the Conversion and Civilization of the Six Nations of Indians, 1642—1776," IV, 289—520; there are many references both in Lydekker and Klingberg; on Johnson's life, see Augustus C. Buell, *Sir William Johnson* (New York: Appleton, 1903); James T. Flexner, *Mohawk Baronet: Sir William Johnson of New York* (New York: Harper, 1959); Arthur Pound, *Johnson of the Mohawks* (New York: 1930).

42. Lydekker adequately reveals the role of Brant; on Brant, see Harvey Chalmers, *Joseph Brant: Mohawk* (East Lansing: Michigan State Univ. Press, 1955); William L. Stone, *Life of Joseph Brant (Thayendanegea)* (Albany: J. Munsell, 1865); Louis A. Wood, *The War Chief of the Six Nations; a Chronicle of Joseph Brant* (Toronto & Glasgow: Brook, 1922).

43. Thomas Secker's sermon (originally, London: Pemberton, 1741) is available in reprint in Klingberg, *Anglican Humanitarianism in Colonial New York,* pp. 213 ff.; for this passage, see p. 224.

44. Klingberg, p. 94; J. D. McCallum, *The Letters of Eleazar Wheelock's Indians* (Hanover, N.H.: Dartmouth College, 1932), Introduction.

45. Quoted in Klingberg, p. 96.

46. Ibid., Ch. 3, pp. 87 ff.

47. de Cost Smith, *Martyrs of the Oblong and Little Nine* (Caldwell, Idaho: Caxton Printers, 1948).

48. E. B. O'Callaghan ed. *Documentary History of the State of New York,* III, 1013—14, 1019—20.

49. Ibid., 1019—20, 1022—27.

50. de Cost Smith, pp. 94—95 and ff.; J. Taylor Hamilton, *A History of the Church Known as the Moravian Church or Unitas Fratrum* (Bethlehem, Pa.: Times Pub. Co., 1900), pp. 142 ff.

51. John T. Hamilton, *The Recognition of the Unitas Fratrum As an Old Episcopal Church by the Parliament of Great Britain in 1749* (Bethlehem, Pa.: Times Pub. Co., 1925).

52. On Moravian Missions in Pennsylvania, see Elma E. Gray, *Wilderness Christians, The Moravian Mission to the Delaware Indians* (Ithaca: Cornell Univ. Press, 1956), Chs. 1—4.

53. Quoted by Rayner W. Kelsey, *Friends and the Indians, 1655 to 1917,* p. 38.

54. *Minutes of the Provincial Council of Pennsylvania,* II (Philadelphia: Pub. by the State, 1852), 17.

55. Kelsey, p. 38 ff.; Charles Evans, *Friends in the Seventeenth Century* (Philadelphia: Friends Book Store, 1875), p. 430; Charles F. Holder, *The Quakers in Great Britain and America* (New York: Neuner, 1913), pp. 505—509.

56. Kelsey, p. 40.

57. Ibid., pp. 44—45.

58. Ibid., pp. 54—59.

59. Lucas, p. 69.

60. T[homas] Rundle, *A Sermon Preached at St. George's Church, Hanover Square, on Sunday, February 17, 1734, to Recommend the Charity for Establishing the New Colony of Georgia* (London: T. Woodward and J. Brindley, 1739), p. 21.

61. Edmund Schwarze, *History of the Moravian Missions among Southern Indian Tribes of the United States* (Bethlehem, Pa.: Times Pub. Co., 1923), pp. 6—14.

62. Ninth ed. (London: D. Dodd, bookseller to S. P. C. K., 1759).

63. Joseph Tracy, *History of American Missions to the Heathen, from Their Commencement to the Present Time* (Worcester, Mass.: Spooner and Howland, 1840), p. 9.

64. *Magnalia Christi Americana*. 2 vols. (Hartford: Andrus, Roberts, and Barr, 1820, first American ed. from the London ed. of 1702), I, 9.

65. Nathaniel Appleton, *A Sermon Preached October 9, Being a Day of Public Thanksgiving Occasioned by the Surrender of Montreal, and all Canada* (Boston: John Draper, 1760), p. 17.

66. Thomas Foxcroft, *Observations Historical and Practical on the Rise and Primitive State of New England, etc.* (Boston: S. Kneeland and T. Green, for S. Gerish, 1730).

67. New Plymouth Colony, *The Compact with the Charter and Laws of the Colony of New Plymouth* (Boston: Dutton and Wentworth, printers to the State, 1836).

68. *Records of the Governor and Company of Massachusetts Bay in New England,* ed. Nathaniel Shurtleff (Boston: William White, 1853), I, 17.

69. The seal is plainly inspired by St. Paul's vision of the man of Macedonia calling, "Come over to Macedonia and help us" (Acts 16:9). Missionary intention is the only possible explanation.

70. *Charter of the Colony of Connecticut. 1662* (Hartford: Case, Lockwood, and Brainard, 1900; same, New Haven: printed for the Tercentenary Commission by Yale University Press, 1933); *Public Records of the Colony of Connecticut, 1636—1776.* 15 vols. (Hartford: Case, Lockwood, and Brainard, 1850—90), II, 8.

71. *Connecticut as a Colony and a State,* ed. Forrest Morgan, I, 243.

72. *Public Records of the Colony of Connecticut,* II, 61.

73. Ibid., I, 531.

74. Ibid., p. 264.

75. Ibid., p. 266.

76. Benjamin Trumbull, *A Complete History of Connecticut, Civil and Ecclesiastical.* 2 vols. (New London, Conn.: Utley, 1898), I, 397—98.

77. Ibid., p. 398.

78. *Records of the Commissioners of the United Colonies,* 10th Sept. 1652, in *Records of the Colony of Connecticut,* III, 478.

79. Wheelock was a "lone wolf" operator who found it difficult to cooperate with others, and it appears that primarily his manner and methods prevented his getting more assistance from the government, rather than opposition to Indian evangelization on part of the legislators.

80. *Records of the Governor and Company of Massachusetts Bay,* I, 384.

81. Ibid., p. 386.

82. The existence of this law is frequently stated, but such a law does not appear in *Records of the Colony of New Plymouth,* ed. Nathaniel Shurtleff (Boston: William White, printer to the Commonwealth).

83. *Records of the Governor and Company of Massachusetts Bay,* I, 209.

84. "Life of John Eliot," *Magnalia Christi Americana,* I, 503.

85. R. Pierce Beaver, "American Missionary Motivation before the Revolution," *Church History,* XXXI, 2 (June 1962), 216—26.

86. Mather, I, 521—22.

87. Commissioners of the United Colonies to Robert Boyle, Governor of the New England Company, Sept. 11, 1668, in John W. Ford, ed. *Some Correspondence between the Governors and Treasurers of the New England Company in London and the Commissioners of the United Colonies in America* (London: Spottiswoode, 1896), p. 18.

88. *Records of the Governor and Co. of Massachusetts Bay,* II, 84.

89. Ibid., III, 6—7.

90. Ibid., II, 134.

91. Ibid., II, 176—77.

92. Ibid., II, 178—79.

93. Ibid., II, 166.

94. Lloyd C. M. Hare, *Thomas Mayhew, Patriarch to the Indians (1593—1682)* (New York: D. Appleton, 1932).

95. William Kellaway, *The New England Company, 1649—1776* (New York: Barnes and Noble, 1962), pp. 93—98.

96. The numerous little "lives" of Eliot have added little to Cotton Mather's brief "Life of Eliot" in Book III of *Magnalia Christi Americana.*

97. *Records of the Governors and Co. of Mass. Bay,* II, 189, also III, 106; Kellaway, pp. 92—93.

98. *Records of the Governors and Co. of Mass. Bay,* II, 258; III, 139.

99. Ibid., IV, 42.

100. Ibid., III, 317; completion of Natick survey, 362—63. 1658.

101. Ibid., III, 192; IV, 137.

102. Ibid., IV, 324.

103. This is intimated at various points in Ford, ed. *Some Correspondence, etc.;* G. P. Winship, *The New England Company of 1649 and John Eliot* (Boston: Prince Society, 1920); and in Kellaway, pp. 33 to 34.

104. A brief description of the tracts will be found in Kellaway, pp. 9—14, 22—23.

105. *Journal of the House of Commons,* II, 949.

106. R. P. Stearns, "The Weld–Peter Mission to England," *Publications of the Colonial Society of Massachusetts,* XXXII, 188—246.

107. *Journal of the House of Commons,* V, 493; see Kellaway for the detailed story of the proceedings through Parliament leading to the passage of the act.

108. *Journal of the House of Commons,* V, 493, 677, 692.

109. Ibid., VI, 271.

110. Charles H. Firth and R. S. Rait, eds. *Acts and Ordinances of the Interregnum, 1642—1660* (London: H. M. Stationery Office, 1911) II, 197—200 — the act in full; see remarks in Kellaway, pp. 15—16.

111. Kellaway, pp. 41—46.

112. George P. Winship, *The Cambridge Press, 1638—1692* (Philadelphia, 1945); Kellaway, pp. 122—34, 150—59.

113. *Records of the Colony of Connecticut,* Vol. III.

114. *Records of the Gov. and Co. of Massachusetts Bay,* IV, 336.

115. Kellaway, pp. 199 ff.

116. Ford, *Some Correspondence,* etc., p. 81.

117. Only 4 out of 14 towns survived the war. See Kellaway, pp. 116 ff.

118. Solomon Stoddard, *Question Whether God Is Not Angry with the Country for Doing So Little Towards the Conversion of the Indians* (Boston: B. Green, 1722).

119. H. Hunter, *A Brief History of the Society in Scotland for Propagating Christian Knowledge* (Edinburgh, 1795).

120. Joseph Sewall, *Christ Victorious Over the Power of Darkness, by the Light of His Preached Gospel* (Boston: Kneeland and Green, 1733), pp. 17, 28; R. Pierce Beaver, *Pioneers in Mission* (Grand Rapids: Eerdmans, 1966), pp. 33—74.

121. The missionaries are instructed to take as examples the existing congregations which grew out of the work of Eliot and Mayhew. Ibid., p. 22.

122. Hopkins, p. 16.

123. Ibid., p. 19.

124. Nathaniel Appleton, *Gospel Ministers Must Be Fit for the Master's Use, . . . Illustrated in a Sermon Preached . . . at the Ordination of Mr. John Sargent, etc.* (Boston: S. Kneeland and T. Green, 1735), p. xiii; R. Pierce Beaver, *Pioneers in Mission,* pp. 75—103.

125. Kellaway, pp. 270—276.

126. The division of support of the missionaries mentioned in this paragraph is not clear. In most instances the New England Company and the S. S. P. C. K. apparently each took part of the salary. Hawley and Moseley were certainly employed by the company. See Kellaway, pp. 266—67.

127. Eleazar Wheelock, *A Plain and Faithful Narrative of the Original Design, Rise, and Present State of the Indian Charity School at Leban, in Connecticut* (Boston: Draper, 1763); *A Continuation of the Narrative. . . .* (Draper, 1765); James D. McCallum, *Letters of Eleazar Wheelock's Indians* (Hanover, N. H.: Dartmouth College, 1932), Introduction; R. Pierce Beaver, *Pioneers in Mission,* pp. 153—183, 211 to 254.

128. Herbert J. Lennox, "Samuel Kirkland's Mission to the Iroquois," unpubl. Ph. D. diss. (Univ. of Chicago, 1932).

Indian Missions
in the New Nation

◆§ When the American Revolution began, Protestant missions to the Indians already had a century and a third of history and experience. The documents of English exploration and colonization coming down from a still earlier period transmitted the tradition that a principal purpose of the entire British invasion of North America had been the conversion of the Indians and the extension of the kingdom of God in the new world. The new nation inherited from the colonial era, and particularly from the New England colonies, a common assumption that the Indian missions were the proper concern of the state and were beneficial to the welfare of the state.

The war sadly disrupted both the support and the maintenance of the missionary programs. It cut off the major source of funds, namely, the remittances from the Society for the Propagation of the Gospel in New England and Parts Adjacent and from the Society in Scotland for Propagating Christian Knowledge.[1] It also practically wiped out local giving. There was no local organization for promotion and collection, and it was not easy for missionaries on the frontiers to solicit funds. Normal living among those persons who frequently gave to missions was seriously affected by military campaigns, occupation by the enemy, inflation, and social confusion. The missions on the frontiers also lay either actually or potentially in the paths of war parties. The Indians were in a state of excitement as both sides sought to enlist their active participation or at least their neutrality. The Anglican Mohawks remained loyal to Great Britain and after the war removed to Canada permanently, thus eliminating the only Anglican mission in the country. The Moravian Indians on the Muskingum were massacred or dispersed by American militia. It seems almost a miracle that the missions survived. But they did survive; and immediately after the war they began to move forward into a new era of expansion and diffusion.

Just as Canada under the French had formerly posed a threat to the British Empire in North America, so it now, in its loyalty to England, was a grave danger to the united colonies. Indians in league with the English were now the same threat to these colonies, especially New England and New York, that they had been during the long course of the French and Indian Wars. The political possibilities of the missions took on a heightened significance in the minds of American authorities. The Iroquois, or Six Nations, within the territory of the colony of New York and on the Pennsylvania frontier constituted the gravest problem. Sir William Johnson had just died. He had been succeeded as Superintendent of Indian Affairs by his nephew, and the Johnson name still had the effect of magic with the Iroquois. Joseph Brant, aided by the Anglican missionary John Stuart, had no trouble in keeping his Mohawks loyal to the Crown.[2] The question was whether or not the other nations would follow their example. The few New England missionaries in the Iroquois country and the Stockbridge Mission might be able to affect that decision in a manner favorable to the Americans.

Samuel Kirkland was at Oneida, currently being paid by the Boston commissioners of both the New England Company and the Scottish Society.[3] Onohoquaga on the East Branch of the Susquehanna River was still a station of the Scottish Society under the direction of the Boston Board, with Aaron Crosby in residence.

Wheelock had practically abandoned his missionaries when he moved to Hanover, N. H., and founded Dartmouth; but some of them, especially Indians, who had worked in the Iroquois country, were available. Samson Occum's Mohegans and Montauks had already begun to prepare to move to the Oneida country, and some of them had knowledge of the Six Nations. The Stockbridges were supposed to have friendly relations and influence with Canadian Indians and some western tribes, as well as with the Iroquois.

Sir William Johnson had with reason suspected that the New England missionaries were New England men first and subjects of the British Crown second. Samuel Kirkland was an ardent patriot, and the Boston authorities at once turned to him. However, the Massachusetts Provincial Congress assigned him an utterly impossible task at the outset. They sent him an address to the Mohawks, asked him to present it to their sachem, Brant, and try to induce the tribe to join the colonists.[4] If they would not come over to the Americans, Kirkland was to use his influence "to keep them neutre." At this very time Brant was serving as secretary to Col. Guy Johnson and trying to destroy Kirkland's influence with the other Iroquois nations. Col. Johnson threatened Kirkland, imprisoned him for a time, and finally drove him from his mission. He was ordered not to return.[5] Johnson and Brant soon had to leave the area, but Kirkland had gone to Philadelphia to interview members of the Continental Congress.

John Adams was impressed with the intelligence which Kirkland brought, and a committee was appointed to confer with him. The result was that the new Commissioners of the Indian Department were ordered to give him $300 to pay the expense of his trip.[6] The committee also recommended that the Commissioners for the Northern Department employ him as their agent to secure the friendship of the Indians and their continued neutrality. Kirkland was the official interpreter at the treaty council at Albany later in the summer, and at that time even the Mohawks promised neutrality.[7] The missionary continued to use his influence with the Indians and to send intelligence to General Philip Schuyler.[8] General Washington gave him high commendation and told Congress that it would be of great advantage to the country if his situation were made "respectable."[9] Thereupon Congress granted him a salary of £65 sterling or $288 8/9 for the next year and an advance of £60 for him to use to "promote the happiness of the Indians and attach them to these Colonies."[10]

The missionary continued to serve Congress through the next year. Although the situation changed and neutrality was abandoned, the Oneidas remained friendly. Intercepted letters revealed the high opinion which the British had of Kirkland's services to the Americans.[11] Kirkland now did double duty as missionary to the Oneidas and chaplain to the troops at Fort Stanwix. General Schuyler recommended that Congress pay him a salary of $444 as missionary and $300 as chaplain and interpreter.[12] He was assigned to General Sullivan's army in the campaign against the Six Nations, reappointed a brigadier chaplain, and instructed to pay as much attention as possible to the Oneidas and other Indians.[13] He continued in service until near the end of the war and then spent some time with his family at Stockbridge. His home and church had long since been destroyed and most of the Oneidas dispersed.[14]

Similarly the Christian Stockbridge Indians were sent with messages of friendship and encouragement to neutrality to the Shawnees of Ohio, the Six Nations, and the Canadian Caughnawagas.[15] Stockbridges also enlisted first as Massachusetts minutemen and then as Scouts in the Continental Army.[16] Congress also used Samson Occum's two sons-in-law as emissaries to the tribes under guise of missionary activity. These were the Mohegan, Joseph Johnson, and the Montauk, Jacob Fowler.[17] The initial success of the employment of missionaries led to an attempt to regularize the situation as established policy.

Congress on Feb. 5, 1776, resolved:

That a friendly commerce between the people of the
United Colonies and the Indians, and the propagation of
the Gospel, and the cultivation of the civil arts among
the latter, may produce many and inestimable advantages
to both; and that the Commissioners for Indian Affairs be
desired to consider of proper places, in their respective
Departments, for the residence of Ministers and school-
masters, and report the same to Congress.[18]

The resolution then continued to instruct the Commissioners for
the Northern Department to inquire on what terms Jacob Fowler
and James Johnson would reside among the Six Nations and instruct them in the Christian religion. About six weeks later another resolution instructed the Middle Department to secure
a minister, a schoolteacher, and a blacksmith for the Delawares.[19]
Whether or not that was done is not evident, but in any case the
Moravian missionaries succeeded in keeping the great majority
of the Delawares neutral and friendly to the Americans until the
terrible massacre of 1782.

Thomas Cushing, on behalf of the Boston Commissioners
of the New England Company, then wrote to the President of
Congress in August, 1776, stating that the missionaries of the
society had been without salary for a year and were in difficult
circumstances.[20] They were Samuel Kirkland at Oneida, John
Sergeant at Stockbridge, and Mr. Crosby at Onohoquaga. Their
continued residence and work at their posts were necessary to
keep the Indians from joining the enemy. Cushing asked Congress in the national interest to allow them their salaries and
promised that if remittances were received from London, the
amount would be refunded. Sergeant also made a separate personal appeal.[21] The request was granted. Eleazar Wheelock also
besought both Congress and General Schuyler for a grant to pay
the expenses of Canadian Indian boys at Dartmouth College.
Schuyler commended the proposal, stating that all the Iroquois
who had studied with Wheelock had remained friendly, except

those immediately under control of the Johnson family.[22] Congress gave him $500.[23] No questions seem to have been raised about the principle involved in these relations. The Continental Congress followed the precedent set by colonial governments.

The greatest missionary casualty of the Revolution was the Moravian mission in the Muskingum valley in eastern Ohio. Plagued by the hostility of frontier settlers, the Christian Indian villages had moved by stages westward across Pennsylvania and had finally been reestablished in the Muskingum valley, supposedly far from white interference. They had flourished and multiplied. Located in a critical position between Detroit and Pittsburgh, the Moravian missionaries had succeeded in keeping most of the Delawares neutral and friendly to the Americans. The British authorities resented this "meddling in public affairs," as they put it, and sent a raiding party to Gnadenhütten in 1781. The missionaries were seized, carried off to Detroit for trial, and then released. The commandant at Detroit thereafter aided and protected them.[24]

The villages had been badly disrupted. While the inhabitants of Gnadenhütten were salvaging what was left of their harvest before going off to join their missionaries at upper Sandusky, a party of American militia arrived. They pretended friendship and then in cold blood slew 90 unresisting Christians begging for mercy.[25] The inhabitants of Schönbrun escaped in time. This evil deed was as senseless and ill-advised as it was wicked, for it drove the whole nation of Delawares into a fury of hate against the Americans. It is one of the most indelible stains on the national honor in the whole long story of treachery and shameful dealing with the Indians. The refugees sojourned for short periods at many places in northern Ohio and Ontario and finally established Fairfield on the Thames River in Ontario.[26]

After the war the state of Pennsylvania granted to the Moravian Church 5,000 acres of land as a token restitution for the losses incurred while the missions had been located in that state.[27]

The church asked nothing for itself, but did petition the Continental Congress for the restitution of the Muskingum lands to the surviving Indians. The petition was filed in 1783, and on May 20, 1785, Congress granted three townships adjacent to the old sites.[28] However, the Delawares opposed the return of the Christians, and new Ohio Indian wars interrupted all efforts at return until after Anthony Wayne's victory at Fallen Timbers.

A long series of actions in Congress followed until the Federal Congress on June 1, 1796, confirmed the grant. However, this was to be a source of great expense and vexation to the Moravian Church. It was far too late to establish an Indian town in eastern Ohio; the original inhabitants would under no circumstances return, having no confidence in the Americans; and the newer stock that did go with Zeisberger was of poor quality. Land-hungry neighbors persuaded the Indians that they were really rich and that the missionaries were withholding their wealth. The leasing of land to tenant farmers brought expense rather than income. Holding the land in trust for a dwindling group of Indians of poor character, the church could find no way to get relief from the burden.[29] Finally Senators Benton of Missouri and Brown of Ohio, apparently acting for the land grabbers, accused the Moravians of misuse of their trust and demanded an accounting to Congress. The church was relieved to get the attention of Congress and in 1822 filed a detailed history of the mission and the land grant, submitted accounts and vouchers which showed that the trust had cost four times the revenue from the leased lands, and asked for relief from their burden. With the assistance of Governor Cass a bill was passed by Congress in 1823 providing for the cession of the land to the United States. The Moravian holding society was reimbursed $6,645.25 for costs of development, the Indians at Fairfield were to receive an annuity of $400, and should they ever return to the United States, this annuity might be converted into a reservation of 24,000 acres.[30]

Once the revolution had come to a successful end and the

country began to settle down to a normal state of life, the greatly
needed organization for the promotion and administration of missions was achieved. There had been some earlier efforts at organization. David Brainerd's visit to Boston just before his death had
resulted in the formation of a society in aid of the mission of
Spencer and Strong to the Iroquois.[31] Then in 1762 an American
counterpart of the New England Company and the Scottish Society was founded in Boston by the members of the two Boston
boards and others. The Massachusetts General Assembly had
granted it a charter, but the King had disallowed the charter on
the protest of the Archbishop of Canterbury, it was said.[32] The
revolution caused the New England Company to transfer its operations to New Brunswick, but the Scottish Society wished to re-
sume aid of the American missions. It named a new Boston board
in 1787. However, nationalism was strong. The Massachusetts
patriots decided that they must form their own society. And so
the men who had been named by the Edinburgh Society, the surviving members of the 1762 group, and others founded the Society for the Propagation of the Gospel among the Indians and
Others in North America.[33] Bishop Etwein that same year, 1787,
also founded the Society of the United Brethren for Propagating
the Gospel among the Heathen, intended as a holding company
for any land which Congress might grant and for gifts from non-
Moravians.[34] The Philadelphia Friends established their Aborigines Committee in 1795.[35] Two union societies of Reformed
and Presbyterian churchmen were next formed in New York
State, the New York Missionary Society in 1796 and the Northern Missionary Society in the State of New York in the following year.[36] The Baptists joined the former for a few years. The
Connecticut Missionary Society and the Massachusetts Missionary
Society were established in 1798 and 1799 respectively.[37] Then
a host of others followed.

The immediate concern of the earliest societies were the
Indians, but more and more the frontier settlements came to be

stressed. Most of the new organizations also declared that the heathen overseas were to be objects of their attention. Actually the promoters of the rising missionary movement had a glorious vision of carrying the Gospel to the whole world. However, the frontier settlements were soon swallowing all the resources of many of the societies. Even before immigration became a factor the occupation of a vast continent was under way, the frontier line was pushing steadily westward, and the population doubled every 20 years. There was a great fear in the older, settled regions that without a tremendous missionary impact upon it the western country would be thoroughly paganized. The demands of the frontier settlements then prevented some societies from undertaking work among the Indians, and none of them was able to send missionaries overseas. A student movement induced action for the foreign missions. The American Board of Commissioners for Foreign Missions was organized in 1810, the General Convention of the Baptist Denomination for Foreign Missions in 1814, and the United Foreign Missionary Society (Presbyterian, Reformed, and Associate Reformed) in 1816.[38] The last merged with the American Board in 1826. These foreign mission boards all included the American Indians as objects of their concern. Then gradually the major denominations created their mission boards and with few exceptions also included the Indians in their responsibility.

Efforts to effect missions to the Indians now multiplied rapidly since there were so many agencies to undertake the work. The Society for the Propagation of the Gospel among the Indians took over support of the remnants of the older New England missions. Answering appeals from the Indians, the Friends undertook educational work among the Tuscaroras and Senecas. The Connecticut Society was unsuccessful in attempting missions to the tribes west of Lake Erie. The New York Society dispatched a mission of two families to the Chickasaws and sent a missionary to the Tuscaroras. The Northern Missionary Society turned to the Tuscaroras and Oneidas, answering the request of the latter that they support Mr. Crosby. Gideon Blackburn began a school for Cherokees under authority of the General Assembly of the Presbyterian Church. The American Board went first to the Cherokees and Choctaws; the Baptists sent missionaries to the Cherokees and the Indians of northern Indiana, while the United Foreign Missionary Society pushed across the Mississippi to the Osages. Others added their efforts and the larger missions expanded their programs.

The enlargement of the Indian mission work was in the main an integral part of the total expanding missionary enterprise of the Protestant churches, which gained steadily in power and scope from the close of the Revolution past the turn of the century and throughout the whole of the 19th century. As part of the larger missionary movement it was the product of the same motivation, namely, glory to God, love of Christ, obedience to the Great Commission, and compassion for souls that were perishing for want of the knowledge of the Gospel. The millennial speculations of the early 19th century added a sense of extreme urgency to the "plucking of brands from the burning." The older pity for the physical state of the Indian continued.

New motives, however, now added interest in Indian missions.[39] As the Indians disappeared from the settled East, many churchmen found it easier to love them at a distance, and they began to feel a concern which had been absent from the thought of the early Puritans. Americans had gravely wronged the Indians in killing them off, seizing their land, and breaking faith with them. Therefore, give them the Gospel as an act of restitution. This sentiment was increasingly presented as a compelling reason for Indian missions even in those two denominations which were so closely identified with the frontier, the Baptists and Methodists. A Baptist report of 1829 called for a "sense of the obligations which we are under to this injured people, whose home and country we possess, [to] redress the wrongs we have committed."[40] A Methodist report said of the Indians: "There are

Indians on our frontier. They have claims upon us not merely as men having immortal souls, but as injured by American Christians. We owe them a vast debt, and our only way to pay them is to send them the gospel!" Moreover, as the Indians disappeared from the eastern regions, the conviction grew that only Christian civilization could save them. Christian civilization was, naturally, British-American culture produced by the Protestant religion. Conversion would produce the desire to share this with fellow Christians, and Christian faith would so transform the Indian's character as to give him the ability to achieve it. It appeared to American churchmen holding these sentiments that they had one and the same duty to the Indians as Christians and as citizens of the United States.

The Articles of Confederation of 1777 vested the management of all Indian affairs and trade in the Congress, and that body set up a Department of Indian Affairs with three geographical subdivisions. The new Constitution of 1787 gave Congress the power to regulate commerce with the Indian tribes, and in 1806 the office of Commissioner of Indian Trade was created. The government dealt with the tribes as if they were independent, sovereign nations on the basis of treaties which were presented by the President to the Senate for ratification. Administration of policy and program was placed in the War Department. A Bureau of Indian Affairs was established in 1824 under the Secretary of War, changed to the Commissionership of Indian Affairs in 1832, and altered to the Department of Indian Affairs in 1834. When the Department of the Interior was created in 1849, Indian Affairs were transferred to it from the War Department.

Henry Knox, the first Secretary of War, had the chief responsibility for shaping an Indian policy for the new nation. He shared many of the opinions of the directors of the missionary societies, and he envisaged a program of civilization carried out through Christian missions as the key to a successful policy. The only alternative which he could see for the Indians east of the Mississippi was extermination at an early date. The course which would presently be followed by him and later by his successors in office was set forth in a report to President Washington on July 7, 1789.[41] He argued that the civilization of the Indians was difficult but not impossible; that it would be costly but still the highest economy in contrast to any system of coercion. Presents and military commissions might be bestowed and all manner of expedients used to attach the aborigines to the nation, but the fundamental program would be the employment of missionaries. Knox stated:

> Missionaries, of excellent moral character, should be appointed to reside in their nations, who should be well supplied with all the implements of husbandry, and the necessary stock for a farm.
>
> These men should be made the instruments to work on the Indians; presents should commonly pass through their hands, or by their recommendation. They should, in no degree, be concerned in trade, or the purchase of lands, to arouse the jealousy of the Indians. They should be their friends and fathers.
>
> Such a plan, although it might not fully effect the civilization of the Indians, would most probably be attended with the salutary effect of attaching them to the interest of the United States.
>
> It is particularly important that something of this nature should be attempted with the Southern nations of Indians, whose confined situation might render them proper subjects for the experiment.

Washington apparently agreed, for the very next month the joint instructions of the President and the Secretary of War to the commissioners for treating with the Southern Indians contained the order "to obtain a stipulation for certain missionaries, to reside in the nation. . . . The object of this establishment would be the happiness of the Indians, teaching them the great duties of religion and morality, and to inculcate a friendship and attachment to the United States." [42]

However, before Henry Knox could proceed with his plan for civilizing the Indians, some Indian wars had to be successfully terminated. The defeats of Harmar and St. Clair on the Ohio frontier were major disasters. Secretary Knox secured through Samuel Kirkland some Stockbridge Indians to go as emissaries to the victorious hostiles on the Maumee River. [43] He also induced the Moravian missionary John Heckewelder to accompany General Rufus Putnam to the same Indians and to a council at Vincennes because of Heckewelder's great influence over the Delawares and Wyandots. [44] Then when a great council was held in 1793 before the Wayne campaign, he sent Heckewelder with the commissioners of the United States to the treaty meeting at Sandusky. [45] Moreover, the Society of Friends secured permission from President Washington to send a delegation of their members to that treaty council in order that they might seek to influence the Indians towards peace. [46] Between the defeat of St. Clair and the victory of Anthony Wayne at Fallen Timbers in 1794 there was great fear as to what the Six Nations might do. General Knox put upon Samuel Kirkland the enormous responsibility of choosing and inviting 50 of the most important sachems and warriors of the Iroquois, including Joseph Brant, if he could be persuaded, to visit the President and officers of state at the capital city of Philadelphia. The missionary was charged with personally conducting the party, which actually numbered 40, and providing for their travel, entertainment, and protection. [47] They arrived at Philadelphia in March 1792 and remained there six weeks. They did not go on the warpath with the western Indians. This was no mean accomplishment on Kirkland's part.

The first tentative step toward the implementation of General Knox's proposed civilization policy was taken in connection with the Iroquois and with the assistance of Samuel Kirkland.

Kirkland had a small school in operation, but he had great plans for expanding it into a high-grade advanced school combining academic and agricultural work along the line of the senior John Sergeant's school at Stockbridge.[48] A girls' school was to be added later. White youths would be admitted also in order to help the Indians learn English. When a council with the Iroquois was held at Painted Post before the Indians were invited to Philadelphia, Kirkland induced Col. Pickering to offer them $1,500 as an annual grant for agricultural purposes, expecting to be able to apply it to his scheme.[49] President Washington recommended it and the Senate gave assent. A grant of $1,500 per year for 21 years was offered for an agricultural educational venture, but it could not be used for Kirkland's project because Knox forbade the teaching of Christianity to those not yet converted.[50] This defeated Knox's own original intention, since teachers and farm mechanics who had the right character and sufficient motivation to participate in the scheme could not be found. Only strong missionary motivation, it appeared, could induce the right kind of persons to devote themselves to the Indians with sufficient permanency and with their welfare in view. Kirkland then endeavored to proceed with his own plan on the basis of help from some of the missionary societies. The Board of Regents of New York chartered his Hamilton Oneida Academy in 1793. It did not fulfill its intended purpose with Indians, but had an honorable career as Hamilton College.

Very little was accomplished towards the civilization of the Indians during the next decade and a half. The army gave help to missionaries as they traveled and settled at their new stations. Gideon Blackburn's Cherokee school received a small amount of aid.[51] About 1810 the meager sum of $100 per year was granted to the Moravian school for Cherokees at Springplace.[52] And then, at length, the establishment of the Cherokee Mission of the American Board of Commissioners for Foreign Missions in 1816 brought the government and missions together in the kind of active partnership which Henry Knox had originally envisaged.

Cyrus Kingsbury began his mission to the Cherokees by a round of consultations with the President, the Secretary of War, and the heads of various departments in Washington in 1816.[53] Reminding them how disastrous to the Indians had been the settlement of the country, he argued that both the dictates of humanity and of the Gospel required that Americans share their blessings with them. Schools were the proper method. Costly and bloody wars would thus be avoided. He presented a plan for an educational enterprise, asking no support for personnel but requesting buildings and the implements of husbandry. He completely won President Madison to endorsement of the scheme. So Kingsbury went south from Washington with an order from the Secretary of War to the agent for the Cherokees for the erection of a schoolhouse and a home for a teacher with such pupils as would board with him. Also there were to be provided two plows, six hoes, and six axes! As soon as a teacher for girls was employed, spinning and weaving instruments would be given. Also other buildings were to be erected as needed. All the property would belong to the government. An annual report must be made to the Secretary of War. Col. R. J. Meigs, the agent, took Kingsbury with him to a council with the Cherokees and Creeks, and there Gen. Andrew Jackson introduced him to the Indians and commended schools to them. The Indians gave their assent and helped to select the site. The Brainerd Mission at Chickamauga was opened next year, and then Kingsbury went on to establish the Eliot Mission among the Choctaws.

The President's message to Congress in January 1818 stressed the urgency of a program for civilization of the Indians. A Committee of the House of Representatives, declaring that "the sons of the forest should be moralized or exterminated," recommended the former.[54] They said, with a burst of oratory, "Put into the hands of their children the primer and the hoe, and they will naturally, in time, take hold of the plow; and, as their minds become enlightened and expand, the Bible will be their book, and they will grow up in habits of morality and industry, leave the chase to those whose minds are less cultivated, and become useful members of society." Mission schools among the Hindus and Hottentots have demonstrated what can be done with primitive people. The government does not have to encounter difficulties such as the missions meet overseas. There are no Bibles or books to be translated into foreign tongues. All that is required is to establish some English schools at small expense. Therefore the committee reported a bill. While the bill was pending, the government extended to the Choctaw mission the same terms as its grant to the Cherokee institution.

The bill did not pass until the end of the next session of Congress, but in March 1819 a permanent "Civilization Fund" was established with an appropriation of $10,000.[55] The act authorized the President "to employ capable persons of good moral character, to instruct the Indians in the mode of agriculture suited to their situation; and for teaching their children in reading, writing, and arithmetic, and performing such other duties as may be enjoined, according to such instructions and rules as the President may give and prescribe for the regulation of their conduct, in the discharge of their duties." It was under this authorization, until repealed in 1873, that the churches and the government joined in a partnership for the elevation of the Indians. The mission boards appeared to be the readily available responsible agencies, and Secretary Calhoun addressed a circular to the agencies that were already engaged or about to engage in the education of the Indians. This document did not specify Christian missions, but since they were the only agencies engaged in the work, it clearly had them in view. The "Circular" of the War Department, dated Sept. 3, 1819, reads:

> In order to render the sum of $10,000, annually appropriated at the last session of Congress for the civilization of the Indians, as extensively beneficial as possible,

the President is of the opinion that it ought to be applied in co-operation with the exertions of benevolent associations, or individuals, who may choose to devote their time or means to effect the object contemplated by the act of Congress.

But it will be indispensable, in order to apply any portion of the sum appropriated, in the manner proposed, that the plan of education, in addition to reading, writing, and arithmetic, should, in the institution of the boys, extend to the practical knowledge of the mode of agriculture, and of such of the mechanic arts as are suited to the condition of the Indians; and in that of the girls, to spinning, weaving, and sewing. It is also indispensable that the establishment should be fixed within the limits of those Indian nations which border on our settlements. — Such associations or individuals who are already actually engaged in educating the Indians, and who may desire the co-operation of the government, will report to the Department of War, to be laid before the President, the location of the institutions under their superintendence, their funds, the number and kind of teachers, the number of youths of both sexes, the objects which are actually embraced in their plan of education, and the extent of the aid which they require; and such institutions as are formed, but have not gone into actual operation, will report the extent of their funds, the places at which they intend to make their establishments, the whole number of youths of both sexes which they intend to educate, the number and kind of teachers to be employed, the plan of education to be adopted, and the extent of the aid required. This information is necessary to enable the President to determine whether the appropriation of Congress ought to be applied in co-operation with the institutions which may request it, and to make a just distribution of the sum appropriated.

In proportion to the means of the government, co-operation will be extended to such institutions as may be approved, as well in erecting the necessary buildings, as in their current expenses.[56]

It is evident that the type of education in view and the manner of government aid proposed are directly in line with the policies and practice inherited from the Eliot-Mayhew mission program, the Stockbridge mission, and Samuel Kirkland's scheme of education.

The *Christian Spectator* printed the circular and introduced it by reprinting, with its own approval, the comment of the *National Intelligencer:*

> Doubtless this appropriation will be more extensively promotive of the object intended by it, as an auxiliary fund, especially in such hands as those in which it is in contemplation to place it, than it could possibly be made, were it constituted an independent one. — The sum is too small upon which to organize a separate system, but, were it ten times its present amount, it is probable that even then, it would be more practically and usefully applied by the men who have gone forth under the impulse of their own humanity, and in the strength of their own means, than it would be by mere undertakers.[57]

The editorial comment thus surmises that the American government officers held a view very similar to that which would lead European colonial administrators in Asia and Africa to subsidize missionary, educational, medical, and other philanthropic work rather than undertake it directly. It was a cheap way to secure expert workers because their salaries would be provided by the missions, and these persons would bring to their task a quality of devotion and zeal which would seldom be characteristic of government employees.

The fund, small as it appears by today's standards, proved to be a tremendous stimulus to missionary efforts. Never before had so much been undertaken for the Indians in so short a period. The act was just about to be passed when two young Princeton

College students, Epaphras Chapman and Job P. Vinal, stopped in Washington on their way to the trans-Mississippi country to scout for a location for a United Foreign Missionary Society mission station. They were overwhelmed with attention, kindness, advice, and aid by officers of the government from the President himself down to minor officials.[58] The society jumped at the offer of assistance to their proposed program. When the act had been passed and the circular issued, the society gave approval and proceeded to ask for the government's cooperation.[59] The Board adopted its own policy statement to implement the intention of the act as well as its own aims and goals. This was an expansion of what was already being done at the American Board's Brainerd Station among the Cherokees, and it established what would now for some period be the accepted pattern.

> The Board have declared it to be their object to promote amongst the Indians not only the knowledge of Christianity, but also of the arts of civilized life. Besides the branches of learning taught in common schools, the boys will be instructed in agriculture, and the mechanic arts, — and the girls in spinning, weaving, sewing, knitting, and household business. They have also resolved that in every establishment there shall be a superintendent and an assistant, who shall be Ministers of the Gospel, a schoolmaster, a farmer, a blacksmith, a carpenter and such other mechanics as shall be found necessary, all of whom come under the general denomination of *Missionary*. This number may be increased as occasion shall require, and at every station there shall be a Physician, by profession; or a person acquainted with the practice of physic.

> They determine also, that in no case should any be taken into this service who should not have a character well established for discretion and piety . . . and that the whole mission family should be governed by the same rules, and, excepting in cases of sickness, should eat at the same table.[60]

Meanwhile, Chapman and Vinal had gone their way by a long route which included a visit to Brainerd with the help of the War Department and the United States Army. They were first commended to Colonel Meigs, the United States agent to the Cherokee nation and Governor of Tennessee, and he in turn commended them to Governor Clarke of Missouri and Major Lewis, agent to the Arkansas Cherokees.[61] Lewis sent with them on their expedition at government expense Capt. John Brown and the government interpreter, Capt. John Miller. This resulted in the selection of the site known as Union.[62] Major Lewis arranged the "talks" with the Indians which resulted in their agreement. Within a few months Colonel McKenney, Superintendent of Indian Trade, informed the society that the chief, counselor, and principal warrior of the Great Osages had come to Washington and were asking for the same treatment given their brethren on the Arkansas River. The society sent the Rev. Dr. Milledoler as their commissioner to confer with the Indians at Washington. It was agreed to send a missionary family to them the following spring. A "family" of 10 men, 15 women, and 16 children was sent to open Harmony station.[63] The society and other missions were soon to learn, however, that the Plains Indians were migratory unlike the eastern Indians, and that within a few years the great majority of a tribe might be located quite some distance from a station which originally appeared to be at the center of their concentration.

Meanwhile a delegation of the Baptist General Convention also called on the President and Secretary of War and came away very happy with an annual grant for their school at Great Crossing, Ky.[64]

The Rev. Cyrus Kingsbury, having established Brainerd and left it to other missionaries, moved on to the Choctaws. He was a man of great vision and tremendous initiative. When General Andrew Jackson and Thomas Hinds, as Commissioners of the United States, were making a treaty with that tribe, Kings-

bury presented to them a plan calling for the establishment of
4 large schools and 32 small ones.[65] One large school and eight
small ones were to be located west of the Mississippi and the
majority east of the River. One large and five small schools were
to be established each year until the number was complete. The
capital investment required for each large school would amount
to $15,000, and $2,000 for each small one. Annual support
would require $5,000 and $1,000 respectively. The large schools
would accommodate 80 to 100 scholars and each small one
20 to 40. The government fund would have to be greatly enlarged if school systems of such magnitude were to be supported
by it. The appropriation was not increased, but Kingsbury continued to build up his school system as rapidly as the American
Board could provide resources and the War Department give
aid. It is evident that the missionary had the approval and co-
operation of the Choctaws because their tribal council assigned
from their government annuity the sum of $2,000 per year for
17 years.

The Secretary of War, J. C. Calhoun, reported to Congress
in 1820 that great strides forward in civilization had been taken
by Cherokees, Choctaws, Wyandots, Senecas, and Shawnees.[66]
The government now amended its regulations to provide for
two thirds the cost of buildings, requiring missions or other
sources to find the other third, and that remained the rule
henceforth.[67] During 1820—21 grants totaling $16,605.80 went
to the Baptist schools at Great Crossings and Valley Towns
(Cherokee); to the Moravians at Springplace; to the United
Foreign Missionary Society for the Osage Schools; to the Amer-
ican Board for the Brainerd and Eliot schools; for tuition of
Indian lads at Cornwall, Conn.; to the New York Missionary
Society for Seneca and Tuscarora schools; to McCoy's Baptist
Mission School at Fort Wayne; to the Presbyterian Synod of
South Carolina and Georgia for a Chicasaw school; and to the
Hamilton Baptist Missionary Society for the Oneida school.[68]

None of these denominational agencies saw anything amiss in accepting government aid and in reporting annually to the government.

This new program for the Indians was given considerable impetus soon after its inception by a report on the state of the Indians made by the Rev. Jedediah Morse.[69] He had undertaken a commission from the Northern Missionary Society in the State of New York and the Society in Scotland for the Propagating of Christian Knowledge to make a tour of investigation. He offered his services to the government also; he was accepted, and the expenses of his trip were paid out of the civilization fund. The Secretary of War commissioned him to collect the fullest information and to make recommendations calculated to ensure peace and contribute to the moral advancement of the Indians.

Morse made an extensive tour among the northern Indians but did not make the expected investigation in the South. However, he gathered information about the tribes all the way to the Pacific coast. This report to the Secretary of War, when printed, ran to 400 pages. Dr. Morse urged that "every movement of civil, military, commercial, and religious classes of the country, in reference to the improvement of the condition of the Indians, should be in unison and harmony; that there should be no interference, or collision, the one with the other." He favored intermarriage *after* the Indians had been educated. "They would then be literally of one blood with us, be merged in the nation, and saved from extinction." He proposed establishment of a "Society for Promoting the General Welfare of the Indians within the United States," and such a society was organized in Washington.[70] He also suggested the founding of an Indian college, and thought that the Foreign Mission School at Cornwall, Conn., might be raised to that status. He commended the object of the civilization fund, and recommended that the plan of the American Board with its education families be substantially followed. Morse believed that the only practical course for the small tribes and remnants was removal and consolidation on prepared land, not wilderness, where they could be educated together. He recommended the establishment of one or more new education families at 19 places or tribes and that these be joined with military posts — a highly dubious suggestion. Morse concluded with the observation that it was "animating in no common degree, that the rulers and law-givers of our favored nation lead in this godlike work." The report greatly encouraged both the national administration and the churches.

There was some opposition at an early date in Congress to continuation of the program, and in January 1824 a resolution of the House of Representatives called for investigation of the expediency of repealing the act of 1819. The committee reported that the measures presently taken were judicious and best calculated to effect the design of the government.[71] The denominations would have done little without financial aid from the government. Missionaries alone accomplished little, but missionaries and schools together brought success. However much the denominations might differ in doctrine and practice, they were one in their wishes for the civilization of the Indians. There was no sectarian motivation in this. Therefore, it was inexpedient to repeal the act.

The American Board memorialized Congress at this time, apparently in order to influence the action, applying for pecuniary aid in the civilization of the Indians.[72] It was argued that "The Indians must be . . . progressively civilized, or successively perish." The only valid objection which anyone had raised was that it would destroy the valuable fur trade. However, the settlement of the country was ruining the fur trade anyway. A very small profit on the lands purchased from the Indians by the government would be enough to support all expenses. The memorial asked the colonizing of the Indians on well-selected lands, the planting of education families among them, and the endowing of a college, since ultimately the Indians would have to be taught and converted by their own people. Let Congress give the means to extend the work. Actually this memorial was principally a statement of Jedediah Morse's ideas, and he was one of the drafters of it.

At this time 21 schools were being supported from the fund.[73] They included American Board 6, Baptist 5, United Foreign Missionary Society 4, Methodists 1, Moravians 1, Presbyterians 1, Cumberland Missionary Society 1, and Roman Catholic 1. Two years later, in 1826, the number of schools had increased to 38.[74] The Protestant Episcopal Church, the Western Missionary Society (Presbyterian), and the Society for the Propagation of the Gospel among the Indians had joined the list of missions. These schools had a total of 281 teachers, 1,159 scholars, and received $13,550 from the government.[75] The Indians themselves were contributing well, and mission giving was considerable. The Indian Department made the following report for 1824—25, showing the amount paid to missionaries by the government and the amount received by missionaries in money, stock, etc., for support of Indian schools:[76]

	1824	1825
From the government	$ 12,708.48	$ 13,620.41
From Indian annuities	8,750.00	11,750.00
From private contributions (money, stocks, houses, etc.)	170,606.00	176,700.44
	$192,064.48	$202,070.85

The great success was in the South among those Indians who were coming to be known as the Five Civilized Tribes, that is, the Cherokees, Choctaws, Chickasaws, Creeks, and Seminoles. The first two were the prize exhibit. They established their own republican government, set up an extensive school system, and made rapid strides in literacy and in agriculture.[77] Conversions were numerous, and the nations were becoming Christian. Not all was uninterrupted progress and harmony, however. The

Creeks ousted the missionaries and asked for a secular school. The mission literature of the time blames hostile government agents for having turned the Indians against the missionaries.[78] The countercharges against missionaries were given in a report of a territorial superintendent. He insisted that missionaries must be capable or kept at home since the Indians were too intelligent to tolerate inferior men. Most missionaries, this critic said, were "without talent, industry, energy, or the proper spirit," and that their "inactive, dronish" habits set a bad example for the Indians.[79] Until the forced removal of the Five Civilized Tribes to Arkansas, the reports were glowing year after year. It was quite a different tale, however, in those areas where the Indians were rapidly dying out or being uprooted and moved again and again. Also among the Indians in the Great Plains it was a very different matter. There the nomadic life completely baffled the missionaries. The mission family would settle near the apparent chief town of a tribe, build schools, and lay out a farm, only to find that the Indians had moved far away.

The churches and missions were most grateful for the assistance which the government rendered, and praised such disinterested and enlightened action. The *Missionary Herald,* for example, declared this generosity to be due to divine influence and acknowledged the encouragement which it gave to workers among the Indians and to Christians in general.[80] Methodist Bishop McKendree noted with approval the aid given by the government and the consequent opportunity provided the church. He stated that educational matters are "perfectly compatible with the duties of missionaries." [81]

If the churches had any qualms of conscience about so intimate a relationship between church and state, one would expect to find the expression of such sentiments most evident among the Baptists. However, no other denomination except the Methodists was so ready throughout the 19th century to rely principally on government support of Indian mission work and do relatively little to get adequate money from the churches.[82] The zealous advocates of the Indian missions constantly fumed about their brethren's being enamored with Karens and Hindus and sending vast sums overseas while they steadily ignored their red brethren at home. The Baptists drew heavily on the civilization fund from the beginning. In fact that great missionary, Isaac McCoy, in 1828 was plainly disgusted with his denomination's lethargy in raising funds and its reluctance to make a public appeal. He said that in the meeting of the board in 1828 "a pretty plain hint was given . . . that Indian stations should be amply supported by the Government." [83]

McCoy's involvement in government affairs was heavy and is illustrative of the extent of the partnership between the church and government. Governor Cass was the chief patron of Isaac McCoy's Carey Mission for the Pottawatomies near Niles, Mich.[84] He provided supplies, used McCoy as subagent in many affairs, and made him head of the commission which went to Kansas to select a site when the Pottawatomies were removed. McCoy served the government as its representative at many treaty councils, and he was joint head with an army officer of an expedition to explore western lands authorized by Congress in December 1827.[85]

The more trouble he experienced in getting money from the mission board the more highly McCoy thought of the government. As soon as he heard of the civilization fund, he applied for assistance, and got it.[86] When he took eight boys to school in the East, the Board refused support, but the fund provided $100 per year.[87] The states of Ohio and Indiana gave him hogs and cattle for his missions.[88] President Andrew Jackson wanted to appoint him superintendent of the civilization fund, but he declined.[89] When first offered a post as government teacher, he refused but later accepted. It was understood that he was holding two distinct jobs simultaneously.[90] On the one hand he was a government teacher responsible to the government, and on the other, superintendent of the Baptist mission, responsible to the mission board. McCoy says that in this arrangement there was no time lost from mission work because the duties were the same. He and apparently some other teacher colleagues received a salary of $400 a year from the government, which they then turned over to the mission board. Thus the government actually paid the salaries of the missionaries, which in most of the missions was supposed to be entirely a church-support item.[91] Later the board, apparently uncomfortable about this arrangement, tried to say that McCoy was really a government employee. McCoy served the government in many matters, but he did refuse appointment as a magistrate with power to enforce the liquor laws because he thought that inconsistent with his missionary status.[92]

The only point at which there was any conflict with government in Indian affairs was in the question of removal. Throughout the first half century and more of the new nation's life there were three general divisions of the country's relations with the Indians: military, commercial, and cultural, and there were political aspects of all three. The government made some use of missions in all three, and in its acknowledged responsibility for the advancement of the Indians in civilization it relied almost entirely upon the missionary agencies of the churches. This partnership with government, involving as it did substantial financial aid, was the most potent stimulus of all to enlargement and maintenance of Indian missions. The indications are that without it Indian missions would have received scant attention from most denominations. The heavy demands made by home mission church extension throughout the vast territory from the Appalachians to the Pacific coast on the one hand, and the attractiveness of overseas missions on the other, might easily have led to complete neglect of the Indians had not the government's challenge and aid kept the mission boards attentive.

NOTES

Chapter 2

1. *American Archives,* 5th Ser., I, 902—903, 1583 — on destitution of the missionaries; William Kellaway, *The New England Company, 1649—1776,* pp. 277 ff.

2. John W. Lydekker, *The Faithful Mohawks* (New York: Macmillan, 1937), pp. 139—89.

3. E. B. O'Callaghan, ed. *Documentary History of the State of New York,* IV, 460; *American Archives,* 5th Ser., I, 903; Herbert J. Lennox, "Samuel Kirkland's Mission to the Iroquois," unpubl. Ph. D. diss. (Univ. of Chicago, 1932), pp. 92 ff.; Kellaway, p. 268.

4. Massachusetts Provincial Congress, April 4, 1775, *American Archives.* 4th Ser., I, 1347, 1349.

5. Ibid., II, 1309—10; Lennox, p. 109.

6. *American Archives,* 4th Ser., II, pp. 1884—85.

7. Ibid., III, 584, 1918.

8. Ibid., V, 772—73, an example; also VI, 762—64.

9. Ibid., III, 852—53.

10. Ibid., III, 1918.

11. Ibid., 5th Ser., I, 867—68.

12. Ibid.

13. Ibid.

14. Lennox, pp. 144—46.

15. Memorial of John Sergeant to Continental Congress, Nov. 27, 1776, *American Archives,* 5th Ser., III, 868—69; also 4th Ser., II, 1002 to 1003; 3d Ser. I, 676, 821, 822—23, 903, 986, 1221, 1235, and II, 87, 476, 1120.

16. Ibid., 4th Ser., I, 1347; II, 315—16, 937, 1049, 1483.

17. Ibid., 4th Ser., IV, 1662; 5th Ser., II, 1362, III, 1604. These two men had been Wheelock's missionaries.

18. Ibid., 4th Ser., IV, 1662.

19. Ibid., 4th Ser., V, 1663.

20. Ibid., 5th Ser., I, 902—903, 1583.

21. Ibid., 5th Ser., III, 868—69, 1583.

22. Ibid., 5th Ser., II, 125.

23. Ibid., 5th Ser., I, 1362.

24. Elma E. Gray, *Wilderness Christians, The Moravian Mission to the Delaware Indians* (Ithaca, N. Y.: Cornell Univ. Press, 1956), pp. 54—68.

25. Ibid., pp. 73—74.

26. Ibid., remainder of book.

27. *American State Papers. Documents, Legislative and Executive of the Congress of the United States,* sel. and ed. Walter Lowrie and Walter S. Franklin (Washington: Gales and Seaton, 1832—61) Class 2, II, 386.

28. Ibid., Class 2, II (17th Congress, 2d session), 372—379: a detailed account of the petition, grant, and subsequent history of the Muskingum River lands, Rev. L. D. De Schweinitz, 1822; Gray, pp. 85 to 86.

29. Ibid.; also Class 8, III, 531.

30. Ibid., Class 8, III, 714—16; Gray, pp. 269—70.

31. Jonathan Edwards, *The Works of Jonathan Edwards, A. M., with an Essay on His Genius and Writing* by Henry Rogers and a *Memoir* by Sereno E. Dwight, 2 vols., 10th ed. (London: Henry G. Bohn, 1845), I, cxliv-cxlv.

32. F. L. Weis, *The Society for the Propagation of the Gospel among the Indians and Others in North America,* p. 4; Oliver W. Elsbree, *The Rise of the Missionary Spirit in America* (Williamsport, Pa.; Williamsport Printing and Binding Co., 1928), p. 49; Kellaway, *New England Company,* pp. 194—96.

33. Weis, op. cit.; Joseph Eckley, *A Discourse Before the Society for Propagating the Gospel Among the Indians and Others in North America* (Boston: E. Lincoln, 1806), Appendix, pp. 25—36; Elsbree, pp. 49—51.

34. Kenneth G. Hamilton, *John Etwein and the Moravian Church* (Bethlehem, Pa.: Times Publ. Co., 1940), pp. 114—24; Society of the United Brethren for Propagating the Gospel among the Heathen, *Proceedings,* Sesquicentennial number, 1937, Foreword.

35. Rayner W. Kelsey, *Friends and the Indians, 1655—1917* (Philadelphia: Associated Executive Committee of Friends on Indian Affairs, 1917), p. 92.

36. *Report of the Directors of the New York Missionary Society, 1st Annual Meeting, 1797,* appended to annual sermon by John M. Mason, "Hope for the Heathen, etc." (New York: T. and J. Swords, 1797); "An Account of the Institution, Progress, and Present State of the New York Missionary Society," *New York Missionary Magazine,* I (1800), 5—15; "A Short History of the Formation and Progress of the Northern Missionary Society in the State of New York," *N. Y. Missionary Magazine,* I, No. 2, 89—109; Elsbree, pp. 51—56.

37. *Panoplist,* XI (1815), 222—224; *N. Y. Missionary Magazine,* I, No. 6, (1800), 434—435; *Connecticut Evangelical Magazine,* I (July 1800), 14; Elsbree, pp. 56—66.

38. Beginnings of the three: Tracy, Joseph et al, *History of American Missions.* American Board histories: William F. Strong, *The Story of the American Board* (Boston: Pilgrim Press, 1910); Fred F. Goodsell,

You Shall Be My Witnesses (Boston: A. B. C. F. M., 1959); Baptist: Robert G. Torbet, *Venture of Faith* (Philadelphia: Judson Press, 1955).

39. For example: *Panoplist and Missionary Herald,* XII (1816), 118 to 121.

40. *Proceedings of the Sixth Triennial Meeting of the Baptist General Convention,* 1829, p. 31.

41. *American State Papers,* Class 2/1, IV, 52—54.

42. Ibid., pp. 65—66.

43. Ibid., pp. 233—35, 322.

44. Ibid., pp. 235, 319—20.

45. Ibid., pp. 340—41.

46. Ibid., p. 341; Kelsey, p. 90.

47. Ibid., pp. 225—226, 231—232; Lennox, pp. 164—65, 167 ff.

48. Joseph D. Ibbotson, *Documentary History of Hamilton College* (Clinton, N. Y.: Hamilton College, 1922), pp. 27—31.

49. *American State Papers,* Class 2, IV, 167—70, 225; Lennox, pp. 171 ff.

50. *American State Papers,* Class 2, IV, p. 235; Lennox, p. 172. Knox: "No attempt should be made to teach the peculiar doctrines of revealed religion excepting those Indians to whom any of its mysteries have been already unfolded."

51. Begun at Hiawasee, Tenn., in 1803 with the assistance of War Dept.: Tracy, p. 66; Clifford M. Drury, *Presbyterian Panorama* (Philadelphia: Board of Christian Ed., 1952), p. 25.

52. Edmund Schwarze, *History of the Moravian Missions among the Southern Indian Tribes of the United States* (Bethlehem, Pa.: Times Pub. Co., 1923), pp. 101, 107. First annual report to government, p. 107.

53. *American State Papers,* Class 2, II, 477—78; Robert S. Walker, *Torchlights to the Cherokees, the Brainerd Mission* (New York: Macmillan, 1931), pp. 16—17.

54. Ibid., pp. 150—51.

55. Approved March 3, 1819. *The Debates and Proceedings of the Congress of the United States,* XXXIV, 15th Congress, 2d sess. (Washington: Gales and Seaton, 1855), 2527.

56. *American State Papers,* Class 2, II, 201.

57. *Quarterly Christian Spectator,* I (1820), 536.

58. United Foreign Missionary Society, *3d Annual Report, 1820,* pp. 4—5.

59. Ibid., pp. 17—18.

60. Ibid., pp. 18—19.

61. Ibid., pp. 5—6.

62. U. F. Miss. Soc., *4th Annual Report, 1821,* pp. 17—21.

63. Ibid., pp. 19—20.

64. The school was discontinued almost immediately. *General Convention of the Baptist Denomination in the United States, 7th Annual Report of the Board of Managers of,* in *Latter Day Luminary,* II, 18 (May 1821), 361. Meanwhile it received $250 annually. General Convention, *Proceedings,* 1820, pp. 290—97.

65. *American State Papers,* Class 2, II, 232—33.

66. Ibid., p. 200.

67. Ibid., p. 273.

68. Ibid., pp. 271—73.

69. Jedidiah Morse, *Report to the Secretary of War of the United States, on Indian Affairs, Comprising a Narrative of a Tour, etc.* (New Haven: G. Goodwin and Sons, and others, 1822).

70. *Quarterly Christian Spectator,* IV (1822), 167; *Missionary Herald,* XVIII (1822), p. 93.

71. *American State Papers,* Class 2, II, 457—59.

72. Ibid., pp. 446—48.

73. Ibid., pp. 457—59.

74. Ibid., pp. 674, 825.

75. Ibid., p. 825.

76. Ibid., p. 669.

77. The Choctaws were generous with their schools. They thanked the American Board for the missionaries in 1820, asked for a school, and said that they had already appropriated for it out of their government annuity $6,000 per year. Kingsbury reported in 1822 that they had given $4,000 toward a school, while the government had given $1,275 and "good people" $8,000. (*Missionary Herald,* XVI [1820], 379—380; XVIII [1822], 377.) It was reported of the Cherokees that they "are rapidly adopting the laws and manners of the whites. They appear to advance in civilization, just in proportion to their knowledge of the Gospel. It therefore becomes all, who desire the civilization of the Indians, to do what they can to send the Gospel among them." (*Missionary Herald,* XVII [1821], 73.)

78. *The Princeton Review,* X (1838), 522—23.

79. Ibid. The editor urges the mission board to investigate the charges.

80. *Missionary Herald,* XVII (1821), 5.

81. Quoted in full in Nathan Bangs, *History of Methodist Missions* (New York: Emory and Waugh, 1832), p. 40 ff. *The Methodist Magazine,* V (1822), 32, states: "Perhaps our Government has done more to encourage and support such exertions than any other under heaven, and if as Christians we do not avail ourselves of this aid, we shall be doubly culpable."

82. General Convention of the Baptist Denomination of the U.S.,

Proceedings, 1826, p. 12; *1829,* p. 31. The *Proceedings* and *Annual Reports* of the Board of Managers together form a series, and from about 1820 into the 1830s they reveal controversy over the alleged starving of American Indian missions in favor of overseas missions, and also manifest dependence upon government funds.

83. Isaac McCoy, *History of Baptist Indian Missions* (Washington: William N. Morrison, 1840), p. 335; see also pp. 115, 151, 159.

84. Ibid., pp. 90, 145—51, 232, 316; Frank Woodford, *Lewis Cass: The Last Jeffersonian* (New Brunswick, N. J.: Rutgers Univ. Press, 1950), pp. 145—46.

85. Ibid., pp. 277, 326; Woodford, p. 145.

86. Ibid., p. 56; later references, pp. 201, 218.

87. Ibid., p. 271.

88. Ibid., p. 128.

89. Ibid., p. 401.

90. Ibid., pp. 145—51.

91. Ibid., p. 153.

92. Ibid., p. 323.

The Missions
and Indian Removal

State and church made common cause in the civilizing and Christianizing of the Indians for two and a half centuries. The state gained political and sometimes even military advantage from its patronage of the Indian mission. The missionary agencies on their part were quite sure that they were contributing to the welfare of the country. Moreover, the missionaries and the directors of their societies and boards were grateful for whatever financial support the state might give, for without it the work would often have been curtailed since the church members gave rather meagerly. Conflict of opinion and interests between missionary forces and government officials was virtually unknown before the second quarter of the 19th century. That is, it did not occur on the higher levels of policy and official relationships, although missionaries and local officers sometimes had personal conflicts. Opposition to certain aspects of government Indian policy along with the championship of Indian rights by churches over against the government developed only over the question of removal. Even then vigorous opposition and intervention during the first half of the century were limited to a very few churches and mission boards. The majority went along with government policy quite wholeheartedly.

White pressure, as the frontier of settlements advanced relentlessly, forced Indians to withdraw involuntarily from their hereditary homelands. Sales manipulated by colonial and then state governments and ratified by treaties took title from them to the satisfaction of the settlers, if not of the Indians. Treaties forced after major defeats, such as the Treaty of Greenville in 1795, opened vast regions to settlement, and the majority of Indians moved out. Some reserved lands were left to remnants of tribes. A precedent was set when the Commissioners of the United Colonies assigned some land to the survivors of the massacred Pequots. New York left portions of its land to the several nations of the Iroquois. However, the land-hungry settlers wanted these holdings, and they meant to have them. The very proximity of white settlement brought rapid disintegration to Indian culture. Large-scale removal was an inevitable, popular demand. An early precedent for attempting to solve the white-Indian tensions and to save the Indian from the bad influence of white neighbors by removal was actually made on the initiative of two groups of Christian Indians themselves rather than by government. However, behind this action, as in all later cases of removal, the ultimate cause was the voracious appetite of the white man for the Indian lands.

The first removals took place immediately after the Revolutionary War. In fact the war had interrupted the first of these. Those Indians, mostly Mohegans, who were the pioneers in the removal experiment were under the pastoral care and influence of Samson Occum.[1] They formed communities in the Connecticut and Long Island towns of Charlestown, Groton, Stonington, Niantic, Farmington, Mohegan, and Montauk. It was thought that the welfare of all would be well served by their consolidation, removal from baneful white influence, and settlement on ample farmlands under their own government in some remote place. Central New York appeared a favorable location. Moreover, it was thought that there within the country of the Six Nations they could exert a powerful evangelistic influence among the Iroquois. Joseph Fowler, who had been a missionary in the region, was the chief agent of the Connecticut and Long Island Indians in carrying through the scheme. The proposal was set forth in 1773. Joseph Johnson, son-in-law of Occum, and Elijah Wampy journeyed to the Oneidas as ambassadors of the seven communities.[2] Thus they made their approach to a tribe largely Christianized. Sir William Johnson gave his approval to the plan. The Oneidas were friendly and agreed to cooperate. They first proposed a tract of 10 square miles, and then in a later council held with a second delegation increased the size of the tract. They adopted the Christians as brethren of the Oneida nation. Samuel Kirkland also assisted the enterprise. The Oneidas' gift to the Mohegans and Montauks was embodied in a deed executed by Sir Guy Johnson, the new Superintendent of Indian Affairs, on Oct. 4, 1774.[3] The new settlement was named Brothertown.

A small number of the Connecticut Indians had already migrated before the beginning of the Revolution, but on the outbreak of war they withdrew to Stockbridge and remained there for the duration.[4] Joseph Johnson kept writing letters to the Governors of New York and Connecticut asking for passports, letters of safe conduct, and travel expense money for his people. Further migration was necessarily postponed until the end of the war. Then in 1784 Occum himself led the first party.[5] Soon the remainder were settled at Brothertown as neighbors and brothers of the Oneidas. When the Oneidas, by the Treaty of Fort Schuyler, ceded their lands to the state of New York, the Brothertown and New Stockbridge tracts were reserved. The deed had been executed by Col. Guy Johnson in 1774, and Occum, wise in the ways of the white men, fortunately had had it recorded. The General Assembly of New York recognized it and in 1789 ordered the Surveyor General to lay out the tract according to the deed.[6] There were some difficulties later, but the General Assembly settled these matters satisfactorily by an act of March 31, 1795.[7]

The Stockbridge Indians should have been in a stronger position than the Mohegan and Montauk remnants, but the war had inflicted extremely deleterious effects on that tribe. Moreover, the Housatonic valley had been settled. Pressures were intense. Some Stockbridges had accompanied the Occum party to Brothertown in 1783. They had conferred with the Oneidas about such a move. Once again the Oneidas were very generous. They adopted also the Stockbridges as brothers and gave them a tract of land adjoining that of Occum's people.[8] The whole of the Stockbridge nation moved from the Housatonic valley to New Stockbridge by stages between 1785 and 1788. John Sergeant, the second of the name, was long in moving his family there, and Occum meanwhile served as pastor.[9]

Neither New Stockbridge nor Brothertown proved to be the hopefully expected refuge where, left to themselves, the members of the Indian Christian community might gain numerical strength in agricultural self-sufficiency. Their Christian unity and solidarity were broken by the incursion of Baptist and Methodist lay preachers. White persons who wanted their land tricked them. There was thievery in both directions and a multitude of mutual irritations between neighbors of the two races. The conditions from which the Indians had sought to escape had entrapped them again. When Dr. Jedidiah Morse visited them in 1820, he advised them to accede to the newly announced government policy and remove still farther to the country west of the Great Lakes.[10] After a few years the two groups did go west, moving by several stages into Wisconsin.[11] Each move brought with it further disintegration and degeneration. Nevertheless, Christian apologists for the missions frequently continued to declare in sermons that, whereas the other New England Indians had all been destroyed, Christianity had preserved the Stockbridges. This was thought to be a strong argument for conducting and supporting Indian missions.

The tide of white settlement flowed relentlessly westward,

driving the eastern Indians back upon those of the hinterland. The campaigns of the Revolutionary War and of the Ohio frontier, ending with Anthony Wayne's victory at Fallen Timbers in 1794, accelerated the movement. Sometimes the interior tribes made way for the newcomers, or the newcomers themselves retired in the face of the advance and fell back upon those beyond the Mississippi. Sometimes there was resistance, and the conflict added to the attrition. The Treaty of Greenville of 1795 confirmed to the United States the cession of the southern and eastern two thirds of the present state of Ohio. The Indians were supposed to be left undisturbed in possession of the land north and west of the treaty line. Far east of the line pockets remained, holding remnants of the old tribes and the large communities of the Iroquois in New York. They were in almost every instance guaranteed possession of their lands by treaties with the colonies, states, and federal government. Yet everywhere white men used every possible stratagem to get that land. Debauchment, trickery, and corruption of the chiefs were incessantly practiced by private citizens. Even the government, being of the people, resorted to all kinds of pressures, cajolery, and attractive promises to induce the tribes to make one cession after another. Any Indian who got title to land of his own had scarcely any chance of keeping it. The population was dwindling, and the Indian seemed as doomed as his ownership of the land.

The mission boards and societies, seeing what was happening, believed that they were engaged in a nose-to-nose race with time to effect the salvation of the Indians. There was tremendous urgency. The United Foreign Missionary Society in its annual report of 1826 declared:

> The Indian is fast sinking into the shades of night. No ordinary effort will snatch these perishing immortals from eternal death. The tide of civilization and avarice is driving them from the home of their fathers. Loud is their call for a resting place, where the Gospel of peace may

surely find them, and where their bones may rest in quiet-
ness. They raise the supplicating eye and stretch forth
the imploring hand to the Great Father, but while they
stretch and while they supplicate, Time, with his strong
right hand, hurries them into the shades of darkness, —
and with his left, directs the invading white to judgment's bar.[12]

In the case of this society the sense of urgency had led to a decision to get the missionary out of a central station to which the
Indian would not come from a distance and to follow him and
live with him. In the case of most agencies, however, it created
a readiness to fall in with an emerging government desire to
concentrate the Indians beyond the Mississippi.

One after another the tribes and remnants lost their lands
and joined the westward trek or remained virtually as beggars
until they disappeared into oblivion. The Greenville Treaty line
was soon obsolete and afforded no protection. Neither did the
celebrated Article IX of the Treaty of Ghent. It had guaranteed
to the Indian allies of Great Britain the possession of their territories as of their status in 1811. President Monroe's administration, hailed by the churches as enlightened, benevolent, and
Christian in seeking to preserve the Indians from destruction by
civilizing them through mission schools, was also distinguished
by establishing the firm policy of removing all the Indians in the
east to the country west of the Mississippi River. Monroe sent
a special message to the Senate on Jan. 27, 1825.[13] The government set out to destroy with its left hand all that it had sought
to achieve with the right. Nearly every school set up in the earlier
years of the one program was destroyed by the other. The cause
of civilization, so loudly acclaimed, was retarded by removal.

The Treaty of Fort Meigs, made in 1817 by Lewis Cass and
Duncan McArthur with seven or eight tribes, extinguished all but
very small claims in Ohio, Indiana, and Michigan. The remnants
left in those areas and all the way east into New York were placed

in an untenable position. The Friends, working among the Iroquois in western New York, found those people so restless that
the work was disrupted, and many were actually going west.[14]
The Brothertown and Stockbridge peoples moved west of Lake
Erie just in time to have to move again to Wisconsin. The remnants south and west of Lake Erie after the treaty of 1817 were
speedily eradicated, the Wyandots alone putting up serious resistance to removal. Consequently the Methodist Mission to the
Wyandots at Upper Sandusky and the new Baptist Carey Mission
at Niles, Mich., were about the first to feel the pressure of President Monroe's removal policy. James B. Finley at the former [15]
and Isaac McCoy at the latter [16] took opposite views of the matter.

From 1817 onward the Wyandots were put under pressure
to move, and this force was intensified in 1824. Missionary Finley reported that the plan projected in that year for transferring
them west of the Mississippi River was "a source of great uneasi-
ness and perplexity, both to the missionaries and the natives." [17]
He wrote:

> After years of toil and suffering, we had succeeded in gath-
> ering a few lambs into the fold of the heavenly Shepherd,
> and how could we bear to see them scattered abroad again?
> If they should be suffered to remain on their reservations,
> and receive proper treatment from the white population,
> we did not entertain a doubt but that ultimately they would
> become completely civilized and Christianized. But their
> removal to distant regions must greatly peril, if it did not
> utterly destroy that hope.

The tribe thereupon sent a letter to the War Department opposing their removal. They said they were happy in Ohio and
pointedly recalled past promises.[18] They declared that they were
"making progress in religion, and in the cultivation of their
lands." They received in reply a letter in the name of the President, accompanied by "a little book" which he was sending them
and which the missionary was to read to them.[19] The President

expected them to find a great deal of reason in the book, and apparently its intention was to persuade them to remove. Nevertheless the letter affirmed that they would never be compelled to give up their homes. This quieted their fears.

Finley made a journey to the east at this time to attend the Methodist General Conference. He went by way of Washington and called on the President and on Calhoun, the Secretary of War, requesting financial aid for the mission. Support for the maintenance of pupils was promised, and a capital grant amounting to $1,333 was given for buildings. Calhoun approved applying it to the church building.[20]

Despite the recent promise, it was only a few months until the question was again raised. The missionary prepared for the Wyandots a document describing their condition and giving reasons why they should not be moved.[21] He argued that the Wyandots' progress in civilization was sufficient reason why they should not be disturbed. He said: "Their present prospect of civilization is very promising; and little doubt can be entertained but, in a short time, these people will be well prepared to be admitted as citizens of the state of Ohio; and to remove them just at this time, contrary to their wishes, would be . . . a most cruel act. It would be undoing what has been done, and throw them again into a savage state." His other arguments were: this was their land, they have been faithful to the United States since the Treaty of Greenville, the Wyandots are more merciful than other Indians, and the government has promised that they would never be moved. "Such strongly plighted faith ought to be most sacredly observed."

There is a letter from Bishop Joshua Soule in the *Methodist Magazine* which corroborates Finley's testimony about the condition of the Wyandots, stating: "It is delightful to notice their manifest inclination to the habits of domestic and social life. . . . Those of the Indians who have embraced the Protestant religion, are generally, if not unanimously, in favor of cultivating

the soil, and of acquiring and possessing property on the principles of civilization."²² The bishop accepts all this as the fruit
of the joint enterprise of the mission and the government in the
program combining civilization and evangelization.

It was Finley's conviction that talk of moving the Indian
to his own land where he would forever be free from encroachment by white men was a flimsy pretext meant to disguise greed
and injustice. The march of the white population would never
cease. If the good of the red man were really desired, he would
be left undisturbed and given protection of the law.²³ Therefore
the missionary used his influence and openly avowed it to prevent the Indians from selling their land and from agreeing to
migrate. He tried to persuade both his brethren in the Methodist Church and government officials that untold evils would result from removal.²⁴

Finley was transferred from the Indian work in 1826. Much
later he reported that after the Wyandots had been removed their
promised western permanent home proved to be only a transient
resting place. He exclaimed: "Thanks be to God, no greedy spec-
ulator can dispossess the poor converted Indian of his vested
rights in 'the better country.' There many of my dear flock were
long since gathered, and there I hope to meet them again."²⁵
It was not until 1843 that the last of the Upper Sandusky Wyandots were compelled to move to Kansas, and then a hundred of
them died within the first year.²⁶

Nathan Bangs was another Methodist who seconded Finley's
views on removal. He pointed out that it overcast the future of
the Indian missions and caused the converts to lose their faith.²⁷
Bishop Soule earnestly tried to promote the cause. Finley never
succeeded in getting much support from the Methodist Church.
A great obstacle to the work was that, unlike other departments
of the church's mission, the Indian missions were left to local
Methodist conference initiative and superintendence while the
national Missionary Society merely received reports and made

grants to the conferences. The conferences were much more responsive to popular sentiment than a national board would be, and run-of-mine Methodists were too much identified with the frontier aims and attitudes to champion the cause of the Indian. The two Methodist missionaries among the Cherokees at the time of removal took a strong stand on behalf of their people and were jailed, having refused to swear the oath of allegiance to Georgia. The Tennessee Conference abandoned its missionaries and publicly chastised them with two resolutions:

> *Resolved,* That whatever may be our private views and sentiments, as men and free citizens, relative to the sufferings and privations either of the aboriginal nations of our country . . . or of the policy adopted and pursued by the State authorities or the General Government, yet, as a body of Christian Ministers, we do not feel at liberty, nor are we disposed, to depart from the principles uniformily maintained by the members and ministers of our Church in carefully refraining from all such interference with political affairs.

> *Resolved,* That however much we may appreciate the purity of motive and intention by which our missionary brethren were actuated, yet we regret that they should have committed themselves and us so far as to render it impossible for us to omit with propriety to notice their proceedings in this public manner.[28]

A few Methodists, including Finley and Soule, might harangue the churchmen about their duty to the Indians, but the Methodist Church at large ignored both the mission and the question of rights. James Wadsworth even claimed that Indian missions were a waste of time and money. He also recommended that the New England remnants be removed from "the mongrel state" of reservation existence and placed in a 60-square-mile tract near Green Bay, Wis., whence might be expected to come "future Homers, Miltons, and Shakespeares."

The Baptists were the most ardent removal advocates among the churches that maintained missions to the Indians. Isaac McCoy was the champion of removal, taking a position just opposite to that of Finley. The government had a powerful ally in him. McCoy was in fact a pioneer in the movement and pressed this policy upon the government. This is one reason why he was so highly regarded by Governor Lewis Cass and the War Department. Where there was conflict of claims and interests, as between the Cherokees and the State of Georgia, McCoy held that the only solution was to give the Indians a land of their own west of the Mississippi where they could exercise sovereign rule.[29] He moved his mission from Fort Wayne, Ind., because of the deleterious effects of having white neighbors. However, he moved his mission only less than a hundred miles, to Niles, Mich., where he established the Carey Mission. He was no more than settled when he decided that he would soon have to face the same situation there.[30] He wrote: "If we remain here it will be only to witness the decline and ultimate ruin of the people of our charge, for no band of Indians has ever thriven when crowded by white population." So within two years of the founding of the Carey Mission, McCoy on June 23, 1822, wrote to Governor Cass, two Congressmen, and several other government officials "on the subject of colonizing the Indians in the West" and requested that they present a memorial to Congress.[31] Taking the view that such colonization should begin with Christian Indians, the missionary also wrote to the board of managers of the Baptist General Convention, urging the adoption of such a policy and dedicating himself to the cause.[32]

The missionary went to Washington to plead for this policy at the meeting of his board being held there in 1824. The members took the position that there was merit in considering and adopting it only if the Secretary of War gave his approval. So McCoy met John C. Calhoun for the first time.[33] To the missionary's great surprise "he not only approved the plan, but argued its practicability, and said that nothing was wanting to insure success, but a right feeling in Congress." McCoy then tried to get the board to present a petition to Congress but met with the argument that it would be better first to prepare the way for a successful application to that body by a campaign through the public press. He did leave Washington with an increased allowance from the education fund and a capital grant for buildings, effected by the Secretary of War. The next year the first trader with a barrel of whiskey arrived at the Carey Mission, and the pastor saw his converts engaging in "a horrid bacchanalian revel." Governor Cass offered to make McCoy a magistrate with power to enforce the liquor laws, but the missionary did not think that to be proper.[34] He was more than ever determined to promote removal. Although he began to see what losses might be caused his mission by such removal, he persisted in believing that the long-term advantages would outweigh the immediate setbacks.

McCoy's next move was the preparation of a pamphlet entitled "Remarks on Indian Reform." He induced the Mission Board to publish this and distribute it free to Congress, government officials, and the general public.[35] The board was now ready to petition Congress, made McCoy its agent to promote the cause in the West, and approached the government to give him a similar appointment.[36] He went to Washington and lobbied on behalf of his plan with President John Q. Adams, Secretary of War Barbour, and 30 members of Congress. It was arranged for him to address the House Committee on Indian Affairs on three separate occasions.[37] The missionary discovered that he had allies with very mixed motives and that many were favoring removal out of greed for the Indian lands. There was much indifference, and many were not interested in Indians because they considered them to be a doomed race. Others thought his scheme impractical because they believed the western plains to be uninhabitable even by Indians. The opposition was principally of two kinds.

Some politicians did not want to see the plains filled with Indians but rather settled by northerners who would vote against the interests of the South. On the other hand there were idealists, like Jeremiah Evarts and the American Board people, who were contending on behalf of Indian rights.[38] He expressed the opinion that such opponents "deserved more credit for the piety of their hearts than for the information of their heads." They probably had a similar opinion of Mr. McCoy.

The efforts to remove the Cherokees and other southern tribes suddenly made removal a national issue of prime importance. McCoy took the stand that Georgia was simply wanting the same rights within her borders that other states possessed. He blamed the government for having granted the same land both to Georgia and the Cherokees. But he dismissed the Cherokee claims and rights by the simple assertion that to have admitted them and to have recognized a nation within the nation would create chaos and ruin the United States.[39] The missionary was then able to satisfy himself with a very simple explanation of all opposition. All of it was "political" — it came from the party out of power.[40] He regretted the controversy but thought it helpful in finally awakening the country's interest in the fate of the Indians.[41] Partisan as he was, McCoy nevertheless had the courage to denounce the brutality and injustice perpetrated by Georgia in the removal of the Cherokees.

In the removal program the government made use of McCoy very practically. He was put in charge of a party to explore Missouri lands in 1828, and twice subsequently the government committed to him the surveying of western lands for tribes which were to be removed.[42] McCoy believed that his written and verbal reports had considerable influence in the shaping of Andrew Jackson's Indian Removal Bill, which was enacted into law on May 28, 1830.[43] Apparently the President thought McCoy should be rewarded for his services and offered to put him in charge of the Education Fund.[44] He refused. Being short of money the missionary did however at that time accept appointment to survey land for the Delawares.[45] McCoy was on a number of occasions bailed out of his financial difficulties by employment as explorer or surveyor for the government. Moreover, he received liberal indemnity for the Carey Mission when the Indians moved, for the sum of $5,700 was agreed to be paid for property in which the government itself had made a considerable investment.[46] Then in 1838 the government made McCoy and the acting superintendent of Indian Affairs, an Army officer, commissioners to hold a council with the Choctaws and make arrangements for the organization of an Indian territory.[47]

McCoy's persistence and his success in winning the approval of high government officials influenced the Triennial General Convention to present a memorial for a removal policy to Congress. Authorized in 1828, it was presented to Congress in November 1829 by Wilson Lumpkin, the Governor of Georgia![48] The policy of relocation was adopted, and McCoy and another missionary, J. Lykins, were sent as agents to Missouri and Arkansas to investigate possible locations. They were authorized to accept any government appointments and assistance offered them.[49] The convention thus officially endorsed the McCoy plan. But there was a division of opinion among the members of the board of managers. The majority of the Baptist constituency was on or close to the frontier, and many Baptists were among those who wanted Indian lands. The greatest influence lay with the few who lived near Boston and were able to attend meetings of the board. The office was near the headquarters of the American Board of Commissioners for Foreign Missions, and the members of the Baptist Board had secretaries and members of the Prudential Committee of that agency as neighbors. McCoy thought those persons, "though they acted with dignified independence, were not a little influenced by" the leaders of that predominantly Congregationalist-Presbyterian organ with their impractical and idealistic philanthropic views.[50] He vigorously combated that influence by enlisting his partisan supporters in barraging the more distant members, who better represented the constituency, with a flood of correspondence. These persons then in turn put pressure on the members who acted in the meetings and thus "produced decisions in accordance with what were supposed to be the views of a large majority." [51]

The convention and the board of managers continued to adhere to the removal policy. When Compere, their missionary to the Creeks, made clear his sympathy for the Indians in the face of forced removal, he offended his Baptist brethren in Georgia. Thereupon the board reprimanded him because he had created embarrassment for the denomination. Moreover, he had "deviated from the path of strict prudence, for missionaries can scarcely have too little to do with the politics of the world."[52] Yet this same missionary organization had countenanced, even ordered, McCoy's lobbying for the removal act, and they had authorized him to accept government appointment and assistance. The board itself had directly lobbied in printing and distributing McCoy's pamphlet. It carried on its missions with government assistance. Besides memorializing Congress it expressed its joy in 1834 in the "wise and benevolent arrangements of the United States," since removal had already achieved "the most beautiful results, and . . . the blessings of salvation . . . and the civilized life are destined soon to wipe away the tears of this long-neglected race." [53] It is incomprehensible in the light of this record how the convention could disavow the political involvements and in 1842 even declare that McCoy had been only a "nominal" missionary whose entire salary had been provided by the government since 1831.[54]

Within a few years the convention was painfully aware of the sad results of the removal program. These included the destruction of mission stations, the grave loss of members, general deterioration of the Indian Christians, and the consequent reduction of government appropriations for missions. The tenth trien-

nial convention in 1841 regretted the decrease in the number of
Baptist missionaries and yet refused to face the facts, stating:

> We rejoice that the descendants of the native lords of the
> soil, after being driven by the influence of the white man
> of a foreign clime, from river to river, from forest to
> forest, over mountains and valleys, have at last found
> a settled home in the regions of the far west, where they
> have a country guaranteed to them by the faith of the
> nation. . . . Here, by the fostering care of the government,
> and the holy influence of religious institutions, they are
> acquiring those habits which are essential to their comfort
> and usefulness on earth, and to their happiness beyond the
> grave.[55]

Their missionary, McCoy, also discovered that the policy
which he had so earnestly and persistently advocated would not
produce all the results for which he had hoped. White settlers
followed the Indians and entered as squatters upon their land.
By 1837 they were endeavoring to lease lands in the Indian
Territory. McCoy vigorously opposed them and considered it
due to his efforts that the government refused to allow the
Delawares to lease their lands.[56] He had argued from the beginning that the Indians must have their own government and
had striven to get an Indian state organized. Intense opposition
was, he reported, of three kinds: the idealists who "adore" the
savage life and want it preserved, the traders who are out to
dupe the Indians, and government agents who feared the loss
of jobs.[57] He might well have added the Five Civilized Tribes,
who had their own government and who did not trust him.
The government used him as an agent in trying to organize the
territory. When McCoy wrote his *History* in 1839, he admitted
the hardships which removal had caused the Indians but, like
his mission board, still persisted in believing that the solution of
all Indian problems would be achieved in Indian Territory.[58]

The identification of the Baptists with the frontier made

them advocates of removal. Yet the identification worked against adequate support of the missions, for which McCoy strove as passionately and persistently as for removal. He and the few enthusiasts for the missions harangued the board and the convention in vain. They talked about injustice, indebtedness for wrongs done, about the soul of an Indian being of equal value with that of a Burman or Hindu, but they sadly concluded that the Indian missions did not have the dramatic appeal of the power, wealth, and large populations found in the Orient.[59] For example, when McCoy attended the triennial convention of 1829 he found that the general report on the missions contained not one word about the American Indians! He saw to it that the error was rectified.[60] Because of the lack of popular support within the denomination the board was driven to a fuller partnership with government and was prone to rely on its grants — even for salaries and buildings — to an extent which would have appeared entirely improper to Congregationalists or Presbyterians. McCoy, for example, had to rely largely on government support from the first grant for the school in 1822 and his appointment by Governor Cass as a government teacher.[61] Other missionaries were likewise appointed. Their salaries were turned over to the mission.[62] Without government aid the mission could not exist.[63] It was openly stated in the annual meeting of 1848 that "it ought to be distinctly remembered that the *pecuniary means* employed in sustaining these missions are furnished, to a considerable extent, by the U. S. Government; thus relieving our treasury from any serious pressure in this quarter. This fact is applicable, especially to four out of the five missions which we have established among the Indians." [64]

There were occasions when the board felt obliged to justify its practice with respect to the acceptance of grants from the government. The *Annual Report* for 1842 states:

> Giving its main attention everywhere to the preaching of
> the word and dissemination of the scriptures, as your Board

does, it has yet in addition sought the establishment of schools as a subsidiary means of good. In the support of these among our own Indians, it has received from time to time, grants from the U. S. government. Our principles and our interest, as a denomination, alike forbid us to become the stipendiaries of any political power. But if any work of our missionaries, which is legitimately their missionary business, be of such a kind that a government needs it and is ready to compensate it, claiming at the same time no control over such missionary beyond this specific work, it is thought that this limited cooperation does not create the right of patronage on the one side, or the sense of dependence on the other. . . . The Board has, in sustaining such schools, expended not only the amount so received, but large additional sums from its own funds.[65]

That same year the committee on appropriations asserted that in the period from 1826 to 1842 the convention had actually spent more on missions, and even on schools, than had been received from the federal government.[66] The whole sum expended on Indian missions was $131,888, of which $72,184 had been given by the government. Of this, $73,197 had been applied to schools, and of that sum the government grants amounted to $53,529. Over a period of 16 years the convention had spent $59,704 of its own money, and out of that figure $19,667 was for schools. The Baptists themselves had put into the Indian mission an average annual sum of only $3,345. The decline in the missions, especially the smaller number of school children, reduced the size of government appropriations in the following period. Nevertheless the annual reports reveal that from 1843 to 1864 the expenditure for Indian work totaled $139,750, and of that sum $69,475 was received in grants from the United States government. The financial record clearly shows the reality and magnitude of the partnership between church and state in the Indian mission of the Baptists.

Even the American Board of Commissioners for Foreign Missions had at first favored removal in theory. This was partly due to knowledge of the terrible attrition experienced by the Indians connected with the three societies which had been absorbed by the American Board. They were the New York Missionary Society, the Northern Missionary Society in the State of New York, and the United Foreign Missionary Society. But it was due still more to one of its prominent and influential members, Dr. Jedidiah Morse, renowned pastor and geographer. He had come back from his inspection of the northern Indians in 1820 a convinced advocate of removal and colonization. He recommended this plan to the Secretary of War, and his report, published as a book, popularized the idea.[67] When an effort was made in Congress early in 1824 to repeal the law authorizing the education fund, the board prepared a memorial to Congress petitioning for much more adequate financial support of the educational scheme.[68] Morse's influence resulted in incorporating into the memorial a section requesting particular attention to colonization of the Indians, collecting them on well-selected lands, one in the North and one in the South, where towns, cities, and states would gradually develop, far from white settlements and under the benign influence of missionary educational families. Morse and three other members of the board presented the memorial to Congress. Jeremiah Evarts at that time was relieved to see the movement for repeal defeated, and at the same time he reported that it appeared as if the recent actions against the Cherokees would not prevail.[69] But Georgia did succeed, and the attack on their beloved Cherokees and the others of the Five Civilized Nations shocked the American Board people into the recognition of the actual consequences of removal. The board, led by its corresponding secretary Evarts, rallied its Congregationalist-Presbyterian-Reformed constituency to a valiant struggle in defense of the rights of the Indians.

The speed and extent of the Cherokees' acculturation to the

way of life of the white population had been amazing.[70] After
the Treaty of Hopewell with the United States in 1785 the
nation had pledged peace. The people settled down to live by
an agricultural economy. When they next fought, it was in the
army of Andrew Jackson against the Creeks and the British.
Following the Louisiana Purchase, some of the tribe had accepted the invitation of President Jefferson to exchange their
land for new territory in Arkansas, and enough responded so
that a western Cherokee nation was established. However, the
nation decided against emigration in 1808. The tribe had already
lost most of its lands when the state of Tennessee was created.
This people was then confined to northwestern Georgia, where
about half the population was to be found, and the adjoining
portions of North Carolina, Tennessee, and Alabama. The state
of Georgia wanted that land. In 1802 the United States government had made a compact with Georgia by which the federal
government was to extinguish the Indian title to the lands as
soon as it might be done peaceably and on reasonable terms.
Despite the Treaty of Hopewell the federal government had then
pressed the Cherokees to accept changes in boundaries by nine
successive treaties.

Meanwhile the Cherokees made remarkable progress in
"civilization." They gave up the blood feud. Agriculture and
the domestic arts flourished. The population increased, whereas
it was rapidly decreasing among the northern Indians. In an
appeal to Congress the chiefs declared:

> The Cherokees have turned their attention to the pursuits
> of the civilized man: agriculture, manufactures, and the
> mechanic arts and education are all in successful operation
> in the nation at this time; and while the Cherokees are
> peacefully endeavoring to enjoy the blessings of civilization
> and Christianity on the soil of their rightful inheritance,
> and while the exertions and labors of various religious
> societies of these United States are successfully engaged in

promulgating to them the words or truth and life from the sacred volume of Holy Writ, and under the patronage of the General Government, they are threatened with removal or extinction.[71]

The coming of the missions had greatly accelerated progress in acculturation. The Moravians established their mission at Springplace in 1801. The American Board mission was admitted by the Cherokee Council in 1816. The Methodist and Baptist missions began about the same time. The first American Board station was Brainerd at Chickamauga in 1817. Then in rapid succession followed Carmel, Creekpath, Hightower, Willstown, Haweis, Candy's Creek, and New Echota, the Cherokee capital.[72] The Baptists and Methodists began in the Valley Towns in North Carolina.

The American Board schools and agricultural projects made the greatest cultural and economic impact. The missionaries soon turned from English to the vernacular, and this added power to the movement. They were wise enough to use the alphabet devised by Sequoia, or George Guess, and soon the larger part of the nation was literate. The mission press, which turned out the newspaper *Cherokee Phoenix* and other literature, was by a wise policy soon turned over to the nation for ownership and operation.[73] The American Board missionaries and the Moravians, however, were slow to admit converts to church membership, while the Baptists and Methodists did not require long and rigorous probation. The Methodist camp meeting had a tremendous appeal. Moreover, most white neighbors who professed to be Christians were Baptists and Methodists, and so through contacts with white neighbors there was considerable assimilation to Christianity as represented by these two denominations, which claimed most members. By the 1820s people were calling the Cherokees a Christian nation. Even the War Department in 1825 recognized that "the Christian religion is the religion of the nation."[74] The progress of the Cherokees and Choctaws was constantly held up before the public in the North and East as proof of the feasibility and expediency of the government civilization program in cooperation with the missions.[75]

The Cherokee nation took a remarkable step on July 4, 1827, when it adopted a national constitution based on that of the United States.[76] However, this inflamed the people of Georgia. In 1828 the legislature passed an act extending the laws of the state over the Cherokee territory within the bounds of Georgia.[77] The next year it incorporated the Cherokee lands into the nearby counties of the state. All Cherokee laws were declared void. Moreover, in that year Andrew Jackson was elected President, and henceforth the Indians would no longer have the protection of the President in their efforts to stand against aggression by the states. When gold was discovered at Dahlonga, the Cherokees were doomed. Andrew Jackson's Indian Removal bill passed Congress in May 1830 despite bitter opposition.[78] Like McCoy, Evarts said the issue had become a question of party politics. Although the friends of the Indians had done "all in their power to prevent the question of Indian rights being made a party question . . . the whole matter is to be settled by the simple fact, 'We have succeeded in making it a party question.' "[79] The act gave the President authority to take steps to effect an exchange of land with any of the tribes.

Meanwhile the state of Georgia was proceeding with brutality to make life so uncomfortable for the Cherokees that they would emigrate. The details of this well-known story cannot be given here except what is necessary to indicate the parts played by the missionaries and the mission boards. These were the people who were blamed by the Georgians and by Jackson's henchmen for the intransigence of the Indians. Jackson informed the Senate in February 1831 that he would not enforce the treaties with the Indians in any particulars in which they might conflict with the claims and wishes of Georgia. Then in March the Cherokee nation's suit against Georgia in the United States

Supreme Court was dismissed on the grounds of want of jurisdiction since the Cherokees were not a foreign nation. It was at
this point that the local missionaries emerged before the eyes of
the country as champions of the Indians, but the leadership of
the American Board had already been long engaged in the cause.

Evarts was a member of many philanthropic and reform
organizations, but defense of the rights of the Indians became
his greatest passion after the general promotion of Christian
missions. He was treasurer of the American Board from 1812
to 1821, secretary and treasurer from 1821 to 1825, and corresponding secretary, or chief executive officer, beginning in 1825.
As editor of the *Panoplist* and its successor, the *Missionary Herald,*
he had a wide reading public among churchmen of many denominations, but he contributed articles also to the secular press.
Tracy's *Memoir of the Life of Jeremiah Evarts, Esq.* is simply
a chronology of Evarts's career made up of extracts from his
voluminous papers. It reveals and documents the dedication of
the man to the cause of Indian rights. Being in poor health
toward the end of 1817, Evarts made a long trip to the South
to avoid the New England winter, "to gain strength by a tour
on horseback," to promote support of the work of the board
among the Presbyterians there, and to see something of the
Indians who were becoming the objects of the newest mission
of the board.[80] His continuous championship of the Cherokees
dates from that visit.

Concern and zeal for the rights of the Cherokees were
awakened in Evarts at the very first intimation in 1819 that
President Monroe's removal policy would be applied to these
Indians.[81] He called for a meeting of the Board's Prudential
Committee to discuss the matter. From that meeting of the
committee the American Board was as fully committed as its
secretary to a defense of the Cherokees and directed against all
efforts to effect their removal. The recommendation of the removal
and colonization plan included in the memorial sent to Congress

in support of the education fund was a temporary deviation due to the personal influence of Jedediah Morse and applied only to the scattered remnants of tribes in the North. Evarts' argument, presented to the committee, was that if the government really wished to protect the Cherokees it could best be done in their homeland. The tide of settlement was flowing across the Mississippi, and there the transplanted people would be hemmed in, infiltrated, and exposed to all the vices of white men. The corresponding secretary at that time, Dr. Samuel Worcester, went to Washington, joined with a delegation from the Cherokee Council, and made representations to the Secretary of War and others. The result was a new treaty recognizing the desire of the majority of the nation not to move.[82] President Monroe visited Brainerd soon after this, expressed satisfaction with the mission, and ordered its enlargement at the expense of the government. Worcester died while visiting Brainerd in 1821, and Evarts succeeded him. A second visit to the Cherokees in 1822 confirmed Evarts in his views. Two years later he made a third visit.

The American Board secretary was willing to credit the good intentions of President Monroe in seeking the removal of the Indians, and apparently he did not strongly oppose the endorsement in the memorial to Congress in 1824 secured by Morse. He did however express "many fears as to the efficacy of the measure" and gave his usual reasons for opposing removal, but said he would "rejoice if these difficulties vanish on experiment."[83] Evarts was in Washington when the first debate began in Congress on the claims of Georgia against the Cherokees and called on the President to urge justice for the Indians, but was unable to speak with the President privately. He wrote to Kingsbury that he could not make his intended visit to the Cherokees and Choctaws. In view of what was happening in Washington he felt that it would be more and more difficult for Indians to live in the old states and that it remained to be seen whether they could even find a resting place on the continent.[84] March

1828 found him again in Washington seeking from leaders in the national administration and from congressmen assurances about certain measures in the proposed bill for removal of the Indians, especially guarantees of adequate protection. He threw his influence against the measure and advised congressmen to oppose it.[85] There was no land west of the Mississippi satisfactory to the Indians, and they would be no more beyond the influence of whites and the aggression of lawless persons than they now were. By the end of December 1828 the outlook was so bad that the Prudential Committee decided he must go to Washington "to make representations respecting the rights of the Indians." He then practically took up residence in the capital.

The constituency of the American Board was flooding Washington with letters and memorials, and Evarts was to be the personal embodiment of their concern.[86] The secretary had a conference with "the General" and found President-elect Jackson extremely concerned about a conflict between state and national interests and consequently unwilling to interpose on behalf of the Cherokees. The Cherokee delegation under John Ross arrived and consulted Mr. Evarts about a petition to Congress. He suggested two changes, which they adopted. He wrote: "I have thought it to be my duty to avow myself a decided friend of the Indians, while I disclaim any authority from them to act as their agent." [87] He continued to lobby on their behalf and as the results of his interviews concluded:

> Next session there will be, I think, much and intelligent debating on this subject; and the result will be, either that Congress will do nothing, and the whites, under the protection of the Southern States, will deal with the Indians as seems right in their own eyes; or everything will be carried headlong, in all branches of the government, against the poor Indians. I have not seen a single man, of any party, who thinks that anything effectual can be done to protect our weak red men of the forest.[88]

Evarts concluded that General Jackson had come to Washington "with a settled conclusion that it would be necessary to deliver the Indians over to the States." Thereupon, in March 1829, he began to prepare a large document on the rights of the Cherokees to lay before the President and his cabinet. He decided, however, that a series of essays appearing in the public press would be more effective. So he began preparing the essays which were published under the signature of William Penn. Pressure was brought upon him to bring his board to approve removal and, as a reward, get more assistance from the government. But he declared: "I do not think we can stand acquitted before God, or posterity, unless we bear a witness against the threatened course of proceeding." [89] The exasperation of the leaders in government was made plain to him and made him aware that he and his colleagues must proceed with caution. Senator Frelinghuysen, of New Jersey, sometime president of the American Board, was his chief advisor and colleague.

It was in July that Evarts sent the first of the essays on "The Present Crisis in the Condition of the American Indians" to the *National Intelligencer.* The first appeared in print Aug. 1. The essays were widely copied by other journals, and they were reprinted in pamphlet form in several other places.[90] Tracy states that Chief Justice John Marshall declared them to be "the most conclusive argument that he ever read on any subject whatever." He described the actual condition of the Cherokees, and he marshalled in their defense all the arguments of facts, law, morality, and religion. The author was soon known and deluged with correspondence. A briefer document, *A Brief View of the Present Relations between the Government and People of the United States and the Indians within Our National Limits,* condensed the information and arguments of the essays. It was prepared for some persons in New York and was widely circulated. Memorials poured in upon Congress. It was not for want of support that the friends of the Indians, led by Senator Frelinghuysen, failed in

Congress to prevent the passage of the Indian Removal Bill. The outcome was predictable after a powerful figure in the capitol said: "Sir, we have succeeded in making the Indian subject a party measure. There may be some chicken-hearted fellows at the North, who will not stand by the party, but we shall carry the measure in both Houses." Evarts wrote and brought in one more memorial from the American Board to Congress before the passage of the bill. When the bill passed, he said to a congressman: "My comfort is that God governs the world; and my hope is, that when the people of the United States come to understand the subject, there will a redeeming spirit arise; for I will not believe that the nation is yet lost to truth and honor."

Evarts had not been in good health for years, and his championship of the Cherokees so exhausted him that it cost him his life. Before he died he composed two more important documents. One was the American Board's memorial to Congress in January 1831. The other was an "Address to the People of the United States, by the General Council of the Cherokee Nation." [91] The council added only the two closing paragraphs. Anson Phelps Stokes describes this as Evarts' most important single service to the Cherokee cause and says that it "will constitute for all time an appealing and authoritative statement of the Cherokee position." [92]

The American Board missionaries acted in the spirit which had animated their board and their secretary. They and the Moravian missionaries held a meeting at New Echota on Dec. 29, 1830. They published their formal resolution and statement.[93] It was signed by nine missionaries of the A. B. C. F. M., two Moravians, and one Baptist, Evan Jones. They declared that they had hitherto kept out of politics, but moral considerations now compelled them to speak out on the wrong done the Cherokees and to ask the sympathy and prayers of all benevolent Americans. Nothing but force could compel the people to remove. Implementation of Georgia's jurisdiction over them would cause irreparable harm. They gave a very convincing description of the progress the people had made. The Methodist missionaries took a similar stand and published a statement, and at least one Baptist was said to be in agreement.[94] This defiance drew from the legislature of Georgia a new law which punished by four years of imprisonment at hard labor any white person guilty of residing in the Cherokee country without having taken an oath of allegiance to Georgia.

Missionaries Worcester, Proctor, Butler, and Thompson were arrested in March 1831. They were, however released on the grounds that they were all agents of the federal government under the civilization program and that Worcester was postmaster at New Echota. Upon appeal from the Governor of Georgia, however, the government disavowed them as agents and removed Worcester as postmaster. Three American Board, one Moravian, and two Methodist missionaries were then again arrested, chained, and treated with indignities. The Methodist McLeod was released as a nonresident and the others eventually let out on bail. When put on trial before the Supreme Court of Georgia on Sept. 16, all but two took the oath and were released. Refusing to take the oath, the Rev. Samuel A. Worcester and Dr. Elizur Butler were sentenced to four years at hard labor. While the Methodists and Baptists disavowed their missionaries' defiance of Georgia, the American Board at its next meeting in November approved the conduct of its men, ordered the Prudential Committee to publish a statement of the facts about the mission, decreed a memorial be sent the President requesting the protection of the missionaries and mission property by the Executive, and called on the churches to pray for the missionaries.[95] The board also appealed the case of the missionaries to the Supreme Court of the United States. The appeal to the President was answered by a curt note from Louis Cass stating that "the President had satisfied himself that the Legislatures of the respective states have power to extend their laws over all persons living within their boundaries, and that, when thus extended, the various acts of Congress, providing a mode of proceeding in Indian intercourse, inconsistent with those laws, become inoperative, he has no authority to interfere. . . ."

The Supreme Court of the United States gave judgment in favor of the missionaries in February 1832. It was ignored by Georgia, but the Governor offered a pardon to the two men if they would meet his terms, but through the board they instituted further proceedings in the Supreme Court. Considering that the issues had been squarely presented to the nation, the Prudential Committee later counseled withdrawal of the suit. Worcester and Butler then in January 1833 informed the Governor that they were withdrawing because of their "apprehension that further prosecution of the controversy under existing circumstances, might be attended with consequences injurious to our beloved country." [96] The two men were released. It is noteworthy that although the board had brought the suit of the Cherokees also to the Supreme Court, all of their other public representations and actions in the course of the year were on behalf of the missionaries. However, it was the consensus that in defending the rights of the missionaries they were defending the rights of the Cherokees and that the cause of the missionaries and that of the Indians were inseparable. Soon after the release of the men the state of Georgia included the mission properties in the lottery for assignment of Cherokee lands. The missionaries were dispossessed and after a short period of concentration at Brainerd moved on to the western Cherokee country across the Mississippi.

The Supreme Court had in the Worcester decision concluded that the Cherokees were a nation under the protection of the United States and therefore free from the jurisdiction of Georgia. Georgia ignored the judgment. President Jackson refused to enforce it. He is supposed to have said: "John Marshall has pronounced his judgment; let him enforce it if he can." The government proceeded with the removal of the Southern tribes by the Army. It is a tale of horrors. [97]

New England in general rallied to the support of the Cherokees and the missionaries. Emerson was the spokesman for liberal humanitarianism in that region. When they realized that they had lost the fight with the national government under Jackson, the New Englanders wanted to make the most of the supposed possibilities provided by removal. The Andover *Biblical Repository* in 1835 asked that the bold experiment be not prejudged. "To take up entire nations of men, and place them several hundred miles from their former seats, with the avowed intention of gradually amalgamating them into one homogeneous mass, or of amicably preserving their national peculiarities . . . is a measure, to say the least, which ought to be watched with the closest attention." [98] It called for prohibition of liquor, extreme care in selection of government agents, protection of Indian lands against all intruders, rigorous control of the fur traders, protection of Indians against Mexicans, and finally renewed stress on Christianization and civilization. [99]

The Methodists throughout the country had little to say. Missionary McLeod's account was published, [100] but the missionaries were disavowed by the Tennesee Methodists, as we have seen. The Baptists rebuked Compere and continued to espouse removal. The Episcopalians at this time were not yet interested in Indians and kept silence. The Presbyterians divided about this time, and the New School portion continued to work with the American Board. They and the Dutch Reformed Church people made a solid front with the Congregationalists. The Presbyterian Synod of North Carolina and the Presbyteries of East Tennessee and Alabama passed resolutions commending the missionaries but said nothing about the Indians. [101] The *Princeton Review*, representing the Old School Presbyterians, however, took the government view or at least failed to oppose it. An editorial of 1838 refers to removal as "a perplexed and painful subject" and affirms that "what is past cannot be undone, nor effectually remedied." [102] The editor considered removal to be no longer a proper subject for discussion. Georgia's position was legally correct. Removal was the only course that could be followed in view of the expanding white population. The United States cannot tolerate the existence of a nation within the nation. If the Indians want to be independent, they must go outside this country. Insistence upon the federal government's restraining of Georgia would have been a violation of states' rights and would have brought on a civil war. The only constitutional power of the government is to regulate trade with the Indians. The nondenominational *Literary and Theological Review* in 1835 carried an article by the writer on Indians, Henry Schoolcraft, in which he praised the brave missionaries in Georgia and urged the churches to give attention to the Indian problem.[103]

The removal controversy focused on the Cherokees and southern tribes. The plight of the northern remnants received scant attention from the American public. But there was one dramatic incident in the North, and it brought the Friends into the public eye as champions of Indian rights. This intervention of the Quakers was to be cited by President Grant as a reason for for calling the Friends into the Indian Service when he inaugurated his "Peace Policy." This affair was the case of the Senaca lands in New York State.[104]

A certain David A. Ogden in 1810 had purchased from previous owners what was known as the "preemptive right" to the lands of the Seneca nation. This was not the legal title to any lands but rather the guarantee to the right to buy those lands whenever the Indians might decide to sell them. This man organized the Ogden Land Company in anticipation of that time. He and his associates quite naturally tried by every possible inducement to persuade the Indians to sell. The success of the government's removal policy in ridding the country east of the Mississippi River of most of the Indians except the Iroquois led the company's officers to expect that Washington would favor, if not openly assist, the eviction of the Senecas. Certain government officials did help, and the company succeeded also in corrupting some of the chiefs. They signed a treaty in 1838 agreeing to the cession of their lands in the state of New York. These chiefs were paid large sums of money. Some of those who were bought were not even chiefs, but they signed. The names of certain persons were added to the list of signatures although they had not authorized their signatures. Less than half the signatures were written on the document in open council in accord with the instructions given by the United States Senate. Worst of all, the chiefs who were the key figures in the transaction had been promised deeds to parcels of land so that they and their families would not have to move. The great majority of the Senecas were aghast when they learned what had happened. But they had no defense against the Ogden Company. When the Friends learned of the wrong that had been done the Senecas, they entered the public arena as their champions.

It was principally the Liberal Friends who waged this battle for the Senecas. The Indian Committees of the New York, Genessee, Philadelphia, and Baltimore Yearly Meetings united in this matter. President Van Buren appeared so convinced of perpetration of a fraud that when he sent the treaty to the Senate he accompanied it with a message stating that the proper conditions in gaining assent of the tribe had not been fulfilled and that there was evidence of bribery. The Friends presented a memorial to the Senate stating all the facts. Despite the evidence the vote resulted in a tie. This was broken when the Vice-President voted for ratification. The Friends made new representations to President Van Buren. He told them that there was now no ground on which he could reject the treaty since the Senate had all the facts before it and was satisfied that the land had been properly alienated to the Ogden Land Company.

There was now no further legal recourse, and so the Friends set out to bring the weight of public condemnation to bear on the company. The story of fraud and bribery was published in the daily press, in magazines, and in widely distributed pamphlets.

It was told by word of mouth. The Ogden Land Company and its political cronies were overwhelmed by a flood of protest. A demand for rectification of the wrong done came from all sides. The outcome was the holding of a conference in 1842 by the War Department, the Ogden Land Company, and the Friends. A compromise was reached. A supplemental treaty was agreed upon by which the company kept the most profitable lands near Buffalo, namely, the Tonawanda and Buffalo reservations, and turned back the Cattaraugus and Allegheny reservations to the Senecas. The Tonawandas, however, refused to leave their land and had to buy title from the company. The Senecas then took from their chiefs the power to alienate land. The land-grabbers got much of what they wanted, but the Indians did not have to stand a total loss.

It then appears that by and large it was only the Congregationalists with their associates in the American Board — the Dutch Reformed and the Presbyterians who would form "the New School" — and the Friends who emerged as champions of Indian rights and foes of removal who were willing to contend even with the federal government and state governments on behalf of the Indians. However, some of the Friends did favor removal. The Orthodox Indiana Yearly Meeting in 1838 asked for sufficient western land for the Indians, to be guaranteed to them forever. They also wanted the Indians then to be represented in Congress by a delegate.[105] The treatment of the Indians will determine God's judgment on America, they felt.

Removal proved to be exceedingly destructive of the progress of the Indians in "civilization," which both the government and the churches professed to desire and foster. It was equally destructive of their growth in the Christian faith. The Indian missions declined steadily as the midcentury approached. There were many reasons, but removal was the chief of them. There still remained a nominal partnership between the churches and the state in Indian missions. Funds were allocated from the educational fund although removal had destroyed the most promising of the schools. The Jackson and Van Buren administrations had disrupted others by drastically cutting the annual grants. Further havoc would be effected by the Civil War, but at its end the civilization program and the education fund were still in existence. A few mission schools were receiving grants. A new expanded partnership between state and church in the mission was about to begin.

NOTES

Chapter 3

1. On Occum, see William DeL. Love, *Samson Occum and the Christian Indians of New England* (Boston: Pilgrim Press, 1899); Leon B. Richardson, *An Indian Preacher in England,* (Hanover, N.H.: Dartmouth College, 1933); Harold Blodgett, *Samson Occum* (Hanover: Dartmouth College, 1935).

2. Blodgett, pp. 149—60; Love, pp. 207—23.

3. Printed in full in Love, p. 223.

4. Love, pp. 231—46; Blodgett, pp. 162—63.

5. Love, p. 247 ff.; Blodgett, Ch. 9, "The Mohegan Migration," pp. 169—99.

6. Blodgett, p. 206, cites *Laws of New York, Reprint,* III, 70.

7. Blodgett, p. 207, cites *Laws of New York,* III, 212, 585.

8. Love, pp. 243—46.

9. Blodgett, p. 192.

10. Jedidiah Morse, *Report to the Secretary of War of the United States, on Indian Affairs, Comprising a Narrative of a Tour, etc.* (New Haven: G. Goodwin & Sons, 1822), pp. 77—78.

11. Herbert J. Lennox, "Samuel Kirkland's Mission to the Iroquois" (unpubl. Ph. D. diss., Univ. of Chicago, 1932).

12. United Foreign Missionary Society, *Annual Report, 1826,* p. 54.

13. *The Addresses and Messages of the Presidents of the United States, etc., from 1789 to 1846,* compiled from official sources by Edwin Williams (New York: E. Walker, 1846), I, 536—38.

14. Rayner W. Kelsey, *Friends and the Indians, 1655—1917* (Philadelphia: Associated Executive Committee of Friends on Indian Affairs, 1917), p. 117.

15. James B. Finley, *History of the Wyandot Mission at Upper Sandusky, Ohio, under the Direction of the Methodist Episcopal Church* (Cincinnati: Wright and Swormstedt, 1840); *Life among the Indians, Personal Reminiscences* (Cincinnati: Curts and Jennings, ca. 1855); also,

Autobiography of Rev. James B. Finley, or Pioneer Life in the West (Cincinnati: Methodist Book Concern, 1855); *Sketches of Western Methodism* (Cincinnati: Methodist Book Concern, 1854).

16. Isaac McCoy, *History of Baptist Indian Missions* (Washington: William N. Morrison), 1840.

17. J. B. Finley, *Life among the Indians,* p. 442.

18. Ibid., p. 443.

19. Ibid., pp. 443—45, the text of the letter.

20. Ibid., p. 366, first application for grant from the Education Fund in 1823; ibid., pp. 243, 445—46; Finley, *History of the Wyandot Mission,* pp. 258, 274, 374—75.

21. Ibid., pp. 446—49.

22. VIII (1825), 33.

23. Finley, *Life among the Indians,* p. 45.

24. Ibid., p. 452. "I have always been opposed to the removing plan, and have honestly told my sentiments to the Indians and others. I used my influence to persuade the Indians not to sell, but remain where they were; for if they were removed to the base of the Rocky Mountains, or beyond them, the white population would follow them."

25. Ibid., p. 453.

26. Wade C. Barclay, *History of Methodist Missions,* II, 125—26.

27. Nathan Bangs, *A History of the Methodist Episcopal Church,* 4 vols. (New York: Lane and Sandford, 1841), IV, 55—61.

28. John B. M'Ferrin, *History of Methodism in Tennessee,* 3 vols. (Nashville: Southern Methodist Publishing House, 1871—74), III, 371 ff.

29. McCoy, p. 41.

30. Ibid., pp. 196—97.

31. Ibid., p. 200.

32. Ibid., p. 201.

33. Ibid., p. 217—18.

34. Ibid., pp. 232, 265, 277.

35. Ibid., pp. 321—23.

36. Ibid., p. 323.

37. Ibid.

38. Ibid., pp. 337—38.

39. Ibid., pp. 38—39, 360 ff.

40. Ibid., p. 378.

41. Ibid., p. 381.

42. Ibid., pp. 326, 343—75, 406, 413, 517.

43. Ibid., pp. 397 ff.

44. Ibid., p. 401.

45. Ibid., 401—406.

46. Ibid., pp. 376, 404.

47. Ibid., pp. 547 ff.

48. Ibid., pp. 385, 395—96; Baptist General Convention, *Proceedings of the Sixth Triennial Meeting, 1829,* pp. 16, 31—32.

49. McCoy, p. 384.

50. Ibid., pp. 360, 377.

51. Ibid., p. 378.

52. Baptist General Convention, *Proceedings of Fifth Triennial Meeting of the, 1826,* p. 13; see also p. 33.

53. Baptist General Convention, Board of Managers, *20th Annual Report, 1834,* pp. 5—6.

54. Baptist General Convention, *Minutes of Board of 1842,* p. 13.

55. Ibid., *Minutes of 10th Triennial Meeting, 1841,* p. 19.

56. McCoy, p. 519.

57. Ibid., p. 529.

58. Ibid., pp. 586—87.

59. Baptist General Convention, *Proceedings of 6th Triennial Meeting, 1829,* "Report of Indian Committee," p. 31; *1847,* p. 20; *1853,* p. 20; McCoy, p. 382.

60. McCoy, p. 382.

61. Ibid., pp. 56, 90, 201, 218; Cass's initiative, pp. 145—51.

62. Ibid., p. 153.

63. Ibid., p. 167.

64. American Baptist Missionary Union, *Annual Report, 1840,* p. 18.

65. Baptist General Convention for Foreign Missions, *Minutes of the Annual Meeting of the Board, 1842,* p. 10.

66. Ibid., p. 14.

67. See note 10.

68. *American State Papers,* Class 2, II, 466—468; American Board of Commissioners for Foreign Mission, *Annual Report,* 1823, p. 14.

69. E. C. Tracy, *Memoir of the Life of Jeremiah Evarts, Esq.* (Boston: Crocker and Brewster, 1840), p. 188.

70. Henry T. Malone, *Cherokees of the Old South, A People in Transition* (Athens, Ga.: Univ. of Georgia Press, 1958), Chs. 4—10; Marion L. Starkey, *The Cherokee Nation* (New York: Knopf, 1946), Ch. 1.

71. Helen H. Jackson, *A Century of Dishonor* (rev. ed., Boston: Little, Brown, 1903), pp. 272-73.

72. AMERICAN BOARD MISSIONS: *Annual Reports* and *Missionary Herald* for the period; Joseph Tracy, *History of American Missions;* Robert S. Walker, *Torchlights to the Cherokees, the Brainerd Mission* (New York: Macmillan, 1931); Sarah Tuttle, *Letters and Conversations on the Cherokee Mission* (Boston: Mass. S. S. Union, 1830); William

E. Strong, *Story of the American Board* (Boston: Pilgrim Press, 1910), pp. 36—47; Starkey, Chs. 2 and 4; Malone, Ch. 7. METHODIST: Wade C. Barclay, *History of Methodist Missions,* Vol. II; Malone, pp. 110—14. BAPTIST: Malone, pp. 106—10. MORAVIAN: Edmund Schwarze, *Moravian Missions among Southern Indian Tribes* (Bethlehem: Times Publishing Co.), 1923.

73. Althea Bass, *Cherokee Messenger* (Norman: Univ. of Oklahoma Press, 1936), ch. on "Cherokee Phoenix," pp. 69—89.

74. Anson Phelps Stokes, *Church and State in the United States,* 3 vols. (New York: Harper, 1950), I, 709.

75. Sermons, tracts, and missionary magazines abound in descriptions and references. See examples: *Missionary Herald,* XXVII (1830), 80—84; XXVIII (1832), 157—58; Tracy, pp. 177—78.

76. *Constitution and Laws of the Cherokee Nation* (St. Louis: R. and T. A. Ennis, 1875).

77. William C. Dawson, ed. *A Compilation of the Laws of the State of Georgia, Passed by the General Assembly since the Year 1819 to 1829, inclusive* (Milledgeville, Ga.: 1831), p. 198; for a detailed story and documents from the point of view of Georgia by its governor, later senator and U. S. Commissioner to the Cherokees, see Wilson Lumpkin, *The Removal of the Cherokee Indians from Georgia,* 2 vols. (New York: Dodd, Mead, 1907).

78. *Public Statutes at Large of the United States,* ed. Richard Peters (Boston: 1854), IV, 411.

79. Tracy, p. 355.

80. Ibid., pp. 110, 119 ff.

81. Ibid., pp. 128 ff.

82. Ibid., p. 130.

83. Ibid., p. 216.

84. Ibid., p. 300.

85. Ibid., p. 306.

86. Ibid., pp. 319—20.

87. Ibid., p. 327.

88. Ibid., p. 328.

89. Ibid., p. 239.

90. Ibid., pp. 336—49.

91. Ibid., pp. 442—48.

92. Stokes, I, 711.

93. *Missionary Herald,* XXVI (1830), 363—64.

94. Ibid., XXVII (1831), 302; see notes 28 and 53.

95. Ibid., p. 362. The course of events in 1831 is reported in this volume, pp. 79—84, 165—66, 248—54, 281—84, 299—302, 332—36, 363—65, and 395—97.

96. Ibid., XXVIII (1832), 18—22, 43—47, 116—17, 400—401; XXIX (1833), 21—22, 109—13.

97. Grant Foreman, *Indian Removal: Emigration of the Five Civilized Tribes of Indians* (Norman: Univ. of Oklahoma Press, 1953).

98. *Biblical Repository and Quarterly Observer,* V (1835), 427—29.

99. The usual prescription, but now Mexicans are added to the sources of evil.

100. D. C. McLeod, letter in *Christian Advocate and Journal, etc.,* V (Aug. 12, 1831), 198.

101. *Missionary Herald,* XXVIII (1832), 47; (1833), 21, note.

102. *Princeton Review,* X (1838), 513, 535, quotation from p. 518.

103. *The Literary and Theological Review,* II (1835), 96—121.

104. The following paragraphs are based on: [Society of Friends], *The Case of the Seneca Indians in the State of New York* (Philadelphia: Merrihew and Thompson, 1840); [Society of Friends], *Appeal to the Christian Community* (New York: 1841); and Rayner W. Kelsey, *Friends and the Indians, 1615—1917* (Philadelphia: Associated Executive Committee of Friends on Indian Affairs, 1917).

105. Indiana Yearly Meeting of Friends, *Minutes, 1838,* p. 17; also from Yearly Meeting, *Address to the People of the United States and to the Members of Congress in Particular* (Cincinnati: A. Pugh, 1838).

Protestant Missions and President Grant's "Peace Policy"

◆§ The western Indians were in constant turmoil in the years immediately after the Civil War. The cause of unrest is easy to discern. It lay chiefly in the repeated removal of the tribes, their difficulty of adjusting to reservation life, nonfulfillment of treaty obligations by the government, the corruption of the Indian Service, the westward rush of settlers with their insatiable appetite for land, and the building of railroads into the Indian country. The resistance of the Indians infuriated those white men to whose aggressive desires the red men were obstacles, while it pricked the consciences of those at a distance from the frontier who were burdened with a sense of debt to the original owners of the land. Public attention was consequently focused on the government's Indian policy with an intensity which had been lacking during the war years. While speculators, exploiters, and land-hungry farmers were demanding Indian removal or extermination, the philanthropists, having seen the abolition of slavery, were now ready to demand justice for the Indian.

The Indian Service was quite generally considered to be corrupt. It was not a humanitarian social reformer but a practical politician, General James A. Garfield, who declared in Congress that "no branch of the national government is so spotted with fraud, so tainted with corruption, so unworthy of a free and enlightened government, as this Indian department."[1] The Indian Service was thought to be completely under the control of the "Indian Ring." An editor of a religious journal asserted: "The truth is that there are three obstacles to the salvation of the Indian — Indian Rings — Western hostility — and the Indian's depravity, and the three ought to be met in the order we have named them."[2] Therefore the reformation of the Bureau of Indian Affairs at headquarters and in the field figured highly in all solutions offered for the "Indian Problem" except the drastic and inhuman one of extermination. The political origin of the corruption was taken for granted; and the notion began to be advanced that an effective antidote to such corruption might be found by the participation of the churches in Indian affairs.

GROWTH OF SENTIMENT
FOR RELIGIOUS PARTICIPATION

Congress in 1865 set up a joint committee to investigate the state of the Indian tribes and their treatment by government agencies. This committee reported in 1867. It laid stress on the decline and degeneration of the Indians, on the aggression of lawless white men as the chief source of war and disturbance, and on the disastrous effect on Indian life through the loss of game lands. It emphasized racketeering by government Indian agents, the demoralization caused by the presence of Army posts, and the need to eliminate abuses by rigorous inspection.[3] The bill by which the committee hoped to implement its proposals made provision for five permanent boards of inspection. Each of these was to be comprised of an assistant Indian Commissioner, an Army officer, and a civilian who was to be chosen from a list of persons recommended by the churches of the country. The bill failed to pass, but the idea of religious participation in Indian affairs gained currency.

The next step came through creation by Congress in 1867 of a special "Peace Commission" charged with discovering and correcting the reasons for hostilities. This body was to establish security along the new railroads and recommend territories into which the Indians might be segregated. The commission included four generals, one of them William T. Sherman. It reported in 1868.[4] The recommendations left open the vexing question whether the Indian Service should be under the Interior or War Department, depending on whether there was to be a policy of extermination or a genuine effort at civilizing the Indians. If it was to be the latter, the War Department was clearly not the proper administrator. The replacement of all superintendents and agents in the service was requested. The President should appoint inspectors reporting directly to him. The Indians should be rigorously segregated in Indian Territory. The commission chided the churches for sending so much money and so many men overseas to Asia and Africa while they neglected the Indians. The Presbyterian *Monthly Record* commended the report and urged its publication in all newspapers, but it took vigorous exception to the remark about missions as ill founded, in bad taste, and untrue.[5] The editor declared that in the period before the Rebellion the Presbyterian Church had spent relatively more on Indian work than on the overseas missions. The American Board of Commissioners for Foreign Missions had by that time spent about $1,250,000 on Indian missions.[6] However, the churches in general were at this time doing little, and the remark of the commissioners did sting the consciences of denominational officers.

Meanwhile the *Weekly Chronicle* of Washington, D. C., in an editorial on Sept. 14, 1867, had suggested that the Friends might be called upon to rescue the service from politics and corruption. The article recalled the faithful keeping of the Penn treaties, the traditional Quaker friendship with the Indians, and especially their educational work with the Senecas. Moreover, they had been effective public champions of the Senecas when wrongs were done them, and they had represented these Indians before the government. The editor suggested that if the Society of Friends could "be induced to take charge of the subject of colonizing the Indian territory, and instructing the Indians, they might prepare them for the inevitable future." [7]

The two branches of the Society of Friends, the Orthodox and the Hicksite, or Liberal, had recently doubled their efforts on behalf of the Indians. Just a few weeks after the appearance of the editorial in the *Weekly Chronicle,* and unconnected with that, the Hicksite Friends held a conference on Indian concerns in Baltimore. It was reported there that prominent statesmen in Washington were talking along the lines of the editorial. This stimulated the assembly to prepare an address to the national government expressing the readiness of the Friends to undertake without compensation such service as would benefit the Indians.[8] The Orthodox Iowa Yearly Meeting about that time appointed a Committee on Indian Concerns and invited the cooperation of other yearly meetings. This led to a Joint Committee representing the entire denomination, which called a conference in Baltimore in January 1869. A memorial was drawn up, and the entire group of delegates went to Washington on Jan. 25 and presented it to President-elect Grant. The very next day representatives of the Liberal Friends also had an interview with the General and expressed similar views. Both delegations were impressed with the President-elect's cordiality, his sympathetic concern for the Indians, and his evident desire to undertake a radically new policy.[9]

The spotlight had been turned on the Friends, but the Episcopalians had become an even more potent force for reform, and others too were exerting influence. For years the Rt. Rev. Henry B. Whipple, Bishop of Minnesota, had been haranguing the President and Congress by personal interviews, letters, and the press. After making his report at the annual meeting of the Board of Missions of his church in 1866, that body had requested a special report on the condition of the Indians. The bishop presented the desired document at the meeting of the board in October 1868. It moved the Episcopalians powerfully to concern and action.[10] Moreover, when the bishop was in New York the previous summer, Peter Cooper asked him to present this report at a meeting at Cooper Union, sponsored by the United States Peace Commission (later called the New York Indian Commission) and attended by many prominent clergy and laymen. Afterwards the General Committee of that organization drew up a memorial to both houses of Congress, using material from Whipple's address. Noting that "the good intentions of Congress towards the Indians" have been frustrated by bad agents and frontier rapacity, this association for the stimulation of public opinion made the suggestion which is probably the origin of the idea behind the establishment of the Board of Indian Commissioners. The memorial said: "To this end we believe it may be necessary to enlist the services of capable and reliable men, independent of political or party bias, who shall not be remunerated from the public treasury, and who shall have no pecuniary interest to serve them from the objects of their appointment." The inclusion of this memorial in the commissioner's report for 1869 indicates such a connection.[11] The reference in Bishop Whipple's autobiography to the Cooper Union meeting having led to "the organization of the Indian Peace Commission" may indicate that the permanent organization of the New York association dated from that event.[12] Cooper was first president, and later Dr. Howard Crosby, president of New York University.

William Welsh, an influential Episcopal layman of Philadelphia and active in mission work, was inspired by Bishop Whipple's report and called a meeting at his residence. A delegation representing the participants at this gathering went to Washington, had an interview with President Grant and other officials on Indian questions, and made a suggestion similar to the New York organization's concerning a civilian advisory board.[13] This must have been soon after Grant's inauguration, when in his address he had stated: "The proper treatment of the original occupants of the land — the Indians — is one deserving of careful study. I will favor any course towards them which tends to their civilization and ultimate citizenship." [14]

About the same time that the Quaker delegations had interviews with the President-elect, Cooper had forwarded to the Indian Office a letter which suggested direct missionary participation in the new peace policy. It had been written by Maj. Gen. W. B. Hazen at Fort Cobb in Indian Territory. The general stated: "I will further say that practical missionaries of good moral character, who should be young and active, of the following avocations, farmers, house-builders, gardeners, fruiterers, and cattle raisers, with such aids as will enable them to instruct in all these branches, can do much in the cause of humanity, and assist greatly in solving the true problem of Indian amelioration." [15]

Protestant concern about Indian policy and Indian rights was thus being registered in Washington in many ways. Moreover, Congress in the summer of 1868 had successfully tested the effectiveness of the use of a religious agency in Indian affairs. It had, without previous consultation with Bishop Whipple, appropriated $45,000 for the relief of the Sisseton and Wahpeton Sioux and placed the disbursement of the fund in the hands of the bishop. He declined; but when informed that no other provision had been made and that the Indians would lose the benefit of the grant, he accepted the responsibility. He sent his friend and old acquaintance of the Dakotas, Dr. Jared W. Daniels, to the Indians as his personal representative. New York and Philadelphia merchants purchased for the bishop goods of high quality at the lowest possible cost. In addition to the direct issue of rations, a work relief system was instituted. The experiment was a great success.[16]

ENLISTMENT OF THE MISSION BOARDS

President Grant was genuinely concerned about the Indian problem. Influenced by the Protestant representations, he was ready to act along some lines recommended by the Peace Commission. His appointment of his military secretary, General Ely S. Parker, a Seneca sachem, as Commissioner of Indian Affairs was not only a reward to a faithful friend and companion in arms but also a token of earnestness in Indian reform. Parker, however, was regarded by the religious forces as a tool of the "Indian Ring." He refused to submit his accounts to the new Board of Indian Commissioners when it was formed, was accused of fraud, and, although acquitted, had to resign.[17] The President's next move was the dismissal of the old superintendents and agents on the reservations and the detailing of Army officers to take their places. The Armed Forces were then being drastically cut back, and thus many officers of the Regular Army could be retained because they would be paid by the Indian Service. However, two superintendencies were excepted from the general order. They were assigned to the Friends. The Northern Superintendency in Nebraska was given to the Liberal branch, and the Central Superintendency in Kansas and Indian Territory assigned to the Orthodox. The Army and the pacifist Quakers might seem strange colleagues, but Grant undoubtedly had as high an opinion of the integrity of the one as of the other. Both could withstand corrupting influences. Many officers and their wives had been staunch friends of the missionaries to the Indians and had supported them. The missionaries frequently voiced appreciation of the officers.[18]

Congress however was loath to lose this vast field of patronage and was jealous of the encroachment of the Executive on its domain. A provision of the Army Appropriation Bill of

July 15, 1870, prohibited the holding of all civil offices by Army officers.[19]

General Parker wrote identical letters to the two denominations of Friends on Feb. 15, 1869, inviting them to submit lists of Quakers qualified for appointment to the superintendencies and agencies in the regions designated.[20] The Friends complied, furnished the names, and set up organization for the work. In June the Orthodox Friends organized their Associated Executive Committee of Friends on Indian Affairs. They appointed Dr. William Nicholson as general agent for field administration. The Liberal, or Hicksite, body set up a Central Executive Committee for supervision of the work.[21] In his first annual message to Congress the following December the President stated: "I have attempted a new policy towards these wards of the nation. . . . The Society of Friends is well known as having succeeded in living in peace with the Indians in the early settlement of Pennsylvania, while their white neighbors of other sects in other sections were constantly embroiled. They are also known for their opposition to all strife, violence and war, and are generally noted for their strict integrity and fair dealings. These considerations induced me to give the management of a few reservations of Indians to them and to throw the burden of the selection of agents upon the Society itself. The result has proven most satisfactory." [22]

The Army officers had to withdraw from the posts in the Indian Service. Congress and the politicians however did not reap the expected reward. The President, on the urging of the new church-related Board of Indian Commissioners, invited the participation of other missionary societies and boards.

THE BOARD OF INDIAN COMMISSIONERS

The House of Representatives and the Senate had been in conflict over the report of the Indian Peace Commission and the treaties which it had negotiated and which had been ratified by the Senate. The House finally agreed to an appropriation for the year 1870, and the Act of April 10, 1869, provided a special fund of $2 million "to enable the President to maintain peace among and with the various tribes, bands, and parties of Indians, and to promote civilization among said Indians, bring them, where practicable, upon reservations, relieve their necessities, and encourage their self-support." [23] The President wanted a civilian board to control or supervise this new program, and it was understood in religious circles that he got this idea primarily from the suggestion made by the delegation from the group which had met at William Welsh's home. [24] Congress was then induced to safeguard the fund from plundering by including in the act a provision authorizing the President "to organize a board of commissioners, to consist of not more than ten persons, to be selected by him from among men eminent for their intelligence and philanthropy, to serve without pecuniary compensation, who may, under his direction, exercise joint control with the Secretary of the Interior over the disbursement of the appropriations made by this act." [25] The initial intention was that this board should have truly effective control, but Jacob D. Cox, Secretary of the Interior, disliked the granting of so great power to a civilian, nonpartisan organ, and with the aid of Senator Fessenden had the bill amended as passed. [26] July 3 the President issued an Executive order to regulate the activities of the new Board of Indian Commissioners. [27] The board, it now appeared, was to have only powers of inspection and advising. It would act through visits of inspection on the reservations, the scrutiny of bids and of goods delivered under contracts, and the auditing and approval of accounts. The members during the first two or more years frequently acted as special commissioners in effecting agreements with Indian tribes and in investigating instances of conflict. No genuinely organic relationship to the Bureau of Indian Affairs or its Commissioner was actually provided. The circumstances of its defeat were written into the enabling legislation and the Executive order.

This Board of Indian Commissioners was in the beginning regarded as representing the churches, but none of the members appear to have been officially nominated by the churches. President Grant probably knew them all personally, and the biographer of one of them said that he regarded Welsh and Brunot "as the leading laymen of the day." The same writer quotes the Secretary of the Interior as stating: "The design of those who suggested the commission was that something like a Christian Commission [i. e., the Civil War organization] should be established, having in view the civilization of the Indians." [28] Most of the appointees had actually been active in the Christian Commission during the war, and some were prominent in the newly emerging YMCA movement. They were wealthy philanthropists, active in their denominations, but they included some with first-hand knowledge of the Indians, like Robert Campbell, the one-time fur trader. Parker, on behalf of the President, sent invitations to nine men of high repute and received their prompt acceptance. When the board was organized May 26, 1869, it included William Welsh, chairman, an Episcopalian; Felix R. Brunot, Episcopalian; W. E. Dodge, Presbyterian; George H. Stuart, Presbyterian; E. S. Tobey, Congregationalist; John V. Farwell, Methodist; Robert Campbell, Presbyterian (?); Henry S. Lane, Methodist; and Nathan Bishop, Baptist. There was no Roman Catholic member, and most Protestant denominations were not represented. It was surely a symbolic rather than an actual representation of the churches. When Welsh discovered that the board was actually without power, he resigned. Felix R. Brunot succeeded him, and Vincent Colyer took his place on the board, becoming its secretary.[29]

This voluntary Board of Indian Commissioners gave itself wholeheartedly to its task, and it is amazing that men with enormous personal responsibilities could devote so great a proportion of their time to its affairs. They traveled far and wide in their inspection of the Service and the condition of the Indians. Their

examination of the accounts saved the government large sums
of money, although for political reasons the Secretary of the
Interior often overruled their decisions. They brought about
more honest bidding. They set standards for goods and saw that
the goods delivered met specifications. Out of their study they
advised the President, the Secretary of the Interior, and the commissioner on policy and procedure. Yet they could do no more
than advise and exert moral pressure, and the politicians could
circumvent their efforts. Irked at being little more than a use-
less ornament of virtue to the administration, the whole board
resigned early in 1874, with the exception of the Friend, John
D. Lang. There was immediately an epidemic of dishonest bidding and delivery of shoddy goods. Complaints were rife. When
the board was "filled up" the following July and August, the
original system was reestablished with what were said to be im-
provements.[30] General Clinton B. Fisk, a Methodist, was made
chairman of the reconstituted board. A. C. Barstow, who was
chairman in 1880, stated at that time: "Originally every member
of this Board was recommended by religious societies; but that
was changed five years ago [i. e., 1875], and Mr. Kingsley, General Fisk, Mr. Stickney, and myself are the only members of the
Board that were originally recommended for appointment on the
Board." [31] Since the Commissioner of Indian Affairs and the Secretary of the Interior took less and less notice of the board's recommendations, it is not surprising that the turnover in membership was great. The second group of "church representatives"
were certainly not of the stature and influence of the first group,
and the later members were not such as to possess the financial
independence nor the public prestige of the initial members.
Because of the "unquestionable integrity, the unflagging enthusi-
asm, and genuine ability" of the original group, as one commen-
tator stated, the Board exerted a helpful influence in the conduct
of Indian affairs.[32] This board continued in existence until 1933.

MISSION BOARDS AND INDIAN AGENTS

There were really two new elements in President Grant's Indian policy. One was official, administrative; the other was nonofficial but encouraged by government. The administrative effort to effect reform and improvement in the service rested on the Board of Indian Commissioners and on the appointment of a new class of Indian agents. These were expected to be nonpartisan individuals, personally devoted to the improvement of the Indians and placed in office under religious sponsorship. But equally important with efficient and honest administration in the President's scheme was the injection of a spiritual dynamic into the process of civilizing the Indians, to be provided by the Christian religion. The missionary societies were expected both to nominate and supervise agents for and to carry on missionary work on the reservations. The experiment with the Quakers had opened the way. The new Board of Indian Commissioners also recommended that all agencies be placed under religious societies.[33] Therefore, when the President had to withdraw the Army officers in 1870, he turned to other denominations. There apparently was idealism in this move as well as a desire to thwart the patronage seekers. Yet it is strange that the man who opposed public funds for sectarian schools, who supported the Blaine amendment, and who in 1875 made the famous exhortation to the veterans of the Army of the Tennessee to "keep the church and state forever separate" should have brought church and state into so intimate an alliance.[34]

The Indian agents and the whole Service at this time had an unsavory reputation, but the new method of nomination was supposed to eliminate seekers of plunder. Bishop Whipple told President Lincoln in 1862: "The Indian agents who are placed in trust of the honor and faith of the Government are generally selected without any reference to their fitness for the place. The Congressional delegation desires to reward John Doe for party work, and John Doe desires the place because there is a tradition on the border that an Indian agent with fifteen hundred dollars a year can retire upon an ample fortune in four years." [35] General Sherman discovered that a politician who had been appointed to an agency "saved" $50,000 within three years out of his salary of $1,500 per year! [36] Dr. Crary, a Methodist, asserted: "If the Government could get the Angel Gabriel to take the Indian superintendency, he could not govern honestly until he would smite with the Almighty's wrath the villainous Indian rings of the frontier and Washington." [37]

Now, however, Commissioner Parker had been able to say in his report for 1870 that in just a few months the Army officers and the Friends together had radically changed the climate of the agencies.[38] Under the Friends, even in such difficult agencies as the reservations of the Cheyennes, Arapahoes, Kiowas, and Comanches, a condition of affairs existed that was all that might be desired under the circumstances.[39] Justified by such evidence the President informed Congress: "I determined to give all agencies to such religious denominations as had heretofore established missionaries among the Indians, and perhaps to some other denominations who would undertake the work on the same terms — that is, as missionary work." [40] Vincent Colyer, secretary of the Board of Indian Commissioners, had already been urging the step for a year, and finally the Secretary of the Interior had proposed it to the President. Commissioner Parker declared that it was not "as a dernier resort to save a dying race, but from the highest moral conviction of Christian humanity" that the President had asked the help of the churches; and he asked the prayers of all good Christians on behalf of the newly appointed agents.[41] The twofold obligation of the boards and societies were, according to the President's intention, the selection and supervision of agents and the maintenance of such missionary work as would lead to the conversion of the Indians and give them the incentive to desire and persevere in achieving civilization as the American people understood that term.

Unfortunately the President's statement did not make the principle of selection clear. While there was no mission work on many reservations and among many tribes, two or more denominations might be at work on others. The President's words could be taken to mean that chronological priority would determine the assignment of any agency. And the Board of Indian Commissioners had suggested that teachers for the new agency schools "should be nominated by some religious body having a mission nearest to the location of the school." [42] Some thought that principle should be extended to agents. Actually the Secretary of the Interior had no notion of how to proceed in the matter, and Vincent Colyer provided him with a map and a list of suggested assignments. [43] Colyer had already overcome the reluctance of some boards.

Secretary Cox sent formal letters of invitation to the Missionary Society of the Methodist Episcopal Church, the American Baptist Home Mission Society, the Board of Foreign Missions of the Presbyterian Church in the U. S. A., the American Missionary Society (Congregational), the Board of Foreign Missions of the Reformed Church in America, the American Unitarian Association, the Protestant Episcopal Church's Board of Missions of the Domestic and Foreign Missionary Society, and to the voluntary, unofficial Episcopalian organization, the American Church Missionary Society. The last declined in favor of the official denominational body. Presbyterians and Episcopalians expressed some doubts about the state-church relationships involved, [44] and the Reformed and Methodist officers saw great practical difficulties. [45] Nevertheless, all agreed to cooperate because the matter seemed so urgent and the end sought so desirable.

The Roman Catholic hierarchy (but it is not known who) was approached through the chief clerk of Interior, and Secretary Cox did not list the agencies assigned to that church in his letter to the Protestants although indicating that they were included in the plan. The Roman Catholic officials claimed, on the basis of the President's statement, some 38 out of 70-odd agencies; and that was a practical mistake in an administration where there were a number of persons of influence hostile to them. They regarded the original assignment of eight agencies, and ultimately of seven, as an injustice. Because of this sense of injury, although accepting the agencies, the Roman Catholics refused to cooperate with the Board of Indian Commissioners or with the Bureau. Fr. Pierre J. De Smet, the famous Jesuit missionary, attended the first meeting of religious representatives with the Board of Indian Commissioners, but there was no Roman Catholic representation after that. The Roman Catholic authorities greatly weakened their case and made compromise difficult by excessive claims, which included the most nominally related peoples, although many claims were indeed justified by recent missionary work, both on grounds of priority and proximity. A running battle was carried on for years with the Commissioner of Indian Affairs and the Secretary of the Interior. The Bureau of Catholic Indian Missions was established in Washington, D. C., with General Charles Ewing as Catholic Indian Commissioner. This bureau proved to be a most effective organ for integrating, supervising, promoting, and financing the Roman Catholic Indian missions. It built up a program of mission work far exceeding the total of all that undertaken by the Protestant organizations. It dealt with government in the matter of the agencies, built up an extensive system of contract schools, and fought for religious liberty on the reservations. A full study of the development of the bureau and its work in connection with the Grant experiment has been made by Fr. Peter J. Rahill in *Catholic Indian Missions and Grant's Peace Policy, 1870—1884* (Catholic Univ. of Am. Press, 1954).

It is unfortunate that Roman Catholics and Protestants at this time held such mutual suspicions and were so hostile toward each other. Much of this was due to the lack of means of communication. Their mutual antagonisms did much to open opportunity for the politicians to wreck the system. Had they been able to make a common front with the government on behalf of Indian rights and improvement, the story might have been different in some respects.

The selection of the Protestant agencies is somewhat strange. The two mission boards with the best claims to priority, continuity, and experience were ignored. The Moravians were never asked. The American Board of Commissioners for Foreign Missions, overlooked at first, was asked belatedly. It was assigned one agency in 1871.[46] The three large regional churches of the South — the Methodist Episcopal Church, South, the Southern Baptist Convention, and the Presbyterian Church in the United States — were completely ignored, although they, despite small mission programs after the war, probably had more Indian members than all other Protestant churches together. These were concentrated among the Five Civilized Tribes. The bitterness of the Reconstruction politics eliminated these three churches from the agencies. The Congregationalist agency invited to take the place (which more logically should have gone to the American Board) was the American Missionary Society although it had no Indian missions at this time. The Reformed Church and the Unitarians had no Indian missions and never established any. Those of the American Baptist Home Mission Society were very small at this time. This society had taken over the Indian missions from its foreign missionary counterpart society only four years earlier, in 1866. Its interest to date had not been in expanding mission work but in securing from the government indemnity for property at mission stations destroyed during the war.[47] The Cherokee Mission was small because the Cherokees had mostly gone with the Southern Baptist Convention.[48] The Methodists had had half a century of experience in Indian missions, but at this time they could count only 9 or 10 missionaries and some 1,200 communicants. The society had little control over these operations because they were under the actual authority of various local conferences, and the society merely made small appropriations. The Methodists had a mission in only 1 of the 14 agencies assigned to them.[49]

The two denominations chosen which, in addition to the American Board, were actively expanding Indian missions were the Board of Foreign Missions of the Presbyterian Church in the U. S. A. and the Board of Missions (Domestic and Foreign Missionary Society) of the Protestant Episcopal Church. The Presbyterians, who now were offered 10 agencies,[50] had seen their program drastically cut down by the Civil War, but they had begun expansion even before the announcement of the peace policy.[51] Then in 1870 they received by transfer from the American Board its Seneca, Ojibway, and half of the Dakota Missions. This was the result of the reunion of the Old and New School Presbyterian denominations and the withdrawal of the latter from the American Board, which thus became Congregationalist almost exclusively.

The Protestant Episcopal Church had followed its Oneida members westward to Wisconsin and then had begun work with other tribes in that state and in Minnesota. Bishop Whipple had also for a decade been carrying on a vigorous mission to the Dakotas or Sioux. Such missions had been carried on by the separate dioceses of the church, but prodded by Whipple and some of his western colleagues the Board of Missions began to take responsibility beginning in 1866.[52] The layman, William Welsh, was especially active in promoting the new program. The board began to exert control and to make appropriations only in 1869.[53]

Three other denominations were given minor participation, but it is not clear whether they were consulted in the same manner as the greater boards. The Sac and Fox Agency in Iowa was listed as Evangelical Lutheran beginning in 1872, and later this was changed to the Southern Ute Agency in Colorado. Warm Springs in Oregon was long listed as United Presbyterian. The

Pueblo Agency in New Mexico and Neah Bay in Washington went to the Christian or Disciples denomination in 1872, and Malheur in Oregon was repeatedly listed as belonging to the Christians. They may have been related to local associations of Disciples of Christ. The General Christian Missionary Society, apparently more concerned about denominational prestige than about starting missionary work, sought through Garfield and Hayes to get an agency assigned on the grounds of its place in frontier life, and its representative first appeared at the annual conference in 1882.[54] It is hard to account for this in light of the earlier assignments. Another Lutheran denomination and the United Brethren tried in vain to get an assignment.[55] However, the denominational rivalry for agencies to which one author makes reference is a gross exaggeration.[56] The societies and boards did not have the resources in men and money to join in the enterprise. What may look like denominational rivalry is much more likely to represent frontier elements, very strong in churches like the Baptists, Disciples, and Methodists, trying to exert local influence from the frontier point of view through the denominational machinery.

The annual conference just mentioned was a meeting of the representatives of the participating societies with the Board of Indian Commissioners, held in Washington or New York usually in January. At a certain point in the meeting it ceased to be official and under the direction of the board and became an informal gathering of the missionary representatives. It was a bit of a jumble, with much talking and exchange of information and no formal business agenda. The mutual exchange was stimulating and encouraging, however. Resolutions adopted at these meetings were intended to influence the Service and Congress, to stir up the church members, and to rally opinion on behalf of the Indian cause. The 1877 resolutions were a commendation of General Grant upon his retirement from the Presidency, an expression "of high appreciation . . . in adhering to this line of benevolent action in the face of misunderstanding and opposition." [57] The resolutions in 1879 were a kind of manifesto of faith in the peace policy in face of political pressures of the opposite sort.[58] Especially problems relating to the agencies were raised here. Long after the severance of the partnership between the government and the churches in 1882 the annual conference continued. It was eventually transformed into the Lake Mohonk Conference on Indian Affairs.

The first task of the missionary societies, from the government's point of view, was the nomination and supervision of agents and assisting them to secure competent Christian employees. The Friends were a year ahead of the other churches in this matter. The Orthodox Friends carefully selected men of their own denomination for the 14 agencies of the Central Superintendency, men of whom they were convinced combined personal integrity, business ability, concern for Indian welfare, and missionary motivation. These men brought to the service a new continuity. Enoch Hoag served for seven years as superintendent and was succeeded by Dr. Nicholson, who during that time had been the supervising general agent for the Associated Executive Committee. Agent John D. Miles remained in office for the whole decade. Although the Orthodox Quakers believed in their agents, they kept them under close supervision as Dr. Nicholson traveled among them and reported to headquarters. Visitation committees frequently appeared at the agencies. A subcommittee of the Executive, composed of members living in and near Washington, provided liaison with the government.[59]

The Hicksite Friends held the Northern Superintendency. A printed circular gave their qualifications for an Indian agent. These were:

> 1. A prayerful heart and a firm trust in the power and wisdom of God, and not in man or military force for guidance and protection.

2. Industry, economy, firmness, vigilance, mildness, and practical kindness and love.

3. A knowledge of farming and gardening, ability to superintend the construction of buildings, and see that the schools are properly conducted.

4. Tact in managing and influencing persons, so as gradually to induce the Indians of the agency voluntarily to join in the various employments of farming and gardening, and in mechanical operations.

5. And high in the scale of qualifications, to be possessed of strict integrity, and to be perfectly reliable in financial matters, and know how to employ with economy and to the best advantage the funds entrusted to him by government for the use of the agency.[60]

These Liberal Friends did not have as well developed a system of supervision as did the Orthodox, but their Central Executive Committee kept general oversight, and numerous delegations visited the agencies.[61]

The Presbyterian Board of Foreign Missions published in church papers appeals for good men.[62] Its officers were conscious of moral responsibility for nominating the "right kind of men," agents who with their subordinate employees should promote, and not hinder, the missionary work. The agent above all others gives the Indians their idea of the American government and renders them friendly or hostile.[63] Consequently the nominees were mostly elders in Presbyterian churches. It was believed that through such men and the new peace policy the way was providentially being prepared for missionary success among the Indians.[64] The secretary, Dr. John C. Lowrie, issued a pamphlet which stressed four essentials in agents: integrity, business capacity, energy, and the power of governing men.[65] He also stressed the fact that agents should be impelled by a higher motivation than salary.[66] The Presbyterians had no field supervision until the Board of Home Missions also entered the Indian mission work.

Then Dr. Sheldon Jackson, superintendent of home missions for the western mountain states and the pioneer organizer of Presbyterianism in the region, managed to keep a sharp eye on Indian matters as well as white church extension.[67]

The Methodist and Baptist churches were much more intimately identified with frontier society. They also had more members than the more cultured and intellectual denominations who wanted to exploit and even exterminate the Indians rather than civilize them. For information they were dependent chiefly on local sources. For these reasons they had much difficulty in their missions. The Methodist Missionary Society had to depend on the local annual conferences for both nominations and supervision. The stamp of approval given agents by the New York staff was a formality. Dr. Reed, the Methodist executive officer, was personally unacquainted with many of the agents whom he approved, even though many of them were ministers. The agencies west of the mountains were fairly well supervised by the California, Oregon, and Washington Conferences, which had permanent mission committees. The small, weak conferences east of the mountains did little with regard either to agents or missions. The Methodists stressed religious interest and motivation in agents because, lacking missionaries, they wanted these men to do evangelistic work themselves; but they were often deceived by the local interests. Referring to all agency staffs Reed stated: "We would like religious, devoted agents, and the same class of subordinates, and I would say that the appointment of subordinates is one of the great things that we ought to look at. A clerk who is irreligious and not at all subject to the agent, would, of necessity, not be inclined to help on the interests of the great movements he might have on hand. The same would be true of the farmer, the blacksmith, schoolteacher, and physician. . . . But where there is not a force of men interested in the civilizing influences we can do but little, because we have no missionary anywhere in those parts." [68] Where rigorous supervision was lacking, local interests could foist an unworthy nominee upon the New York office. Frequently the agent was a minister on conference assignment.[69]

The Domestic Committee of the Episcopal Board of Missions undertook the nominating function only after the President had agreed to the stipulation "that the agents so appointed are to be wholly free from the control or interference of politicians." [70] But such assurance was more readily given than maintained. The General Convention in 1871 created a Standing Committee on Indian Affairs comprised of six prominent laymen, with William Welsh as chairman.[71] Its function was to supervise the agents, to produce such civilizing aids as the government did not provide, and to invoke the assistance of the government and the courts in protecting the Indians. Welsh and his committeemen made trips of inspection and supplied the agents with cattle, oxen, and sheep for their wards. The committee became the Commission on Indian Missions with 50 members. It was under the Domestic Committee of the Board of Missions and was later reduced to 12 members.[72] With the consecration of William Hobart Hare as Bishop of Niobrara especially for the Indian jurisdiction, there was added even more powerful supervisory control.[73]

The Reformed Church in America, having no churches near its agencies, was faced with grave difficulty in choosing agents. It tried to select for the remote Arizona posts men who had lived on the border for some years, had experience with Indians, and "had led a consistent Christian life in the midst of the temptations peculiar to our sparsely settled territories." [74]

The American Missionary Association, which at one time held as many as 10 agencies, was sought out by many applicants, most of whom it eliminated as deficient. The secretary regarded this as "thankless work" which nevertheless might provide men who would show the spirit of Christ toward their charges.[75] He warned that an Indian agency was no sinecure and that it should be undertaken only by a thoroughly competent and self-sacrificing man. He endorsed the qualifications of an agent as set forth in an article in the Springfield, Mass., *Republican:* executive capacity, judicial knowledge, business ability and experience, diplomatic skill, high moral character, ability to endure hard work, and ability to carry onerous responsibilities and bear injury to reputation.[76] During the first years Rev. E. P. Smith, agent for the Chippewas of the Mississippi, with consent of the government acted as field secretary of Indian Missions for the association until he became Commissioner of Indian Affairs in 1873.

The small salary and the isolation of certain posts were major obstacles to securing and keeping the kind of agents desired by the churches and the government. The officers of the boards had a high opinion of the influence of white women among the Indians and especially upon the Indian women.[77] Therefore they wanted married men as agents, and both agent and wife had to have missionary motivation to serve at $1,500 a year at a remote agency and pay their moving expenses. For decades the agents had lived on graft, not salary. There were mistakes in judgment from time to time, and some agents gave way to the inevitable pressures, especially when their nomination had been due to local frontier interests. Bishop Whipple thought that some mission executives were occasionally lax. He said: "Wherever churches entered heartily into this work, it was a success. Where they used their position to provide places for friends, it was a pitiable failure." [78] The vast majority of agents were able, devoted, and honest. In order to get the right kind of men, some of the societies supplemented the salary from their own funds. Thus the American Missionary Society added "some thousands of dollars." [79] It petitioned Congress to raise the salaries in 1871.[80] Dr. Reed, the Methodist executive officer, confessing the difficulty of getting the right agents at the low salary, said that they could get men who would try to live on the salary, but that these men could not pay the cost of transporting their families to their posts.[81] Isolation was sometimes worse than financial pressure. The agent at the Colorado River Apache Agency wrote to Dr. Ferris of the Reformed Church: "Send out someone to join me to keep me from barbarism." [82] Year after year the mission boards, the Board of Indian Commissioners, the Commissioner of Indian Affairs, and the Secretary of the Interior asked Congress to increase the salaries, but in vain.

POLITICAL INTERFERENCE

The Board of Indian Commissioners was quick to observe under the new system "a manifest improvement in the agencies." [83] The Commissioner of Indian Affairs reported in 1873 that the scheme was working with increasing satisfaction and that the societies, knowing better what was expected, were making better selection and doing better supervision.[84] However, in stark contrast to such approbation in the first years is the statement of the Commissioner in 1882 that one great cause of retardation among the Indians was the difficulty of securing the right kind of agents who would furnish precept and example. "If the agent is an *honest, industrious,* and *intelligent Christian* man, with physical ability and disposition to endure hardship and courageously encounter difficulty and disappointment, or in other words, if he is morally, mentally, and physically above the average of what are considered good men, he will work wonders among these wards of the nation." [85] But, he added, such men were seldom secured. The explanation is not that the societies picked poor agents but that the system had been largely nullified by political pressures and by the ability of the Indian Office to circumvent the efforts of the societies and the Board of Indian Commissioners.

Those who assume that the missionary societies simply were not able to nominate the right kind of men as agents, because of troubles and complaints during the last half of the program, have misinterpreted the facts and have not read sufficiently the records of the missionary boards. Most of the agents who got into trouble were not chosen by the boards. One of the easiest means of getting rid of the agents appointed with approval of the boards was to blacken their reputations by tarring them with the same old stick of former days. Politicians and the local partisan press would force many out of office by raising charges of fraud and corruption. E. P. Smith had warned the American Missionary Association about the attacks which would be made on their agents, especially if they should be missionaries. "The missionaries run the risk of reputation as well as life, for the men whom they displace follow them with slander and abuse, and the good men want to feel that this Association has enough confidence in them to sustain them and not to believe any charges until they are disproved." [86]

Smith himself provides an excellent example. He had resigned the pastorate of a Congregational church at Pepperill, Mass., in order to enter the service of the U. S. Christian Commission during the war. He was superintendent of its western division and later field secretary of the commission. Following the war he entered the educational service for freedmen carried on by the American Missionary Association, being first district superintendent at Cincinnati and then director of the entire program in the South. Grant's peace policy challenged him, and he volunteered for Indian service. He was appointed Indian agent for the Chippewa and Pilager tribes in Minnesota and there won the commendation of Bishop Whipple.[87] There he built up a solid reputation for high achievement and saved the government more than half a million dollars in the exposure of one case of fraud.[88] His concern for the timberlands as the cause of white avarice and aggression made him want to sell off all the timber, invest the proceeds, and save the denuded lands for the Indians.[89] It was over timber contracts that charges were later to be brought against him. While agent in Minnesota, E. P. Smith also served as field secretary for the Indian missions of his association.[90] He was made

Commissioner of Indian Affairs in 1873, to the great delight of the churches, and was regarded as their choice for the post.

Since he was so obviously the living symbol of the Peace Policy itself, Smith was singled out for marked abuse by the Indian Ring. Eventually charges of fraud were brought against him. A newspaper in Minnesota published accusations, and some local interests persuaded William Welsh of their truth. Welsh then brought charges.[91] The writer of his obituary later wrote: "The merciless opposition which he met from designing men, who sought to profit at the expense of the Indians, exhibits one of the saddest phases of our republicanism."[92] The secretary of the American Missionary Association and editor of the *American Missionary* resolutely defended Smith, declared that all who knew Smith's personal affairs were assured that he had never received a cent of profit from Indian affairs, and called for a full investigation.[93] The special commission appointed to investigate and try the case was unable to understand Welsh's "peculiar mental state" and the multitudinous errors in the alleged facts presented by him. More important, Welsh refused to present what was supposed to be the incriminating evidence. Smith was completely cleared, and the evidence was published in a book by the Department of the Interior.[94] When Columbus Delano resigned as Secretary of the Interior, Smith also resigned his post. He was publicly vindicated by being elected president of Howard University, a post which could have been awarded him only if he were free from the cloud of suspicion raised by Welsh's charges. The American Missionary Association asked him to undertake a field investigation of its mission work in West Africa.[95] He died of African fever, as it was called, on shipboard near Fernado Po, on June 15, 1876, and was buried at Old Calabar.[96]

The Board of Indian Commissioners protested unjustified charges against the church-nominated agents, declaring that wholesale condemnation of men chosen with greater care than any other class of government officers was rank injustice.[97] The agents compared favorably with any group of businessmen in the country.

There were less dramatic and even more effective ways by which the politicians could arrange matters to their satisfaction. Between the Indian Office, the Department of the Interior, and the Senate there was often long delay in acting upon nominations with the expectation that in the interval economic pressure would force the withdrawal of the nominee. Then also those in power in Washington and local political circles would seek either to cozen or to force the religious societies to nominate their candidates. Scores of persons went to Washington to lobby for the jobs, and the politicians would try to coerce or inveigle the mission secretaries into approving them. Local frontier church members, who had no sympathy for the Peace Policy, could often be made a front for these persons. Sometimes there was direct interference. Bishop Hare was greatly distressed in 1878 when the Army on orders from the Secretary of the Interior forcibly removed several agents in whom he had confidence. Enemies of the missions thereupon vilified the bishop.[98] The Baptist executives reported to the Home Mission Society that their consent to an appointment had been forced by the Commissioner of Indian Affairs. They spoke of the sentiment of all the societies, stating: "General dissatisfaction was felt by the Societies, because competent men, whom they had nominated, were often set aside for unknown men, who, in many instances, had no sympathy whatever with the Societies in their efforts to evangelize the Indians. If these men turned out badly, as sometimes happened, the Societies, whom it was generally supposed they represented, suffered reproach."[99]

The Orthodox Friends did not feel such pressures as early as some of the others, and when this did happen, they withdrew from the scheme of supposed cooperation after an interview with President Hayes had brought a verbal agreement but no actual improvement. The Associated Executive Committee in 1879 informed the President of its withdrawal from every form of official relationship.[100] Two of the Quaker agents remained in service until 1884 and 1885, but otherwise even teachers were dropped from employment.

The indignation of the other boards and societies was raised to the boiling point by the administration of E. A. Hayt as Commissioner of Indian Affairs. He was disliked by Protestants and Roman Catholics alike.[101] The general sense of frustration erupted into open protest in Hayt's presence at the annual conference in January 1880.[102] The Unitarian executive officer, Dr. Rush R. Shippen, protested that the very devotion of agents to the Indians was used against them. A certain agent had been appointed without Unitarian approval on the ground of urgency and the man's excellent qualifications, but he had so outraged the Indians that they had killed him. The Unitarians had not considered him to be their man.[103] Subsequent nominations had been ignored. There was objection to the appointment of ministers by the Unitarians. It came out that the Secretary of the Interior had said that "the tendency was to nominate broken-down ministers for the service, and that the exigencies of the service required very strong, executive business men." This led to an uproar, and it was especially offensive to the Methodists, who frequently appointed ministers. Dr. Lowrie interposed that the Presbyterians never appointed ministers, but not because they would not make good agents. The Baptists reported having had forced upon them by the Commissioner a man who later was discovered to be an imbecile. Then it came out that both the Orthodox Friends and the Reformed Church had withdrawn. The conference then drew up a resolution which was taken to the President asking for an understanding. The boards offered to submit with each nomination the testimonials on which it was based.[104] Assurance was given that there would be a return to the original procedure.[105]

There was however no lasting improvement in the situation.

The boards were not asked for nominations during Garfield's short administration, when Secretary Kirkwood had vowed that "he was going to run the thing." [106] Then President Arthur's Secretary of the Interior, H. M. Teller, also announced that he would not consult the religious bodies. He informed Dr. Reid of the Methodist Missionary Society: "I know no reason why government officials should be selected for one class of government employment by religious bodies and not for all." He had the effrontery to add a statement that could certainly be disputed, that "since the religious bodies have been allowed to select agents, some of the grossest frauds have been known in Indian Affairs. The frequent changes made in these appointments is sufficient evidence that mistakes were frequent, and my own observation has convinced me that no benefit accrued to the service by this method of selection." Teller's letter of Aug. 5, 1882, wrote off the whole policy which had been initiated by President Grant, revealed his smallness of character, and insulted Grant himself. He made the astounding assertion that he had no idea of the meaning of the term "Peace Policy"! "You mention the peace policy of the government as if it were connected with and dependent upon the scheme of selecting agents. I do not think that there is any connection between the two. I do not know what you mean by the peace policy of the government, and therefore I am unable to say whether I agree with you on that point or not." [107] Thus the Peace Policy was terminated and the participation of the missionary societies ceased.

A judgment of considerable merit was passed on the experiment by Bishop Whipple in 1877. He said: "Much has been said of the 'Peace Policy.' It has been unduly praised by its friends and unjustly condemned by its enemies. We have no Peace Policy. In every essential feature our Indian system has been unchanged for fifty years; it is based upon the intercourse law of 1832. . . . Despite all the evils and conflicts of an unreformed Indian policy, more has been done [through Grant's scheme] for the civilization of the red man than at any period of our history." [108] Rather interestingly that "realistic" critic of Indian policy, General Francis A. Walker, who had been made Commissioner of Indian Affairs after Parker solely to provide him with a salary while he completed the national census, also agreed that the "sole Indian policy of the United States deserving the name was adopted early in the century." He declared that "to throw upon a dozen religious and benevolent societies the responsibility of advising the executive in the appointment of the agents of the Indian service is not a policy." [109] He gave a kind of left-handed compliment to the effort, however, when he remarked that, while it was usual to sneer at "Quaker sentimentality," posterity would be far more sentimental over the fate of the Indian than any present Quaker or philanthropist, and that "the United States will be judged at the bar of history according to what they shall have done in two respects, by their disposition of negro slavery, and by their treatment of the Indians."[110] A vigorous defense was made by the New York *Times* after Custer's defeat. It read in part: "From all sides come denunciations of what is called in terms of ascending sarcasm, 'the peace policy,' 'the Quaker policy,' 'the Sunday-school policy.' . . . What is meant by the 'Quaker policy' which is thus bitterly assailed? If it means anything, it means the policy of justice and humanity. Whatever may have been the faults of the present Administration, history will credit it with at least having made the attempt to treat the Indians fairly." [111]

MISSION WORK

The second obligation of the mission boards was to undertake intensified and expanded missionary work. All of them understood this to be a major challenge, accepted it, and made plans, although a few never initiated Indian missions.[112] All these societies had great difficulty in securing ministers for missionary service and in obtaining sufficient funds. It was far easier to recruit well-qualified women than ordained men.[113] Overseas missions

had greater appeal. The Reformed Church was unable to establish missions, and the Baptist work expanded very little.[114] The
Unitarians regarded the ministers whom they nominated to agencies as being their missionaries in a mission of Christian concern
and humanitarianism, and from time to time expressed a futile
desire to enlarge the work.[115] The Friends carried out their sense
of missionary obligation through their agents and agency employees. They all did evangelistic work, and so did visiting teams
of Friends. The Osage Agency in 1874 is a good example. The
agent, Mr. I. T. Gibson, conducted two services each Sunday, and
active evangelists among his employees were four ministers, four
elders, and many members of the Society of Friends, while eight
visitors had also done some evangelistic activity.[116] The Friends
operated largely through the schools to which they appointed the
teachers who were paid by the government. They supplemented
the government's grants to the schools, and each school received
supplies of books, clothing, and other items from some yearly
meeting to whose care it was assigned. The schools in the Central
Superintendency increased in the decade following 1869 from
4 to 15, and pupils from 150 to about 1,000.[117] After withdrawal
from the cooperative plan the Friends instituted more traditional
missionary methods and continued to build upon the foundations
laid in the 1870s.[118]

The annual statistics provided by the Commissioner of Indian Affairs are very imperfect. But poor as they are they give
some notion of the increase in mission work in the period. The
1869 tables indicated only 15 Protestant missionaries, 10 schools,
17 teachers, and 594 pupils.[119] The 1873 report revealed (after
elimination of the Cherokees, etc., not included in 1869) 69 mission schools (in addition to government schools), 86 teachers,
2,690 pupils, and 30 church buildings. Among all the Indians
there were reported 74 missionaries, 90 church buildings, and
7,419 members of Protestant churches.[120] The total expenditures
for mission work by eight societies in 1876 were $93,096.68.

The difficulties of the Methodists, indicated above, continued, but the work grew. In 1870 they had 9 missions, 5 churches, 8 missionaries, 27 native local preachers, 532 church members and 177 probationers, and expenditures of $3,540.[121] Their editor lamented in 1873: "It is true we are doing something, but our faces wear no glow of self-satisfaction at our success among the lowly wards of our government." [122] Their highest figures are those of 1877, when there were 22 missions, 17 churches, 20 missionaries, 41 Indian local preachers, 2,394 members and 532 probationers, and, strangely, appropriations of only $2,950.[123] Only the California, Oregon, and Washington Conferences vigorously promoted their missions. There were few full-time missionaries; most Indian churches only got occasional visits from preachers itinerating among the white churches. There had to be great reliance, therefore, on agents who were ministers and did evangelistic work along with their official duties.[124] The outstanding one among them was "Father" James H. Wilbur at the Yakima Agency in Washington.

The American Board completely withdrew from the Indian missions at the close of this period, turning over its Dakota mission to the American Missionary Association in 1882 on the grounds that the Sioux Christians were now mature and could well be associated with a home mission agency. Previously the American Missionary Association had established small missions in 1873 in Wisconsin and Minnesota,[125] and at the Skokomish Agency in Washington, where the Rev. Cushing Eells, father of the agent and former missionary to the Spokans, did voluntary service.[126] Within two years the Rev. Myron Eells began a long-term pastorate there under regular appointment.[127] A sense of comity inhibited the association from starting work on some of its agencies where others — Episcopalians, Roman Catholics, and Methodists — had missions.[128] There was a genuine interest on part of the association's constituency, and almost every issue of the *American Missionary* after 1870 carried a variety of items about the Indians. The association gave its church and mission at Red Lake, Minn., to the Episcopalians.[129] Aside from a scholarship program for Indian youths at Hampton Institute, there was no large-scale expansion until reception of the Dakota mission.

The Presbyterians at the inception of the peace policy had missions among the Chippewas and Ottawas in Michigan, Omahas in Nebraska, Creeks and Seminoles in Indian Territory, and newly among the Navajos in New Mexico and Winnebagos in Nebraska. Nineteen missionaries were in service.[130] Then the American Board's Seneca, Ojibway, and Dakota missions were taken over in 1870—71. That same year Henry S. Spalding reestablished the long-suspended Nez Percé mission at Lapwai, Idaho; and missionaries were sent out to try approaches to the Zunis, Utes, and Jaccarilla Apaches.[131] Through the efforts of the Presbytery of Santa Fé the missions in that area were transferred to the Board of Home Missions.[132] At the close of this period in 1882 another small mission had been begun among the Iowas and Sacs in Kansas, and three new ones were designated for opening when personnel could be found.[133] New missionaries were commissioned every year: 5 in 1871, 11 in 1872, 10 in 1873, 8 in 1874, 4 in 1875, 5 in 1878, 5 in 1879, 10 in 1880, 16 in 1881, and 9 in 1882. However, the turnover was great, and in 1882 the total force was comprised of 13 ordained ministers, 1 unordained man, and 27 women. The Indian native staff included 9 ordained ministers, 14 licentiates, and 14 lay teachers and evangelists. There were 1,275 communicants. Expenditures for that year were $23,786.70.[134] It should be noted that a heavy death toll was partly responsible for the rapid turnover in mission personnel under the various societies.

The acceleration of the Episcopal Church's Indian work was astounding.[135] Presented with the challenge by the government, Indian missions ceased to be a diocesan responsibility and came under control of the Board of Missions.[136] The general convention of 1871 put the Indian missions on the same level as other do-

mestic missions and created the Standing Committee on Indian
Affairs.[137] The House of Bishops at the same time established the
missionary jurisdiction of Niobrara for the Indian work, covering
most of South Dakota.[138] With the subsequent election and
consecration of Bishop William Hobart Hare in January 1873,
a new enterprise of some magnitude was truly under way. Other
bishops delegated to him the jurisdiction of the Indians in their
areas: the Santee Sioux in Nebraska, Shoshones and Bannocks in
Wyoming, and the Oneidas in Wisconsin.[139] The Standing Committee became the Indian Commission, with Col. E. C. Kemble as
executive officer.[140] However, Kemble became one of the new
government inspectors and was succeeded by the Rev. R. C. Rogers.[141] An Indian Hope Association was soon organized in Philadelphia to provide books and supplies and send women workers
to the Indian women.[142] There were already six such active local
associations in 1874.[143] The Dakota mission was greatly expanded, and some efforts were begun with the Cheyennes, Arapahoes, and Kiowas in 1880 on the Darlington and Anadarko
Agencies.[144] The Episcopal Church sent out 80 new missionaries
from 1871 through 1882, and in that time 20 Indians were made
deacons and 2 of these ordained priests.[145]

The missionary work of this period was carried out on the
same basic assumption which had been held ever since the days
of the Mayhews and John Eliot in the 17th century, namely, that
"evangelization" and "civilization" were the two primary goals
and that they must be effected simultaneously. The inevitable
product of evangelization was believed to be civilization, the Gospel bringing the desire for and persistent effort toward the Anglo-
American culture which was the very flowering of the Gospel.
Progress in civilization, on the other hand, was expected to lead
the Indian to the acceptance of Christianity. Education was by no
means a mere "bait." Methods were determined by these two
aims, and great stress was consequently laid on schools and
literature.

THE QUESTION OF RELIGIOUS LIBERTY

A number of problems in church and state relations was raised by the participation of the churches in the peace policy. One of grave importance includes the questions of religious teachers in government schools, government aid to mission schools, and the place of mission schools in the whole governmental system of education. Perhaps the most serious issue was that of religious liberty, a fundamental right of all American citizens. Was it the right of the Indian wards of the government as well? Neither the Protestant nor the Roman Catholic missionaries and officials were really concerned about the Indian's right to maintain and defend his own religion, and they were fighting more for freedom of action by the missionary agencies. There is a rare statement in a letter from the missionary, Dr. Thomas S. Williamson, to John V. Farwell of the Indian Commissioners, saying that the government has no right to interfere in the religious beliefs of the Indians, but "it can and ought to be done by instruction in Christianity through missions." [146] For a time the Indians were refused even liberty of choice between Christian churches. When Red Cloud and his band appealed for Roman Catholic missionaries to serve them and Fr. McCarthy was expelled from Pine Ridge, there was a denial of religious liberty.[147] Similarly when the Protestant Sioux at Devil's Lake asked for ministers, and their own Dakota kinsmen, Daniel Renville and his wife, were sent them by their own native missionary society only to be expelled, there was again a denial of religious liberty.[148]

When a mission board accepted assignment of an agency it was expected to carry on mission work as well as to nominate the agent. Did this mean that such a denomination had exclusive right to the agency assigned to it? Were missions already there henceforth to be excluded? It was soon ruled that this was not the case. But might any other denomination enter an agency after assignment, even if the assigned church did not begin mission work? Home mission boards were accustomed to denominational imperialism and competition in the churching of the country as the frontier moved westward. Foreign mission boards, however, observed comity overseas. This was a form of voluntary cooperation which fixed territorial responsibility for evangelism and guaranteed noninterference in specific areas held by priority of occupation or by mutual agreement. Comity was always voluntary, except where a colonial government had the policy of separating Roman Catholic and Protestant missions. The peace policy resulted in what looked for a time to be state-imposed comity. There was scarcely any conflict over territory by Protestant agencies among themselves because men and money required for expansion were too scarce. Hence competition in missionary activity was largely a matter of Protestant-Roman Catholic rivalry. Unfortunately this was a time when these two branches of the church were mutually suspicious and hostile.

There were a few instances of friction among Protestant societies over assignment of agencies causing interference with mission work. A Hicksite Quaker agent withdrew funds from a Presbyterian boarding school for the Omahas, and the Presbyterians feared this was the first step in forcing them out. They closed their Winnebago mission because it was believed impossible to continue under the Liberal Friends.[149] The American Board similarly feared the consequence of the assignment of all the agencies where the board had missions to the Episcopalians, whom they regarded as interlopers and violators of comity. They resented the opening of churches and schools at the very places where they were established while there were thousands of Dakotas elsewhere to whom no missionary had yet gone. Translations and linguistic tools were borrowed without credit. The Episcopalians interfered with discipline in their churches by too readily receiving disaffected communicants and laymen who wanted pay for services, they said.[150] Now they feared elimination. One agency, Sisseton, was then transferred to the American Board.[151] However, soon afterwards that board turned it over to the American

Missionary Association, which nominated all the other Congregationalist agents. The board was well satisfied with the Quaker agent at Santee.[152] Happily, within a few years the American Board and Episcopal missionaries were working together in friendship. Bishop Hare made full acknowledgment of indebtedness for translations and linguistic aids.[153]

There were no other instances of friction between societies cooperating in the peace policy; but as the years passed some others wanted agencies. The evidence seems to indicate that they were more interested in the prestige of the nominating power than in mission work. Then, too, the three great churches of the South with their many Indian members came more clearly into view, the Disciples of Christ wanted recognition, and the Moravians expressed a willingness to take one agency.[154] After some delay, partly due to fear on the part of Methodists and others that the change would allow the Roman Catholic Church opportunity to take control of too many agencies, the participating boards and societies in 1880 asked for a general redistribution.[155] Two years later they called for a conference of all denominations that might be interested in redistribution, but it was then too late, for the scheme had been abandoned.[156]

There were some flagrant cases of denial of freedom to Roman Catholic missionaries on some Protestant agencies. For example, a Presbyterian agent whom his church considered to be one of the very best endeavored to prevent a priest from saying mass and teaching at the Nez Percé agency in 1873; but the most outrageous case of injustice and maltreatment was at the Methodist agency of Round Valley, Calif., the following year.[157] Behind the opposition to Roman Catholic missionaries in many cases was resentment by both agents and missionaries when priests forbade children to attend government or mission schools.[158]

The Catholic Indian Bureau had long been campaigning for the opening of all agencies on the ground of religious liberty, but had made little progress.[159] Then occurred an event which brought Congregationalists and Presbyterians into the fight. The Dakota Christian Indians had organized their own Dakota Missionary Society, and an Indian minister, the Rev. Daniel Renville, was the missionary. Some of the Christians moved to Devil's Lake, and they appealed for a minister. The society sent Renville and his wife, both Sioux Indians. As Dakotas, it would seem that they had a right to receive Dakota rations. The rations were refused them, and the agent, who did not thwart them in any other way, notified Washington and asked what to do with them. He was ordered to expel the minister and his wife.[160] Commissioner Hayt replied: "It is against the rule of the Indian office to allow teachers of one denomination to intrude on the field held by another."[161]

The Dakota Missionary Society quite naturally protested to the Commissioner against the exclusion, and the American Board endorsed the appeal.[162] After Hayt's ruling the Society took its appeal to the Secretary of the Interior, Carl Schurz. The Presbyterian Board likewise protested through its secretary, Dr. John C. Lowrie. Schurz referred the matter to the new Commissioner, Trowbridge, who then canvassed the missionary societies on the question. It is amazing that six gave unqualified approval to the ruling, two were noncommittal, and one favored removal of all restrictions. Schurz therefore reiterated the ruling; but Trowbridge told Stephen R. Riggs that the ruling would not be made retroactive.[163] Riggs then voiced the feeling of the missionaries, the Christian Dakotas, and the American Board in calling for the abandonment of the scheme of collaboration if exclusion were involved. He exclaimed: "The Indians have rights in this matter which we are bound to respect."[164] The Prudential Committee of the American Board protested that "the plan was devised to increase and not to diminish the forces at work, not to put restrictions upon religious liberty, but to stimulate all denominations of Christians to effort on behalf of the Indians."[165] Several Presbyteries in Iowa and Nebraska asked abandonment of the plan.[166] Thus prodded, the General Assembly of the Presbyterian Church took a petition to President Hayes, stating: ". . . we would strongly insist upon giving to the Indians the same religious liberty which we claim for ourselves; that reservations should be open to all religious societies who sincerely work for the elevation of the Indians."[167] The Presbyterian and American Board secretaries took this matter to the next annual conference in 1881 and, despite some pleas for delay, secured endorsement of the Presbyterian memorial. A delegation was directed to make this known to the Secretary of the Interior.[168]

Secretary Schurz speedily reversed the former ruling and decreed: "In future, in all cases, except where the presence of rival organizations would manifestly be perilous to peace and order, Indian reservations shall be open to all religious denominations, providing that no existing treaty stipulations would be violated thereby."[169] Thereupon the Congregationalists exulted: "In response to the representations of the officers of the American Board, seconded by those of many other societies, the Secretary of the Interior has this day, February 11, revoked the obnoxious ruling of the Indian Department, by which ruling no religious denomination could engage in any missionary work unless the agency of that reservation had been assigned to that denomination. Hereafter no agent can send our missionaries away from Devil's Lake, or from any other field in which they are clearly called to labor."[170] While the American Board officers claimed the victory, the Roman Catholics, some of whom had regarded the whole peace policy as a Protestant venture in church-statism,[171] looked upon this as their victory. They had indeed contributed much towards its achievement.[172]

THE DISSOLUTION OF THE PARTNERSHIP

Even after Secretary Teller excluded the mission boards from participation in the administration of the agencies, collaboration in education continued for another decade. The dissolution came about largely as the result of a Protestant-Roman Catholic conflict over the Indian schools.

Two active and influential Protestant churchmen occupied key positions in the Bureau of Indian Affairs during the administration of President Benjamin Harrison. One was the Commissioner of Indian Affairs, a Baptist minister, the Rev. General Thomas J. Morgan. The other was the Superintendent of Indian Schools, the Rev. Daniel Dorchester, a Methodist clergyman. Commissioner Morgan was especially influential in effecting the dissolution of the partnership.

Thomas Jefferson Morgan had organized and commanded a Negro brigade in the Army of the Cumberland. He had earlier served as a subaltern under Colonel Benjamin Harrison, who had recommended him for rapid promotion and who apparently thereafter retained a high opinion of him. After the war Morgan studied for the ministry at Rochester Theological Seminary and was ordained in 1869.[173] Then after a pastorate of less than a year at Brownsville, Nebr., the young man became president of Nebraska (State) Normal School at Peru. He left that post in 1874 to join the faculty of the Baptist Union Theological Seminary at Chicago as professor of homiletics, but soon exchanged the field of preaching for the chair of church history. Meanwhile President Grant had appointed Morgan to membership on the Board of Visitors of the United States Military Academy at West Point, and his alma mater, Franklin College, awarded him the LL. D. degree. Seven years later he exchanged his professorship in the seminary for the presidency of the New York State Normal School at Potsdam, but after only two years accepted a similar post as head of the Rhode Island Normal School at Providence. Dr. Morgan was a popular speaker and preacher and a strong advocate of education for the Negro. When Benjamin Harrison was elected President, Morgan was strongly recommended for the position of United States Commissioner of Education, but Herbert Welsh of the Indian Rights Association urged upon Harrison his appointment as Commissioner of Indian Affairs, and at the President's request he accepted.[174]

It was apparent from the outset that Dr. Morgan and the Roman Catholic mission officers were mutually antagonistic. The Roman Catholic forces attempted to block the appointment of Morgan and then to prevent its confirmation through pressure upon the Senate's Committee on Indian Affairs. He had dared to attack the contract school system immediately after accepting the appointment. Questioned by the Senate's Committee, Morgan compromised and declared that he would observe the status quo but would resist expansion of contract schools. He was then confirmed.[175] From that first encounter there was almost open warfare. Morgan was described by his opponents as "the most outspoken official champion of opposition to the Catholic education of Indian youth," and it was charged that he "bulldozed" the Catholic Indian Mission Bureau.[176] They called him a bigot, and he did make nasty comparisons between Roman and Protestant missionary work. In defense he claimed that after failing to induce the President to remove him the Roman Catholic party attempted to destroy his reputation, that upon entering office he found the whole Service infiltrated with their agents, and that the Superintendent of Indian Schools (before Dorchester) was a Roman Catholic zealot.[177] The Commissioner held that the Roman mission schools refused to conform to government standards, to render itemized accounts, and resented inspection, while their hierarchy were using public funds to further missions rather than education. The conquest of the Indian schools through tax money would be the first step in taking over the entire public school system of the nation. An anonymous letter in the New York *Sun* on June 28, 1891, denounced Commissioner Morgan's policy, and it was traced to the Catholic Indian Mission Bureau. The Commissioner demanded an apology and refused to give an interview to its officers, and thereafter he refused to speak with that "insolent and infamous Bureau of Catholic Indian Missions." [178]

The *Fifty-eighth Annual Report of the Commissioner of Indian Affairs, 1889,* had to go to press early in the autumn, and although Dr. Morgan had just entered office and was still unconfirmed in the appointment, he issued his personal platform in that report, dated Oct. 1. He declared that the reservation system belonged to a vanished state of things and must soon cease to exist. He approved the outing system at Carlisle School, by which the Indian youths spent four months of the year living with white families. He wanted the Indians converted into "intelligent, honest American citizens, self-respectful and self-helpful." [179] However, the new and the controversial element was in an appended "Supplemental Report on Indian Education," dated Dec. 1. It was actually a statement which Morgan had presented before the Lake Mohonk Conference of the Friends of the Indian held Oct. 2—4. [180] The conference had approved the plan, and it had been given publicity. The government was no longer to leave the education of Indians primarily to voluntary, private agencies, especially churches. A compulsory, systematized, and comprehensive plan of Indian education conforming to the laws of the several states was to be established. It would begin with children in early years, employ only the English language, offer industrial training, and provide even higher education for those qualified. It would tend toward the breaking up of tribes by bringing children together out of many tribes, and it would stress individuality. There was to be coeducation. The government-controlled and -directed system would attempt to include "the influence of the home, the Sabbath school, the church, and religious institutions of learning."

A speaker at the Lake Mohonk conference declared:

The plan laid before the Conference by General Morgan last year, as a plan, leaves absolutely nothing to be desired. It is perfect, it is ideal; but just there is the trouble — it is only an ideal. If Commissioner Morgan could stay Commissioner, or if any party or policy of appointments under the federal government had a guarantee of permanence, all would be well. I would hold up both hands for taking over to the Commissioner the whole work for him to do.[181]

Doubts were directed toward government stability, not toward Morgan's plan. His next annual report stated that this plan had been endorsed by the National Education Association, the American Institute of Instructors, the New York State Teachers' Association, the Lake Mohonk Conference, and the Indian Rights Association.[182] He also stated:

> There is also a growing popular recognition of the fact that it is the duty of the Government and of the several States where they are located, to make ample provision for the secular and industrial education of the rising generation, leaving the churches free to prosecute with renewed vigor their legitimate work of establishing and maintaining religious missions. By this harmonious and yet separate activity of the Government and of the churches all of the Indians will eventually be brought into right relations with their white neighbors, and be prepared for the privileges and responsibilities of American Christian citizenship.[183]

Commissioner Morgan's scheme of government education struck at the support of both Protestant and Roman Catholic schools although there were far more of the latter. Had he not made this a crusade for what were increasingly being recognized as Protestant principles and against Roman Catholic practice, Morgan could hardly have gotten the overwhelmingly favorable response and support from the Protestant mission leaders. They believed him when he declared: "The battle I fought was a battle for the integrity of the American public school system, and to have surrendered my position would have been treason to the cause of free education."[184] The secretaries of the mission boards had confidence in Morgan and listened with believing ears when he told them about discrimination against Protestant schools under the previous Superintendent of Indian Schools and about continuing intrigue. Therefore they were more and more ready to follow him, even at considerable cost to their agencies because the cost to the nation seemed too great. When General Morgan left office at the end of the Harrison administration, he became corresponding secretary of the American Baptist Home Mission Society, and thus he himself joined the ranks of the secretaries. The power of his voice was magnified, and his editorship of the *Baptist Home Mission Monthly* gave him a ready forum for his views. Moreover, Dr. Morgan took to the lecture platform, especially under the sponsorship of the American Protective Association, and his influence rapidly increased with Protestant rank and file churchmen and with the general public.

It is evident that Protestant views about the desirability of the partnership of mission boards and government in Indian education were rapidly shifting in the early 1890s. The pressure exerted by the National League for the Protection of American Institutions tipped the scale toward the decision which was already inevitable. It is not easy to believe that the influence of such an organization could have been the decisive factor, but it did force the decision already pending. This organization, popularly known as the American Protective Association, or the A. P. A., was a manifestation of rabid agrarian American nativism, violently opposed to immigration and to the Roman Catholic Church. It supported the Republican Party and sought to identify the Democratic Party with the Roman Church. It claimed to be able to deliver a million votes. Protection of "the common school system" was its great war cry, and it sponsored a sixteenth amendment to the Constitution which would make more explicit the separation of church and state. It made a major issue of government support of the Indian mission schools, and it called upon every Protestant denomination and every participating mission board to renounce and condemn the practice.[185]

Being thus squarely challenged, and being already convinced, one board after another took action. The statistical table accompanying the letter of the A. P. A. was enough to frighten many a board secretary and his board of directors and to induce them to give up the grant which their agency had been receiving in view of what appeared a real threat by Rome. This revealed that in a period of eight years ending in 1893 the Catholic schools had received $2,355,416 out of a total of $3,767,951 for all schools, including Lincoln and Hampton Institutes and some nonchurch schools. The eight Protestant agencies listed had together received a total figure of only $938,977.[186] The letter to the boards stated:

> We earnestly appeal to your patriotism. . . . The pecuniary loss which would thus be sustained in assuming the entire care and support of your mission schools among the Indians would be light, as compared with the advantages which would ensue from such a sacrifice in the establishment of a correct principle of public policy.[187]

The version of this letter received by the Protestant Episcopal Church urging action pointed out that opposition to "sectarian appropriations by the National Government for Indian Education" had then been voiced by almost all the mission boards in the country engaged in Indian missions and by the national judicatories of the Methodist Episcopal Church, the Presbyterian Church in the U. S. A., the United Presbyterian Church, and a number of small denominations.[188] The Board of Missions of the Episcopal Church then, in the course of the general convention of 1892, adopted resolutions refusing further acceptance of subsidies and approving the proposed constitutional amendment.[189] The Methodists, Presbyterians, and the American Missionary Association all took such action in 1892.[190]

During the next few years there was considerable debate on the subject in Congress. Then the Appropriation Act in 1895 determined that financial aid would be limited to existing contract schools only, not to exceed 80 percent of the amount previously granted.[191] The next Congress on June 7, 1897, cut the figure for that year to 50 percent and terminated the practice by stipulating that "it is to be the settled policy of the government to hereafter make no appropriation whatever for education in any sectarian school." [192] It did allow 40 percent of the 1895 sum to be awarded in 1898 to existing contract schools at places where nonsectarian schools could not be provided. The 1899 Appropriation Act affirmed that it now made the "final appropriation for sectarian schools." [193] The ancient partnership of church and government was officially dissolved and repudiated by both the United States Congress and the Protestant mission boards.

Even after this official termination there were lingering vestiges of collaboration. Denied government funds, the Roman Catholic mission directors turned to the Indian tribes and got many of them to make contracts with the mission schools and to request the government to pay those schools out of funds belonging to the tribe and held by the government or due the tribe under treaty stipulations. Through the following years such tribal trust funds and treaty annuities drastically diminished and less and less was available to schools in that manner. Very few Protestant schools made such contracts. Similarly, rations due under treaty stipulations, which children would have received at home with their parents on the reservations, were given to the schools in which the students were enrolled. Continuing mission schools were subject to inspection, and they had to meet a considerable number of requirements. Mission buildings had been erected on land assigned to but not owned by the mission, and title remained with the tribe or government. Congress in 1922 authorized the Secretary of the Interior to issue a patent to any religious organization engaged in mission or school work on a reservation prior to Sept. 21 of that year for not more than 160 acres actually occupied and used for mission or school purposes. Here and there reminders of the ancient partnership of church and state are still to be found, but that relationship passed with the very last year of the 19th century.

NOTES

Chapter 4

1. Laurence F. Schmeckebier, *The Office of Indian Affairs, Its History, Activities, and Organization,* pp. 48—49, cites 40th Cong., 3d sess., *Congressional Globe,* p. 1881.

2. *American Missionary,* XVII (January 1873), 9.

3. Schmeckebier, pp. 50—51, cites 39th Cong., 2d sess., S. rep. 156, pp. 3—8.

4. Report to the President by the Indian Peace Commission, Jan. 7, 1868, in *Report of the Commissioner of Indian Affairs,* 1868, pp. 26—50.

5. *The Record of the Presbyterian Church in the U.S.A.,* XIX (March 1868), 68. Soon to change title to the *Monthly Record,* etc.

6. Statement by Dr. Treat in *Report of the Board of Indian Commissioners, 1871,* p. 166.

7. Rayner W. Kelsey, *Friends and the Indians, 1655—1917,* p. 165; also, *Friends Intelligencer,* XXIV (1867), 514.

8. Kelsey, pp. 165—66.

9. Ibid., pp. 166—67.

10. Board of Missions of the Protestant Episcopal Church, *Proceedings of the Annual Meeting, 1868,* pp. 9—11, 22, 147—68; Henry B. Whipple, *Lights and Shadows of a Long Episcopate,* pp. 521—48.

11. *Report of the Commissioner of Indian Affairs, 1869,* pp. 95—96.

12. Whipple, p. 262.

13. *Handbook of the Church's Missions to the Indians,* p. 39; *American Missionary,* XV, 10 (October 1877), 222.

14. James D. Richardson, *A Compilation of the Messages and Papers of the Presidents* (1898 ed.), VII, 8.

15. *Report of the Commissioner of Indian Affairs, 1869,* p. 97.

16. Ibid., pp. 326—30; Whipple, pp. 285—88.

17. See full statement in *American Missionary,* XV, 10 (October 1871), 220—24.

18. For example: *Missionary Herald,* LXXII (August 1876), 266. The Presbyterians began their mission to the Navajos of New Mexico in 1868 largely through the efforts of the wife of General Alexander, Board of Foreign Missions of the Presbyterian Church in the U.S.A., *Annual Report, 1869,* p. 11.

19. Schmeckebier, p. 55; cites 16 Stat. L., 319.

20. Kelsey, p. 168; text in full.

21. Kelsey, pp. 170—72, 187.

22. James D. Richardson, *A Compilation of the Messages and Papers of the Presidents,* VII, 38.

23. Schmeckebier, p. 56; cites 16 Stat. L., 40.

24. Ibid., pp. 56—57.

25. *American Missionary*, XV, 10 (October 1871), 222.

26. Elsie M. Rushmore, *The Indian Policy During Grant's Administrations*, p. 19.

27. *Report of the Commissioner of Indian Affairs, 1869*, p. 96; *Report of the Board of Indian Commissioners, 1869*, pp. 4—5.

28. Charles L. Slattery, *Felix Reville Brunet*, p. 143; *Report of Commissioner of Indian Affairs, 1869*, pp. 43—44.

29. *Report of the Commissioner of Indian Affairs, 1869*, pp. 4, 44—45; Rushmore, p. 20.

30. *Report of the Commissioner of Indian Affairs, 1877*, p. 9.

31. *Report of the Board of Indian Commissioners, 1879*, p. 110.

32. Rushmore, p. 25.

33. *Report of the Board of Indian Commissioners, 1881*, p. 6.

34. See A. P. Stokes, *Church and State in the United States*, II, 68.

35. Bishop Whipple in a letter to the President of the U.S., *Lights and Shadows of a Long Episcopate*, p. 511.

36. Slattery, p. 145.

37. *Missionary Advocate*, XXVI, 2 (May 17, 1870), 7.

38. Address before the American Missionary Association, published in a supplement to the *American Missionary*, XV, 12 (December 1871).

39. *Report of the Commissioner of Indian Affairs, 1870*, pp. 9—10.

40. Richardson, VII, 109—10; *Report of the Commissioner of Indian Affairs, 1870*, p. 10.

41. *Report of the Commissioner of Indian Affairs, 1870*, p. 10.

42. Ibid., 1869, p. 50.

43. *Report of the Board of Indian Commissioners, 1870*, pp. 5, 96, 98.

44. See remarks of Lowrie and Welsh in *ibid., 1871*, pp. 171, 176.

45. Ibid., *1870*, pp. 4, 137; Wade C. Barclay, *History of Methodist Missions*, III, 327.

46. American Board of Commissioners for Foreign Missions, *Annual Report, 1871*, pp. xx—xxi.

47. American Baptist Home Mission Society, *Annual Report, 1866*, p. 20; *1867*, p. 13; *1868*, p. 14.

48. Ibid., *1876*, p. 10.

49. *Report of the Board of Indian Commissioners, 1879*, p. 96.

50. Ibid., *1871*, p. 171.

51. Board of Foreign Missions of the Presbyterian Church in the U.S.A., *Annual Report, 1869*, pp. 6—11.

52. Board of Missions of the Protestant Episcopal Church, *Proceedings, 1866,* p. 94; *1868,* pp. 9—11, 16, 22, 147—68.

53. Ibid., *1870,* p. x.

54. *Report of the Board of Indian Commissioners, 1879,* p. 107; Loring B. Priest, *Uncle Sam's Stepchildren,* p. 32.

55. Priest, p. 32; see his documentation, p. 259.

56. Ibid., p. 28 ff.

57. *Report of the Board of Indian Commissioners, 1876,* p. 75.

58. Ibid., *1878,* pp. 127—28.

59. Kelsey, pp. 170—87.

60. Rushmore, pp. 34—35; quotes from Alice Fletcher, *Indian Education and Civilization,* p. 682.

61. Kelsey, pp. 187—97.

62. *Presbyterian Monthly Record,* XXI (October 1870), 227; XXIII (December 1872), 379—80.

63. Board of For. Miss., Presbyterian Church in the U. S. A., *Annual Report, 1871,* p. 21.

64. Ibid., p. 71.

65. *Report of the Board of Indian Commissioners, 1879,* p. 101.

66. Ibid., *1871,* p. 171.

67. Robert L. Stuart, *Sheldon Jackson;* Arthur J. Lazell, *Alaskan Apostle, The Life Story of Sheldon Jackson.*

68. *Report of the Board of Indian Commissioners, 1879,* p. 97.

69. Barclay, III, 327, footnote.

70. Board of Missions of the Protestant Episcopal Church, *Proceedings, 1870,* pp. x—xi; *1871,* pp. 12—13; *Spirit of Missions,* XXVI (February 1871), 49.

71. Protestant Episcopal Church, *Journal of the General Convention, 1871,* pp. 177, 186, 191—92, 233, 253, 379, 388.

72. Board of Missions of the Protestant Episcopal Church, *Proceedings, 1877,* pp. xxvi—xxviii, xxxiii—xxxvi; *Spirit of Missions,* XXXVII (1872), 25—26, 33—34.

73. Hare was the one hundredth bishop consecrated in the church, and the circumstances of his calling and consecration were interpreted as constituting a new epoch in the history of that church. *Spirit of Missions,* XXXVIII (1873), 98.

74. Board of Foreign Missions, Reformed Church in America, *Annual Report, 1871,* p. 167.

75. American Missionary Association, *Annual Report, 1878,* p. 33.

76. *American Missionary,* XXII, 11 (November 1878), 325—26.

77. See for example, *Report of the Board of Indian Commissioners, 1871,* pp. 165, 170; the Indian Commissioners had similar ideas, see *1872,* p. 28.

78. Whipple, p. 551.

79. *Report of the Board of Indian Commissioners, 1871,* p. 168.

80. *American Missionary,* XV, 12 (December 1871), 273—74.

81. *Report of the Board of Indian Commissioners, 1873,* p. 184. The Board of Indian Commissioners also recognized that transportation costs were a major obstacle to securing good men for subordinate jobs. *1873,* p. 25.

82. Ibid., *1871,* p. 167.

83. Ibid., p. 20.

84. *Report of the Commissioner of Indian Affairs, 1873,* p. 9.

85. Ibid., *1882,* p. 4.

86. *American Missionary,* XVII, 12 (December 1873), 280.

87. Ibid., p. 273.

88. Ibid., XX, 10 (October 1876), 236.

89. *Report of the Commissioner of Indian Affairs, 1871,* pp. 590, 593.

90. American Missionary Association, *Annual Report, 1871,* p. 65.

91. *Report of Commission Appointed by the Secretary of the Interior to Investigate Certain Charges Against Hon. E. P. Smith, the Commissioner of Indian Affairs.*

92. *American Missionary,* XX, 10 (October 1876), 236.

93. Ibid., XVIII, 6 (June 1874), 134; vol. XIX, 9 (September 1875), 198.

94. *Report of Commission Appointed by the Secretary of the Interior to Investigate Charges Against Hon. E. P. Smith, the Commissioner of Indian Affairs.*

95. *American Missionary,* XX, 2 (February 1876), 26; 8 (August 1876), 177—79.

96. Ibid., 9 (September), 193; 10 (October), 235 ff.; 11 (November), 244—45.

97. *Report of the Board of Indian Commissioners, 1878,* pp. 4—5.

98. Managers of the Domestic and Foreign Missionary Society of the Protestant Episcopal Church, *Report, 1877—78,* p. 476.

99. American Baptist Home Mission Society, *Annual Report, 1880,* p. 36.

100. Kelsey, p. 185.

101. P. J. Rahill, *The Catholic Indian Missions and Grant's Peace Policy,* p. 290.

102. *Report of the Board of Indian Commissioners, 1879,* pp. 98 ff.

103. *Report of the Executive Committee of the American Unitarian Association, 1878,* p. 12.

104. *Report of the Board of Indian Commissioners, 1879,* p. 107 to 108.

105. American Baptist Home Mission Society, *Annual Report, 1880,* p. 36.

106. *Board of Indian Commissioners, 1881,* p. 87: General Fisk's report of conversation with Garfield and Kirkwood.

107. Ibid., *1882,* p. 53.

108. Whipple, pp. 551—52.

109. Francis A. Walker, *The Indian Question* (Boston: Osgood, 1874), p. 104.

110. Ibid., pp. 145—46.

111. An editorial from the New York *Times* reprinted in the *American Missionary,* XX, 8 (August 1876), 185—86.

112. For typical responses, see: Methodist Missionary Society, *Annual Report, 1872,* p. 135; *Presbyterian Monthly Record,* XXI (October 1870), 227; Board of Foreign Missions of the Presbyterian Church U. S. A., *Annual Report, 1871,* p. 21; American Board of Commissioners for Foreign Missions, *Annual Report, 1870,* p. xx.

113. Board of Foreign Missions, Presbyterian Church U. S. A., *Annual Report, 1881,* p. 11; Board of Missions of the Protestant Episcopal Church, *Proceedings, 1874,* pp. 153—54, 169.

114. References are scarce in the *Annual Reports* of the B. H. M. S. and the *Baptist Home Mission Monthly.* There were some references to a "debt" to the Indians. *Baptist Home Mission Monthly,* I, 1 (May 1878), 4; II, 3 (March 1880), 39.

115. *Report of the Executive Committee of the American Unitarian Association, 1874,* pp. 54—55; *1874,* p. 11; *1875,* p. 16; *1876,* p. 10; *1877,* pp. 7—8; *1878,* pp. 11—12.

116. *Report of the Board of Indian Commissioners, 1879,* p. 71; Kelsey, p. 179.

117. R. W. Kelsey, *Friends and the Indians,* p. 176.

118. Ibid., p. 184.

119. *Report of the Commissioner of Indian Affairs, 1869,* p. 154.

120. Ibid., *1873,* pp. 332—47.

121. Methodist Missionary Society, *Annual Report, 1870,* p. 120.

122. *Missionary Advocate,* New Ser., I, 6 (June 1873), 88.

123. Methodist Missionary Society, *Annual Report, 1877,* p. 177.

124. Barclay, III, 327—28.

125. American Missionary Association, *Annual Report, 1873,* pp. 92—96.

126. Myron Eells, *Father Eells* (Boston: Congregational S. S. and Pub. Soc., ca. 1894).

127. American Missionary Association, *Annual Report, 1875*, p. 67; Myron Eells, *Ten Years . . . at Skokomish* (Boston: Congregational S. S. and Pub. Soc., 1886).

128. *Report of the Board of Indian Commissioners, 1873*, pp. 76—77.

129. American Missionary Association, *Annual Report, 1877*, p. 12.

130. Board of Foreign Missions of the Presbyterian Church U. S. A., *Annual Report, 1869*, pp. 6—11.

131. Ibid., *1871*, pp. 18—21.

132. Ibid., *1878*, p. 11.

133. Ibid., *1882*, p. 11.

134. Ibid., pp. 98, 100.

135. *Spirit of Missions*, XXXIV, 1 (January 1869), 3—6, an iddication of the upsurge.

136. Board of Missions of the Protestant Episcopal Church, *Proceedings, 1870*, pp. x—xi; *1871*, pp. 12—13; *1872*, p. 15.

137. Protestant Episcopal Church, *Journal of the General Convention, 1871*, pp. 177, 186, 191—92, 233, 254, 379, 388.

138. Ibid., pp. 102, 349, 352, 361.

139. M. A. de W. Howe, *The Life and Labors of Bishop Hare, Apostle to the Sioux;* Board of Missions of the Protestant Episcopal Church, *Proceedings, 1873*, pp. 11—12, also pp. xl, 133.

140. The annual report of the commission reveals the progress of the work. It is included in the *Proceedings* of the Board of Missions: *1872*, pp. 14—24; *1873*, pp. 11—21; etc.

141. Board of Missions of the Protestant Episcopal Church, *Proceedings, 1873*, p. 13.

142. Ibid., *1872*, p. 17; *Report of the Board of Indian Commissioners, 1871*, p. 176.

143. Ibid., *1874*, pp. 22—23: Boston, Philadelphia, New York, Providence, Baltimore, and Fairfield County, Conn.

144. *Handbook of the Church's Missions to the Indians*, p. 134.

145. Ibid., pp. 299—304, 322—23.

146. *Report of the Board of Indian Commissioners, 1871*, p. 155.

147. Rahill, pp. 276 ff.

148. *Missionary Herald*, LXXVI (September 1880), 345—46.

149. Board of Foreign Missions of the Presbyterian Church in the U. S. A., *Annual Report, 1870*, pp. 7—8.

150. American Board of Commissioners for Foreign Missions, *Annual Report, 1871*, pp. xx, 89; *1875*, pp. 68—69; *Presbyterian Monthly Record*, XXIII (June 1872), p. 176.

151. Ibid., *1871*, pp. xx—xxi, 89.

152. Ibid., *1872*, p. 82.

153. Board of Missions of the Protestant Episcopal Church, *Proceedings, 1875*, p. 138.

154. *Board of Indian Commissioners, 1879*, pp. 115 ff. Conference journal of 1880 reveals first invitation to Southern churches. The Southern Baptist secretary was present. He came also the next year along with a representative of the Disciples. *1881*, pp. 84 ff.

155. *Report of the Board of Indian Commissioners, 1879*, p. 108.

156. Ibid., *1881*, p. 84.

157. Rahill, pp. 113, 146—49.

158. See, for example, Board of Foreign Missions, Presbyterian Church in the U.S.A., *Annual Report, 1873*, p. 14; *1874*, p. 11.

159. Rahill, pp. 273 ff.

160. *Missionary Herald*, LXXVI (September 1880), 345—46.

161. Ibid., p. 346.

162. American Board of Commissioners for Foreign Missions, *Annual Report, 1878*, p. xxxix.

163. *Missionary Herald*, LXXVI (September 1880), 346.

164. Ibid., loc. cit.

165. ABCFM, *Annual Report, 1880*, p. 93.

166. Ibid., loc. cit.

167. *Report of Board of Indian Commissioners, 1880*, pp. 98—99.

168. Ibid., pp. 99—114, discussion and action.

169. *Missionary Herald*, LXXVII (April 1881), 129.

170. Ibid., March, p. 87.

171. *Address of the Catholic Clergy of the Province of Oregon to the Catholics of the United States on President Grant's Indian Policy, etc.*, p. 7.

172. Rahill, esp. pp. 273 ff.; *Report of the Board of Indian Commissioners, 1881*, pp. 74—75.

173. For Morgan's career see *Dictionary of American Biography*, XIII, 187—88; *National Cyclopedia of American Biography* (1899), p. 54; "Memorial Services" in *American Baptist Home Missions Monthly*, XXIV, 11 (November 1902), 294 ff.; *Baptist Encyclopedia* (1881), pp. 815—16.

174. Indian Rights Association, *Seventh Annual Meeting, 1889*, p. 110; Morgan, Thomas J., "Indian Contract Schools," in *American Baptist Home Mission Monthly*, XVIII, 12 (December 1896), 393.

175. Indian Rights Association, *Proceedings of Eighth Annual Meeting, 1890*, p. 80.

176. *American Catholic Quarterly Review*, XXV, 97 (January 1900), 156—59.

177. Thomas J. Morgan, *Roman Catholics and Indian Education* (Boston: American Citizen Co., 1893), pp. 6—8.

178. Ibid., p. 9; U.S. Commissioner of Indian Affairs, *60th Annual Report, 1891*, pp. 162—63.

179. U.S. Commissioner of Indian Affairs, *58th Annual Report, 1889*, pp. 7—8.

180. Ibid., pp. 93—97; Lake Mohonk Conference of the Friends of the Indian, *Proceedings of the Eighth Annual Meeting, 1890*, p. 59.

181. Lake Mohonk Conference, *1890*, p. 70.

182. U.S. Commissioner of Indian Affairs, *59th Annual Report, 1890*, p. viii.

183. Ibid., pp. vi—vii.

184. Thomas J. Morgan, *Roman Catholics and Indian Education*, p. 14.

185. Humphrey A. Desmond, *The A. P. A. Movement* (Washington: New Century Press, 1912).

186. Protestant Episcopal Church, *Journal of the General Convention*, 1892, p. 418; Morgan, op. cit., Morgan's apology also gives these figures.

187. Ibid., pp. 417—18.

188. Ibid., pp. 416—19.

189. Ibid., p. 419.

190. Presbyterian Church in the U.S.A., *Minutes of the General Assembly, 1892*, New Ser. XV, 45—46; Methodist Episcopal Church, *Journal of the General Conference, 1892*, pp. 167—68; American Missionary Association, *46th Annual Report, 1892*, pp. 12, 14.

191. Stokes, II, 289.

192. Ibid., pp. 289—90.

193. Ibid., p. 290.

Protestant Missionary Views on Government Indian Policy During the Grant and Hayes Administrations

᯲§ The protagonists for Indian rights among American Protestant churches in the half century before the Civil War were the American Board of Commissioners for Foreign Missions and the Society of Friends. The American Board was then the missionary organ of the Congregationalists and the New School Presbyterians. It had attained its preeminence as a champion of Indian rights through its valiant efforts to defend the Cherokees and Choctaws against aggression by the state of Georgia and removal by the national government. The Friends had similarly sought to aid the Senecas. Episcopalian and American Board missionaries and officials had also tried to secure justice for the Dakotas during the Civil War period. However, it was not until after the war and during the Reconstruction era that a broader common front developed among the Protestant churches on behalf of the Indian cause. This came about through the participation of a number of mission boards and societies in President U. S. Grant's "Peace Policy." [1]

The objectives of the peace policy were the pacification of the Indians through just and fair dealing, the appointment of able and honest Indian agents devoted to Indian improvement and nominated by the religious societies, settlement of the tribes on reservations and within Indian Territory as far as possible, fostering their progress in "civilization" through education, and thus neutralizing them as an obstacle to white settlement of the western country. The President mentioned citizenship as the ultimate goal for the Indians. The government expected the participating missionary societies to conduct mission work vigorously so that the Christian religion might become a potent spiritual force in the civilizing process. Since they believed that they had been offered active and responsible partnership in the government's Indian affairs, the missionary agencies became both vocal defenders and critics of the policy. They simultaneously championed the cause of Indian rights before the public.

INDIAN RIGHTS

The first task of the churches was to try to convince the public and many members of the frontier churches that the new policy of civilization was a valid and practicable alternative to the popular demand for extermination. The new policy must have a chance to prove itself. Extermination was inhuman and unchristian. The Indian was a man, not a beast, and Christ offered salvation to him as well as to all other men.[2] However, every Indian uprising, every account of a "massacre," real or manufactured, every instance of resistance to aggression and injustice brought new demands for repression, removal, and even extermination from a large part of the populace, especially in the West. The rank-and-file frontier church member was likely to hold the same views as his unchurched neighbor. The mission boards endeavored to awaken both the Christian conscience and the national conscience. One editor lamented: "It is still an open question with Christian people whether the bullet or the Gospel is to settle the fate of the Indian — whether extermination or redemption is our duty towards him." One heard such remarks as: "The rule for the Indian is six feet and a bullet." "Give them the Gospel, but begin with powder and ball." "General Crook is better than General Howard." [3] It was the common feeling that Indians are outlaws, savages with no rights which white men are bound to respect.[4] The missionary forces tried to conquer these exterminationists and simultaneously arouse friends of truth by presenting evidence that there were more murders of Indians by whites than of whites by Indians, that stories of massacres were often fabrications, and that Indian wars were usually due to injustices perpetrated by the settlers and to broken promises by the government.[5]

Then there were those who believed that the Indian was doomed to destruction by natural circumstances and that government policy should assist and not hinder that desired end.[6] Confronting this view, the American Board affirmed that the Indians are not dying out and that "the Christian people of our country have no longer any right to cherish the hope, even so faintly, that the 'Indian Question' is going to be settled by the 'visitation of God' through the agency of disease. We will not believe that they *ever* felt that it should be settled by extermination." [7] Another Congregationalist agency nevertheless feared the imminent destruction of the Indians by another means. "It is still a question whether the Indian tribes can be delivered from border ruffians, whisky, and violence, and brought thoroughly under the influence of Christian agents and Christian missionaries, and thus be saved from final extinction." [8] Anything other than a faithful application of the new policy would clearly lead to extermination.[9] And to those who did not hope for such extinction but rather feared its inevitability there went out an urgent call to support both the government's peace policy and missionary expansion, since "these Indian missions are the sole refuge of the heathen tribes, so long neglected and cruelly oppressed, against foes that seek to destroy both body and soul. Brethren, let us not fail to give them our most faithful prayers and offerings, remembering that *time is short!*" [10] The Baptists dared to assert that "the wild Indian is deteriorating and dying out, while the Christianized Indian is improving and increasing." [11]

The officers and directors of the missionary societies had little hope of awakening the consciences of the "border ruffians" and the corrupt political "Indian rings" of Washington and the frontier communities, which like vampires lived off the Indian Service and by exploiting Indian helplessness and lack of legal protection. The Indian rings could, however, be thwarted and Indian rights protected if the hands of the good people of the frontier could be strengthened and enough people throughout the country induced to bring sufficient pressure upon Congress to enact needful legislation. The motivation for missions to the Indians was the same as that with respect to all heathen peoples, namely, glory to God, love and obedience to Christ, and compassion for perishing souls. Important added motives for battling for Indian rights as well as for evangelization were a sense of grave "indebtedness" to the Indians and the vindication of the national honor. In the missionary circles of the churches many hearts and minds were genuinely burdened with a sense of national guilt because Indians were dispossessed from lands once all theirs, treaties solemnly made were lightly broken, and the long record of exploitation and injustice was ignored.[12]

The little that was being done on the Indians' behalf was all too meager. "When, however, it is remembered how the red man has fared at our hands, and how he has been pushed back before the tide of civilized life, till he has had no abiding home left, it is but a poor return we are making, in the form of Christian love and labor, to prepare them for the home Christ has provided for all the troubled and the weary." [13] At this time the frontier was advancing from the Pacific coast as well as from the prairies, and the Indian was being ground between millstones from which there was no escape. This made the feelings of guilt and urgency all the stronger.[14] Consequently there was an expectation that the United States was about to be judged at the bar of history.[15] The nation that had oppressed the black man now seemed willing to cheat the red man. But as Lincoln had the honor of giving liberty to the Negro, so Grant was now to be credited with devising a plan of honest dealing with the Indians and of attempting their moral and material elevation.[16] Let the nation therefore back it with prayer, with pressure on congressmen, and with contributions to the mission boards.

There were also people who would not respond to arguments about debt and honor. They might be reached if it could be demonstrated that policies of either extermination or repression were excessively costly and that the taxpayer would benefit from the peace policy. And so the missionary societies spread that word far and wide. Indians were expensive. Even feeding them on reservations costs $5 million each year; but that was cheap compared with military operations. Simply compare it with the expense of the Sioux and Florida Wars of 1852 and 1854, which for each Indian warrior killed in battle had cost the government a million dollars and the lives of 25 whites, since the Indian does not die unresistingly.[17] The Florida War had cost 1,500 lives and $50 million; but that was relatively cheap, since for each warrior *engaged* in the fighting this figured out at only one white life and $33,000. The Sioux War of 1852—54 had cost hundreds of lives and $40 million, while the Oregon War of 1854—55 ran to $10 million. Fifteen or twenty Indians were killed in the Cheyenne War of 1864—65 at a total cost of $35 million plus the destruction of lives and property in the frontier settlements. The clash with the Cheyennes again in 1867 cost another $40 million. The Sioux War of 1867 cost over $10 million. Military repression of the wild Apaches required $100 million during the 20 year period from 1846 to 1866. It was currently costing the government some $2 million in cash to the Army just to restrain them. During the 50-year period ending in 1876 it cost the government $12.5 million per year for military operations. Contrast all this expense with the fact that not one cent was needed for military purposes to keep the civilized Cherokees, Creeks, Choctaws, and Seminoles in order! [18] All the Indian schools that would ever be needed would cost far less than one year's military appropriation, and at least two missionaries could be maintained at what was required just for the salary and maintenance of a single soldier and his bayonet.[19]

Employing such arguments and reporting constantly on the success of schools and various projects in civilization, the missionary agencies endeavored to create interest in and gain support for the new peace policy. They cried: "The churches of the land must arouse the consciences of the American people more and more, until it shall be impossible to return to the old ways of Indian fraud and cruelty." [20] They regularly commended the President on success of the plan and urged its continuance and development.[21] Expressions of approval along with exhortations to support appeared frequently in the church press, and the periodicals carried many items of news about the Indians.[22] The Episcopal Indian Commission for a few years published a special periodical entitled *The Church and the Indians*. Numerous pamphlets were also published.

There was quite naturally constant recourse to that favorite ecclesiastical device, the resolution. The boards and societies passed resolutions commending or reproving the government, demanding protection of Indian Territory, the application of law to the Indians, the grant of land in severalty, or a dozen other specific matters.[23] Regional presbyteries, synods, associations, and conferences were induced to do the same.[24] Sometimes even a national church assembly would take similar action, such as the General Assembly of the Presbyterian Church in the U. S. A.[25] These resolutions would be printed in church papers and forwarded to the administrative officers of government and Congress. Resolutions eased the consciences of the resolvers, but their ultimate purpose was the prodding of Congress to action and the restraining of local western governments. They represented an effort to stir up the constituency of each denomination to the end "that the members will do all in their power to make the Indian question a pressing question, until the attention of Congress is so secured and held to it that the legislative enactments necessary to bring about these changes may be completely accomplished." [26]

The annual conference of the representatives of the mission boards and societies with the Board of Indian Commissioners provided the opportunity for common action in resolutions by all the participating agencies. Resolutions were adopted each year and forwarded to the President, the Secretary of the Interior, and the Commissioner of Indian Affairs. If the matter were considered sufficiently urgent, a delegation would present the document personally. The resolutions ranged from a warm commendation of President Grant upon his approaching retirement to a rather full commentary on policy and program in 1879.[27]

However, as one writer baldly confessed: "If resolutions and memorials could have saved the American Indian, he would long ago have been lifted into blessedness. But, unfortunately, reports of committees and expressions of favor from benevolent societies are but a poor substitute for either manly justice or Christian beneficence." [28] Local groups working to educate public opinion and bring influence to bear on local politicians and on Washington were desirable. Interdenominational Indian rights associations with various titles and modeled after the New York Indian Peace Commission were therefore established in a few places, including New York, Boston, and Oregon.[29] The Episcopal Church sponsored numerous local Indian aid associations in large cities.

The associations supplied agents and missionaries with books, clothing, medicine, and other material and undertook public education on Indian affairs.[30] This church also called on its clergy to disseminate information and to form an association in each parish.[31] The Friends organized similar associations which supplied agents and schools and gained the public ear.[32] There was at least one large-scale effort by church women to make some impact on Congress. Bishop Hare in 1882 referred to a strange scene in the Senate the previous spring when several western senators were "lashed almost to fury by the simple reading of a petition of one hundred thousand church women praying that the Government would keep its promises to the Indians and extend to them the protection of the law." [33]

No other denomination in this period was so well organized to work for Indian rights and influence policy as the Protestant Episcopal Church. Immediately upon accepting the responsibility for nominating agents, the general convention in 1871 created a Standing Committee on Indian Affairs comprised of six laymen, with William Welsh as chairman, "to operate with the Board of Missions by supervising the secular work of the agencies under their care, by providing such civilizing agencies as the Government does not provide, and by involving the aid of the Government, and, if need be, the assistance of the courts, in protecting the rights of the Indians." [34] This committee soon became the Commission on Indian Missions of the Episcopal Church, with a membership of 50 persons. That number was unworkable and reduced to twelve.[35] This commission had a commissioner, first Col. E. C. Kemble and then the Rev. J. C. Rogers, resident in Washington, keeping watch over affairs there as well as visiting reservations and promoting the mission work. A subcommittee, headed by Senator Stevenson of Kentucky, was appointed to watch the course of legislation and to bring the influence of the church to bear wherever possible.[36] The commission did excellent service, but it appeared that there was need of an official organ of the church which would be solely concerned with the matter of rights. Moreover, to the Episcopalians the critical issue appeared to be the protection of law. Therefore the general convention of 1877 created a joint committee of three bishops and three deputies "On Securing For the Indians the Protection of the Law." [37] This committee reported in 1880 that the matter was highly complicated. It was necessary to secure parallel legislation by the Federal Government and the states. The Indians east of the Mississippi were already protected by state laws, but those west of the Mississippi were not. Moreover, the state and territorial legislatures were made up of the kind of settlers who exploit and oppress the Indians, and no desirable legislation could be expected from them. There would have to be total reliance upon federal law for the western Indians. [38] The committee was enlarged so as to be comprised of three bishops, three presbyters, and three laymen. It was to continue to seek effective legislation and to report from time to time. Bishops H. B. Whipple and W. H. Hare were constantly active in promoting the cause of Indian rights and welfare within their respective dioceses, throughout the Episcopal Church, and in Washington. They wrote letters, had personal interviews with the President and other administrative officers, and used the press extensively. [39]

The missionary societies placed their chief hope for sound policy and effective legislation in the Board of Indian Commissioners when it was established by Congress and the President in 1869 and composed of wealthy philanthropists who were regarded as representing the churches. [40] The original Board resigned in 1874 because neither the Service, the Administration, nor Congress paid heed to its reasonable recommendations. The second group, supposedly also representing the churches, was not as influential and able. After 1875 the fiction of church representation was abandoned. The Board had less and less influence. Both active laymen and officers of the boards turned with new hope after 1882 to the voluntary Indian Rights Association.

It is difficult to say what effect the efforts of the churches achieved in the shaping of policy and the winning of Indian rights during this period. Certainly they succeeded in making the matter truly one of public interest. The churches were not again to be so vocal on Indian rights until the decade of the 1950s.

CIVILIZATION, THE ALTERNATIVE TO WAR AND EXTERMINATION

The Indians were an obstacle to white settlement. Even where their lands were poor, whites were certain that they wanted them. The Indians had lost their game lands and were being segregated on reservations where the government had to feed them in idleness. Unable to adjust to such a life, resentful at broken treaties and repeated removals, provoked by atrocities and wrongs inflicted by the settlers, or rather by the "border ruffians," the Indians could be expected to break out in frequent rebellion, with bloody reprisals. The government was faced with two practical questions, according to General Francis A. Walker, Commissioner of Indian Affairs: What shall be done with the Indian as an obstacle to the progress of settlement and industry? What shall be done with him as a pensioner on our civilization when and so far as he ceases to oppose or obstruct the extension of railroads and of settlement? Walker's answer to the first was to strike him down with the Army; to the second, to confine him to reservations and somehow keep him there. In either case the Indian's only hope was submission.[41] President Grant's peace policy was built upon the assumption that there was another possibility than extermination or sullen submission in degrading idleness. It was the Indian's voluntary acceptance of civilization and his emulation of the white man in living by his own labor. Secretary Schurz said: "If the Indians are to live at all, they must learn to live as white men!"[42] But could Indians be civilized? Every annual report of the Commissioner of Indian Affairs, of the Board of Indian Commissioners, and of each participating mission board offered ample proof through detailed accounts of progress on the several reservations. The condition of the Five Civilized Tribes in Indian Territory and then the Dakotas or Sioux at Santee, Sisseton, and later elsewhere were the prize exhibits.

At the beginning of the program the national government agreed with the missionary societies that the churches must add the one indispensable ingredient which the government could not provide if the Indians were to become civilized. This was the Christian religion. Both in the 17th- and 18-century efforts and in the early 19th-century missions to the Indians, as well as in the overseas missions to primitive peoples, the missionaries had assumed that the Gospel brought civilization in its train, while civilization disposed such people to accept Christianity. The same assumption held now. Dr. John C. Lowrie declared: "The object of the missionaries is to give them the gospel, and civilization will follow as the result. . . . The gospel first, then civilization. The order should not be reversed. This doctrine is ground upon which we should all stand." [43] William Welsh said: "If the Government will turn its attention to checking the white violations of the law, the religious bodies can tame and control the Indians." [44] Moses N. Adams, agent for the Sisseton and Wahpeton Sioux, wrote in 1872: "There seem to be no obstacles in the way of their civilization, except such as are common to all Indian tribes, and which the gospel of Christ and Bible civilization can meet and remove." Among the common obstacles he listed ignorance, idleness, prodigality, hunting, fishing, smoking, babbling, tattling, love of spirituous liquors, riding horseback from house to house, and polygamy! [45] Christianity would replace these characteristics and pursuits with others more desirable. Most important, the Gospel would awaken individualism and the desire for a home and sanctified family life.

E. P. Smith, the Commissioner of Indian Affairs, who during his brief tenure truly represented the churches, stressed the necessity of bringing the incentive of Christian faith and life through

men and women who embodied it themselves and who would
serve as friendly exemplars — Christian agents and missionaries.
He stated in his *Report* for 1874:

> . . . I desire to reiterate my conviction of the entire
> feasibility of Indian civilization, and that the difficulty of
> its problem is not so inherent in the race character and
> disposition of the Indian — great as those obstacles are —
> as in his anomalous relation to the Government, and in
> his surroundings affected by the influence and interest of
> the white people. The main difficulty, so far as the Gov-
> ernment is concerned, lies in the fact that the Indian's
> deepest need is that which the Government through its
> political organization and operations, cannot well bestow.
> The first help which a man in barbarism requires is not
> that which can be afforded through a political party, but
> that which is offered by a fellow-man, wiser than himself,
> coming personally and extending a hand of sympathy and
> truth. No amount of appropriations and no governmental
> machinery can do much towards lifting an ignorant and
> degraded people, except as it works through the willing
> hands of men made strong and constant by their love for
> their fellow men.

> If, therefore, it shall be possible to continue the sym-
> pathy and aid of the religious people of the land in this
> work, and to rally for its prosecution the enthusiasm and
> zeal which belong to religion, and also if it shall be pos-
> sible to procure the enactment of such laws as will recog-
> nize the essential manhood and consequent capabilities
> and necessities of the Indian, and to provide reasonably
> adequate appropriations . . . every year will witness a steady
> decrease of barbarism. . . .[46]

The chief question connected with the policy of civilization
which agitated the churches was whether or not the Bureau of
Indian Affairs should be transferred from the Department of the
Interior to the War Department. Frontier forces were constantly

pressing for such a move, and it was repeatedly proposed in Congress. There was general agreement among missionaries that the presence of military posts inevitably resulted in the demoralization and degradation of the Indians in their neighborhood.[47] Even those missionaries who testified to the high quality and interest of many officers protested that the Army was not a fit teacher of civilization.[48] Bishop Hare's desire to use the Army as a police force to assist the agents on the reservations to control or expel obnoxious white intruders and to protect peaceful Indians against their lawless fellows brought him much criticism.[49] It was common knowledge that the Roman Catholic Church in the main favored the proposed transfer, and that further strengthened the opposition by Protestants who believed that church to be working against the whole peace policy.[50]

The anticipated transfer was opposed in 1873 by the New York Indian Commission and by the boards at the annual conference in 1874.[51] When the proposal was again made in 1876, the American Board protested: "If they are the children — the wards — of the government, it should be careful not to answer a cry for bread with *lead,* or when they ask for fish to give them scorpions. Your Committee rejoice that the President is still devoted to a peace policy; and regret, that while in professed accord, the Legislative department of the government should for a moment, against the united voice of the best Indians, have thought of promoting it by a transfer to the War Department." [52] At the same time the Dakota vernacular *Word Carrier* protested against this action by men who hate Indians.[53] Bishop Whipple spoke and wrote against it.[54] The Baptists declared in 1878 that such a transfer "would be a mistake alike in morals and economy, and unworthy of the character of the American people." [55] The House of Representatives had just then passed a bill making the change in administration, but the Senate, instead of passing it, appointed a joint committee for study and report on the subject, and the House agreed. While the report was awaited the Indians had become greatly agitated at the prospect of the transfer.[56] The Congregationalists observed that the majority of the members of the joint committee represented the western communities which desired the change. They objected that the Indians did not want it. The Army also did not want the responsibility, but acceded after the joint committee had made the responsibility a point of honor. So, because the powerful Indian ring wanted it, the bill would probably become law unless the President intervened.[57] The bill was defeated, and a little later the Presbyterians expressed satisfaction over its defeat.[58]

There was sentiment for an independent Indian Department of cabinet rank, but the religious societies never undertook a vigorous campaign on behalf of the proposal. Dr. Lowrie of the Presbyterian Board raised the issue at the annual conference of 1874, and in the general convention of the Episcopal Church in 1877 it was proposed that the church advance the suggestion for an independent Indian Bureau with a Cabinet officer as chairman, the Commissioner of Indian Affairs as the executive officer, and two Army officers and two civilians as members.[59] Bishop Whipple proposed directly to President Grant that an independent department be established "with one of the best men in the nation at its head." [60]

RESERVATIONS, REMOVAL, INDIAN TERRITORY

The missions, with the exception of the American Board and some Episcopalians, were heartily in favor of the official policy of concentrating and segregating Indians on reservations. There was a nostalgic remembrance of the 17th- and 18th-century mission stations with their Christian villages and of the prosperous stations among the Five Civilized Tribes. Not the voluntary wandering of the Indians but white pressure had destroyed them. The Indians of the prairies had been utterly baffling. An expensive station with a large mission family would be located at or near what was supposed to be the chief seat of a tribe, only to discover that the tribe soon moved away to some remote place, leaving the station isolated. Most mission agencies therefore deemed "schools and missions impracticable until the Indians are collected on reservations"; and they welcomed this action of the government.[61] Immobilized, the Indians could be "reached." There they could also be protected against white aggression and be taught to work. The editor of the *American Missionary,* approving in the main General Walker's suggestion of concentration, stated: "The true policy is, we believe, to provide a suitable number of reservations, where the efforts of the Government, seconded by the Christian sentiment of the country, may create oases in the sight of cognate tribes, who shall be drawn towards them by affinity, and the opportunity of bettering their condition. The blessing of God on earnest Christian labor must do the rest." [62]

Bishop Whipple and many Episcopalians favored reservations, and the bishop would have placed all the Indians in Minnesota on the White Earth Reservation, those of the Pacific coast on two reservations, and all the remaining tribes in Indian Territory.[63] His colleague, Bishop W. H. Hare, could regard a reservation only as a necessary evil or temporary expedient; and the American Board missionaries held the same view, urging that any reservation be terminated before it interfered with attainment of citizenship.[64] Bishop Hare thought the reservation to be "a gravelstone in the machinery of our political and social life" and that segregation thwarted the attainment of the desired civilization.[65] He denounced the system in strong terms:

> The present system, by which, too often, reservations of thousands upon thousands of acres are a vast common, in which any man scratches a piece of land where he will, and where beef, flour, sugar, coffee, etc., are doled out to vicious and virtuous, indolent and industrious alike, is a monstrous evil, which should be tolerated not a day longer than is absolutely necessary. Even were our taxpayers willing to endure it, we have no right to inflict it

upon the Indians, who ought to receive from us a useful and not a pernicious training; nor have we any right to rear a race of paupers to be a curse to our whole Western country; nor any right to fight God's good law that man shall labor, and that if any man will not work neither should he eat.[66]

Repeated removals were held to be bad for Indian morale, injurious to progress in civilization, as well as acts of bad faith.[67] Treaty stipulations should be faithfully met so long as treaties existed, and provisions should be promptly issued in such manner as caused the Indian the least inconvenience and interruption of labor.[68] The Baptists protested in 1882 that at the moment thousands of Indians were in danger of starving because Congress had failed to make appropriations for supplies. Officials of the United States were calling upon the Army to keep the Indians on the reservations and make them "starve quietly." [69] However, the inclusion of tomahawks, scalping knives, and other tools of war in supplies was viewed as abhorrent.[70]

Nearly all of the boards and societies favored the plan of concentrating the Indians as far as possible within Indian Territory, and they all wanted the Indians there protected against contacts with the whites. The Presbyterian secretary, John C. Lowrie, had long advocated such a measure before the beginning of the peace policy. "It would facilitate the spreading of the Gospel by the different missionaries among the tribes, and they would advance rapidly towards civilization, soon being able to stand side by side with the whites." [71] The American Board missionaries and Bishop Hare were of a different opinion. These lone objectors held that such a policy would prevent Indian contact with the right kind of whites, would be injurious to progress, and would long delay the absorption of the Indians into the national society.[72] The others believed that, segregated in Indian Territory, the Indians could be beneficially isolated from contact with bad white people, christianized, and protected in their development toward civilization and citizenship. They were not to be isolated for the protection of Indian culture; the intended end was the very opposite.

The Friends protested the Army's failure to remove white intruders. Dr. Nicholson stated: "If the Territory is opened to settlement by the whites, the policy of congregating the Indians there with a view to their civilization will prove futile. The class of white men that precedes true civilization are worse than Indians, being land-grabbers, who desire to gain possession of the land to sell it to those who shall become the earliest settlers of the country. They will corrupt and demoralize the Indians in every way, and their fate is certainly sealed whenever this class of white men are turned loose upon them." [73] The Quakers fought every effort to open the country or to organize it as a regular United States territory or to admit it to the Union as a state.[74] The Indians had been solemnly promised this land free from all intrusion, and their title was not simply that of original possession, which had been extinguished by conquest, but that of legal conveyance by the United States.[75] Speaking for the churches the Board of Indian Commissioners insisted that any law passed for organization of the territory must be agreeable to the Indians.[76] Separate societies also stressed the requirement of Indian consent.[77] As late as 1883 the Board of Foreign Missions of the Presbyterian Church was protesting the incursion of 100,000 settlers a year, holding that the organization of a state and expropriation of the land were not yet inevitable and that the Indians, having clear title to their land, could alone determine what was to be done with it.[78]

INDIVIDUALISM, HOMES, LAND IN SEVERALTY

Congregationalists and Episcopalians, while demanding faithful keeping of treaty stipulations until expiration or voluntary surrender, deplored the concept behind the treaties, which required that the Indians be treated simultaneously as sovereign powers and as wards of the nation and dealt with as tribal units rather than as individuals.[79] The treaty system was one of the most fearfully and wonderfully concocted systems human stupidity had ever devised.[80] Treaties with tribes maintaining tribal relationships should give way to personal rights.[81] The action of Congress in decreeing that no more treaties be made was, therefore, applauded.

Individual responsibility was prerequisite to progress in civilization and to citizenship, and it invariably began with the desire for a true and settled home. The *American Missionary* stated:

> Before the Indian can become civilized, the conditions of civilization must exist. For him at present these are scarcely possible. No mere tribe can attain to a civilized state, yet the tribal relation is fostered and perpetuated by our policy. Such agencies of a civilized life as civil courts, town meetings, common schools, railroads, telegraphs, etc., these are simply impossible so long as tribes of men are forced or permitted to wander over vast territories to which they have no other title than that of a tribal occupancy. The prime condition of a home is an exclusive title to the land upon which it stands and from which its support can be drawn. Without a home, a high civilization is impossible, but our policy has been to discourage, and too often render impossible, the creation of a home by the Indian.[82]

There was a conviction common to all societies that homemaking depended upon the granting of homesteading rights and title to land in severalty to individual Indians. Land in severalty, civil law, and citizenship, regarded as relatively inseparable, were the most persistent notes in statements throughout the entire period. Let the Indian have the same right to personal possession of his land as any American citizen or immigrant.[83] After the Sioux uprising of 1862 and consequent location on reservations the American Board missionaries had resumed their emphasis upon homemaking and farming and had fostered a movement of Christian Indians to form separate agricultural communities. The Episcopal missionaries followed in this effort. This venture was costly to the Indians because they not only received no help from the government but had to forswear their tribal relationships and give up their annuities. Moreover, they had to pay a heavy fee for homestead rites and were subject to long and discouraging delays in getting title to their lands. They had to learn a new way of life. They had none of those resources of industrious German and Scandinavian immigrants, who nevertheless got into debt and lost their farms. Yet they persisted.[84] And their persistence was taken as proof that Indians could do the same. Equal rights with citizens and immigrants were asked for them, as well as aid in initially acquiring livestock and implements equal in value to what they would have received as reservation Indians.[85] Since Indians can easily become herdsmen, William Welsh suggested giving them cattle and goats as the first step.[86] It was thought that the government could stimulate agricultural homesteading by providing a market and by purchasing a part of its supplies from the Indian farmers.[87] The passage of the Dawes Act granting severalty was hailed as the reaching of a glorious milestone, but it brought new problems and greater opportunity for despoiling the Indians of their lands.

CIVIL LAW AND CITIZENSHIP

The missionaries and their supporting societies were convinced that the civil law could be of far greater protection to the Indians than segregation on a reservation. The law would be both protector and educator. Non-tax-paying Indians, without status before the law, could not testify against whites who wronged them; and the law did not follow white lawbreakers into the reservations because the agents had no police in their service. The impact of American civilization caused the Indian culture to disintegrate. Bishop Hare warned: "Civilization has loosened, in

some places broken, the bonds which regulate and hold together
Indian society in its wild state, and has failed to give the people
law and officers of justice in their place." [88] Thomas S. Williamson, missionary to the Dakotas, said that the two great hindrances
to progress were the Indian religion and the absence of law. [89] The
chiefs did not by custom have the function of punishing murderers
and robbers. Consequently, while the Indians suffered terribly
from white offenders, they suffered ten times more from themselves. The church-related Board of Indian Commissioners in
1871 observed: "When they have adopted civilized costume and
civilized modes of subsistence, we owe it to them, and to ourselves,
to teach them the majesty of civilized law, and extend to them its
protection against the lawless among themselves." [90]

The winning of civil law for the Indians held such high
priority that the Protestant Episcopal Church created a special
committee to seek it from both the federal and state governments. [91] The American Board missionaries, remembering the
voluntary civil governments among the Cherokees and Choctaws,
with whom their Board had been associated of old, fostered similar
voluntary systems among the Dakotas, beginning with the "Haz-
elwood Republic" of 1856. [92] They regarded the later developments with pride, and were certain that these prepared the participants for the application of the common law of the land.
They asked it repeatedly. [93] The other boards and societies all
made similiar recommendations. [94]

The secretary of the Dakota Mission of the American Board
made the statement:

> The success also of the republican idea, where every man
> is a unit of society, is verified, as at the Santee Agency.
> It would seem needless to mention this were it not true
> that there are still influential advocates, in government
> circles, of the theory that you can only treat the Indian as
> a member of a clan. It is the belief and experience of your
> missionaries that this is a profound error, and that it lies

at the bottom of the government's acknowledged ill success in many cases. This theory, that the Indian is an
Indian and to be treated in a way peculiar to himself, forever hedges him round, and really pledges the whole power
of our government to keep him from becoming anything
but an Indian after all. No wonder that many have become disgusted and have broken away from reservations;
or that others have grown despairing and have gone on
the war path. The theory of the government is radically
and wholly wrong. You must disintegrate the clan if you
would elevate the man. And then nothing should bar
them from all the rights and responsibilities of American
manhood, as fast as they are able to assume them.[95]

And the chief of these rights and responsibilities is American citizenship. Citizenship would be the crown of the whole process of
civilization and the keystone in the arch of Indian rights. The
boards and societies raised their voices in chorus demanding it.[96]
Riggs reported: "A title to property in severalty and the rank of
a citizen have a wonderful charm for [the Indians]." [97]

EDUCATION

Effective education was quite generally believed to be the
key to civilization, citizenship, and Christianization alike. As long
as the Indians were not citizens, the several states of the union
had no obligation to provide them with schools. The boards and
societies held that, until the states should make such provision,
it was the duty of the federal government to provide general education equivalent to the common school system.[98] If the government were not inclined to bear the expense outright, it held
enough property and funds belonging to the Indians to meet all
the expenses of their schooling and industrial training.[99] The
extensive school systems of the Five Civilized Tribes provided
such a precedent. The Presbyterians early in the program supplemented the salaries of some teachers because they were too
low, but expected to discontinue the practice just as soon as the

government did better by the teachers.[100] The Friends in Kansas
and Indian Territory expected to work entirely through agency
schools, to which they appointed Christian teachers through the
agents. They avowed: "When a school is opened it is for the
purpose of imparting to the pupils a knowledge of Christianity,
as well as of the ordinary rudiments of education, it being considered that merely instructing them in the ordinary elements of
learning would avail but little unless they are led to a higher life
than that to which they have been accustomed in their wild condition." [101] The Baptists said education adds permanence and power
to Christian influences.[102]

The proper missionary supplement to the government agency
day school was the boarding school. The Presbyterians in the
early phase of the peace policy program believed it proper to continue the earlier practice of having the government bear the cost
of buildings (to which it retained title) and two thirds the maintenance of the pupils, while the mission paid the salaries of the
teachers.[103] The Methodists, however, were willing to accept a
government grant for their school at Fort Peck and supplement
it with their own funds.[104] The Baptists too were willing to depend largely on government funds for "the Indian university,"
which was to become Bacone College at Tahlequah, later moved
to Muskogee.[105] But the general practice became that of the Congregationalists, of the Presbyterians formerly associated with the
Dakota Mission of the American Board, and of the Episcopalians
in providing building, teachers, and supplies from mission funds
and receiving rations for the pupils from the government. The
boarding school was intended to remove the pupils from home
associations for periods long enough to wean them from tribal
customs, to teach them "civilized" ways, and to introduce them
to Christian life and doctrine.[106]

Bishop Hare explained his concept of such schools in these
terms:

The ideas which governed me in laying out the whole

boarding-school work of the Jurisdiction were, that the schools should be plain and practical and not calculated to engender fastidious tastes and habits, which would make the pupils unhappy in, and unfitted for, the lowly and hard life to which their people are called; that, as the Indians have not been accustomed to labor, the school training should be such as would not only cultivate their intellect, but also develop their physical functions and teach them to do well the common acts of daily, humble life, such as sawing, sweeping, etc., etc.; that in order to do this and also for the sake of economy, the schools should be self-serving; i.e., that the scholars should take care of themselves and of rooms, beds, china, lamps, etc., etc., in, or connected with, the houses in which they live; and that the scholars should have such training in the responses and music of the Services that they should form the nuclei of Christian congregations where they have not been gathered, and valuable auxiliaries where they are already in existence.[107]

This close relationship of practical agriculture with allied crafts for the boys and for the girls domestic crafts with elementary school subjects was a feature of both mission day and boarding schools.[108] The boarding school was thought to be more effective than the day school in teaching English, and all of the societies, except the Congregationalists, Presbyterians, and Episcopalians, believed that all instruction should be in English.[109] The Presbyterian secretary had originally held that view but had been led to change it after he became acquainted with the Dakota Mission taken over from the American Board. The missionaries of the three boards working among the Dakotas insisted that the pupils taught only in English learned that language by rote and did not really understand it. Genuine progress in education and in Christianity depended on an effective introduction in the vernacular. Pupils literate in and learning through the vernacular could then easily learn English and truly comprehend it. Even if the desired goal was proficiency in English, the vernacular was the indispensable means to it.[110] Even Hampton and Carlisle graduates were said to be deficient in the comprehension of English. Yet in the end English was necessary for citizenship.[111]

The American Missionary Association was enthusiastic about sending students to Carlisle, especially to Hampton (its own creation), and to its schools for freedmen in the South, but recognized that adequate schools on the reservations were necessary.[112] Bishop Hare was pleased with Hampton and sent advanced students there.[113] The American Board wanted the country to realize that Hampton and Carlisle could never educate the Indian children of the country, and that schoolhouses by the thousands would have to be built and maintained throughout the Indian country.[114] Its missionaries also believed that Indian education must be self-propagating. They trained native teachers for the work and regarded the mission as only "the energizing power." [115]

GENERAL STATEMENTS OF POLICY

Pronouncements and statements were usually on specific points, and general statements on policy were infrequent. The Hicksite Friends gave the government a simple 7-point statement in 1869 advocating faithful and liberal keeping of treaty stipulations, no more removals of Nebraska tribes, no more sale of reservation lands for the present and later only under strict control, hospitals for each reservation, industrial schools and English instruction for all children, and competent instruction in agriculture and lumbering with provision of teams and tools.[116] The Dakota Mission of the American Board adopted a document in 1877, which the Board endorsed.[117] It affirmed that Indians are men with the same wants and impulses as others; demanded civil law; compulsory education in books, agriculture, and mechanic arts, so that "no more Indians be raised"; accepted the reservation system as a temporary expedient to be abandoned before interfering with attainment of citizenship; the right to land titles;

establishment of a "true Indian Civil Service"; and affirmed the teaching of Christianity as indispensable to civilization, enlightenment, and education. The annual conference of 1879 adopted a rather full statement.[118] It asked retention of the Indian Bureau under the Department of the Interior, the granting of land in severalty, provision of civil law, and a common school system. Bishop Whipple made frequent reports and pronouncements along these lines.[119] The General Assembly of the Presbyterian Church in the U. S. A. addressed a memorial to the President and Congress in 1880, which was adopted by the annual conference of 1881 and taken personally to the President. It called for American education, American homes, American rights, and American citizenship for the Indians.[120]

THE GOAL, INTEGRATION

Most of the religious societies or their representatives seem never to have made specific statements as to what they expected as the final result of the peace policy, but some degree of integration seemed implicit in citizenship. However, those Episcopalians, Congregationalists, and Presbyterians vocal about Indian affairs clearly looked to its fruit being the integration and absorption of the civilized Indian citizen into the general American society and economy. Bishop Hare spoke for others than himself alone when he deprecated any policy or program which, "if permanently maintained, would tend to make Indian life something separate from the common life of our country: a solid foreign mass indigestible by our common civilization." [121] The American Board, with integration in view, promoted fraternal intercourse between the Dakota churches and the frontier home mission churches and welcomed the mutual confidence which resulted. In the end it could be said that at least some of the frontier churchmen supported the mission boards in their efforts for the Indians because "certainly there are many in the settlements whose nightly sleep is sweeter because of this cordon of Indian churches around them, always ready to shield them from the wild men of the prairies." [122]

NOTES

Chapter 5

1. Peter J. Rahill, *The Catholic Indian Missions and Grant's Peace Policy,* for the Roman Catholic story and preceding chapter for Protestants.

2. American Board of Commissioners for Foreign Missions (hereafter ABCFM), *Annual Report, 1870,* p. xx; *1877,* p. xxxiii; *American Missionary,* XXXV, 1 (January 1881), 73; American Missionary Association (hereafter AMA), *Annual Report, 1878,* p. 7.

3. *American Missionary,* XVII, 1 (January 1873), 9.

4. AMA, *Annual Report, 1878,* p. 7.

5. Board of Missions of the Protestant Episcopal Church (hereafter BMPEC), *Proceedings, 1868,* pp. 9, 147—68; *American Missionary,* XX, 8 (August 1876), 185—86; XXXIII, 12 (December 1879), 398; [New York] Indian Peace Commission's memorial printed in *Report of the Commissioner of Indian Affairs* (hereafter RCIA), *1869,* pp. 85—96; and material gathered by church-related members of the Board of Indian Commissioners, for example, *Report of the Board of Indian Commissioners* (hereafter RBIC), *1871,* pp. 62 ff.; *1874,* p. 215.

6. ABCFM, *Annual Report, 1870,* p. xx.

7. Ibid., *1878,* p. xxxix.

8. AMA, *Annual Report, 1873,* p. 8.

9. Ibid., *1875,* p. 17; Methodist Missionary Society (hereafter MMS), *Annual Report, 1872,* p. 135.

10. *Spirit of Missions,* XXXVII (1872), 220.

11. American Baptist Home Mission Society (hereafter ABHMS), *Annual Report, 1877,* p. 12.

12. Ibid., p. 12; *Baptist Home Mission Monthly,* II, 3 (March 1880), 29; IV, 4 (April 1882), 12; *American Missionary,* XXXIII, 12 (December 1879), 396—400; *Spirit of Missions,* XXXVII (1872), 339 to 340.

13. ABCFM, *Annual Report, 1867,* p. 15.

14. Ibid., *1876,* p. xl.

15. *Spirit of Missions,* XL (1875), 568—69.

16. *American Missionary,* XIV, 1 (October 1871), 227—28.

17. Ibid., XVI, 11 (November 1872), 254; XX, 3 (March 1876), 64; AMA, *Annual Report, 1875,* p. 17.

18. *American Missionary,* XX, 3 (March 1876), 64.

19. *Missionary Herald,* LXXIV, 2 (February 1877), 38.

20. AMA, *Annual Report, 1872,* p. 9.

21. Some examples: ABCFM, *Annual Report, 1875,* p. xliii; *1877,* pp. xxxvii—xxxviii; AMA, *Annual Report, 1871,* p. 22; *1881,* p. 45; *American Missionary,* XXXII, 4 (April 1878), 102—103; Board of

Foreign Missions of the Presbyterian Church in the U.S.A. (hereafter BFMPCUSA), *Annual Report, 1871*, pp. 20—22; ABHMS, *Annual Report, 1881*, pp. 33—34.

22. BFMPCUSA, *Annual Report, 1877*, p. 10; *1878*, p. 12; AMA, *Annual Report, 1879*, pp. 6—7; ABCFM, *Annual Report, 1877*, pp. xxxvii to xxxviii. The Unitarians were not able to stir up much interest in a subject that was "less interesting than discussions of the origin of the universe." *Report of the Executive Committee of the American Unitarian Association, 1876*, p. 10.

23. Examples: AMA, *Annual Report, 1879*, p. 7; *1881*, p. 15; *American Missionary*, XVI, 4 (April 1872), 79; XXXV, 12 (December 1881), 403; ABHMS, *Annual Report, 1881*, p. 34; *1882*, p. 15; BFMP-CUSA, *Annual Report, 1879*, p. 11; Protestant Episcopal Church, *Journal of the General Convention, 1877*, pp. 74, 145, 450—55.

24. *RBIC, 1872*, p. 174.

25. Ibid., *1881*, pp. 77—79.

26. AMA, *Annual Report, 1879*. p. 7.

27. *RBIC, 1876*, p. 75; *1878*, pp. 127—28.

28. ABHMS, *Annual Report, 1883*, p. 19.

29. *American Missionary*, XV, 2 (February 1872), 33; *RCIA, 1869*, pp. 95—96.

30. BMPEC, *Proceedings, 1872*, p. 17; *1874*, pp. 22—23; *RBIC, 1871*, p. 176.

31. Ibid., p. 17; *RBIC, 1871*, p. 176; *1874*, pp. 22—23.

32. *RCIA, 1870*, pp. 246—47.

33. *Spirit of Missions*, XLVII (1882), 372.

34. Protestant Episcopal Church, *Journal of the General Convention, 1871*, p. 192, 233, 254.

35. BMPEC, *Proceedings, 1872*, pp. 14—24; *1873*, pp. 11—21; *RBIC, 1871*, p. 176.

36. *RBIC, 1871*, p. 176; Protestant Episcopal Church, *Journal of the General Convention, 1874*, p. 126.

37. Protestant Episcopal Church, *Journal of the General Convention, 1877*, pp. 122, 130, 287.

38. Ibid., *1880*, pp. 451—55.

39. H. B. Whipple, *Lights and Shadows of a Long Episcopate*, numerous references; M. A. DeW. Howe, *Life and Labors of Bishop Hare*. Bishop Hare in a report mentions "my not infrequent conferences with the President, the Secretary of the Interior, and the Commissioner of Indian Affairs." BMPEC, *Proceedings, 1875*, p. 136.

40. *RBIC, 1879*, p. 110; *RCIA, 1869*, pp. 4, 43—45.

41. *RCIA, 1872*, pp. 2—9.

42. *American Missionary*, XXXVII, 4 (April 1883), 105.

43. *RBIC, 1871*, p. 171.

44. Ibid., p. 181.

45. Ibid., *1872*, pp. 191—92.

46. *RCIA, 1874*, pp. 16—17.

47. *RBIC, 1871*, p. 163; *American Missionary*, XVI, 4 (April 1872), 79—81.

48. *Missionary Herald*, LXXII, 8 (August 1876), 266.

49. Howe, pp. 115—20.

50. Rahill, pp. 120, 160, 204—205, 271.

51. *RBIC, 1873*, pp. 201, 207.

52. ABCFM, *Annual Report, 1876*, pp. xl—xli.

53. *Missionary Herald*, LXXII, 8, (August 1876), 266.

54. Whipple, pp. 552, 559—60.

55. ABHMS, *Annual Report, 1878*, p. 40; also *1880*, p. 36.

56. *RBIC, 1878*, pp. 9—10. The commissioners list seven major reasons and six minor ones why the transfer should not be made.

57. *American Missionary*, XXXIII, 1 (January 1879), 13.

58. BFMPCUSA, *Annual Report, 1879*, p. 11.

59. *RBIC, 1873*, p. 201; Protestant Episcopal Church, *Journal of the General Convention, 1877*, pp. 144—45.

60. Whipple, p. 560, also p. 545.

61. *RBIC, 1871*, p. 172; *1872*, p. 194; *Missionary Advocate*, XXVI, 2 (May 17, 1870), 7.

62. *American Missionary*, XVII, 6 (June 1873), 124.

63. Whipple, p. 560.

64. Howe, p. 54. ABCFM, *Annual Report, 1877*, p. xxxviii; *1878*, p. xxxix.

65. *Report of the Board of Managers of the Domestic and Foreign Missionary Society of the Protestant Episcopal Church, 1879—1880*, p. 417.

66. Ibid., *1877—1878*, p. 445.

67. *RBIC, 1871*, p. 8; *RCIA, 1869*, pp. 119—20; AMA, *Annual Report, 1878*, pp. 6, 33; ABCFM, *Annual Report, 1879*, p. 55.

68. *Spirit of Missions*, XLVII (1882), 285—287.

69. ABHMS, *Annual Report, 1882*, p. 15.

70. Some persons thought that the supplying of tobacco was almost as bad as tomahawks!

71. *RBIC, 1871*, p. 171; *Presbyterian Monthly Record*, XXII, 2 (February 1871), 48—49.

72. ABCFM, *Annual Report, 1876*, p. 89; Howe, pp. 54—55.

73. *RBIC, 1871*, p. 163.

74. Ibid., *1872*, p. 151.

75. Ibid., p. 11.

76. Ibid., *1873*, pp. 4—5.

77. ABHMS, *Annual Report, 1880*, p. 35.

78. *Presbyterian Monthly Record*, XXXIV, 2 (February 1883), 49—50.

79. *RCIA, 1873*, p. 3. E. P. Smith spoke with authoritative voice for Congregationalists.

80. *American Missionary*, XXXIV, 10 (November 1880), 376.

81. Protestant Episcopal Church, *Journal of the General Convention, 1877*, pp. 144—45; *American Missionary*, XXXIII, 12 (December 1879), 400; XXXIV, 9 (September 1880), 264; XXXIV, 10 (November), 368; ABCFM, *Annual Report, 1879*, p. 93; AMA, *Annual Report, 1877*, p. 98, etc.

82. XXXIV, 6 (June 1880), 169.

83. AMA, *Annual Report, 1877*, p. 98; *1878*, p. 33; *1879*, p. 7; *American Missionary*, XXXIV, 11 (November 1880), 369; ABCFM, *Annual Report, 1876*, p. 91; BFMPCUSA, *Annual Report, 1879*, p. 11; ABHMS, *Annual Report, 1882*, pp. 15—16; *RCIA, 1870*, pp. 203—206; *1873*, p. 4; *RBIC, 1871*, pp. 8, 165, 181.

84. ABCFM, *Annual Report, 1876*, p. xl; *1879*, pp. 90, 95; *1881*, p. 86; *RCIA, 1870*, pp. 235—39.

85. *RBIC, 1872*, pp. 174—75; ABHMS, *Annual Report, 1881*, p. 34.

86. *RBIC, 1871*, p. 181.

87. Ibid., *1873*, p. 207.

88. BMPEC, *Proceedings, 1877*, pp. 145—46.

89. *RBIC, 1871*, pp. 155—56; see also *1872*, pp. 190—91.

90. Ibid., p. 8.

91. Protestant Episcopal Church, *Journal of the General Convention, 1877*, pp. 74, 122, 130, 287; *1880*, pp. 450—55.

92. Riggs, Stephen R., *Táh-Koo Wah-Kán or the Gospel Among the Dakotas* (Boston: Congregational S. S. and Pub. Soc., 1869), pp. 362 ff.

93. ABCFM, *Annual Report, 1876*, p. 89; *1877*, p. xxxviii.

94. AMA, *Annual Report, 1873*, p. 33; *American Missionary*, XXXV, 12 (December 1881), 403; BMPEC, *Proceedings, 1877*, pp. xv to xvi; *Missionary Advocate*, XXVI, 2 (May 17, 1870), 7; BFMPCUSA, *Annual Report, 1879*, p. 11; *RBIC, 1881*, p. 78.

95. ABCFM, *Annual Report, 1879*, p. 93.

96. AMA, *Annual Report, 1879*, p. 7; *1881*, p. 15; *American Missionary*, XXXIV, 9 (September 1880), 264; 11 (November), 370; XXXVI, 12 (December 1880), 405; ABCFM, *Annual Report, 1875*, p. 69; *1878*, p. xxxix; ABHMS, *Annual Report, 1881*, p. 34; *1882*, p. 16; *RBIC, 1881*, pp. 77—79; *RCIA, 1869*, p. 120.

97. ABCFM, *Annual Report, 1876,* p. 91. See petition of the Dakota Indians to Washington. *Annual Report, 1877,* p. 74.

98. BFMPCUSA, *Annual Report, 1871,* p. 23; *1875,* pp. 9—10; *1876,* p. 9; *1879,* p. 11; AMA, *Annual Report, 1878,* p. 33; *RBIC, 1878,* p. 127.

99. ABCFM, *Annual Report, 1882,* p. lv.

100. BFMPCUSA, *Annual Report, 1875,* pp. 10—11.

101. *RBIC, 1871,* p. 162; R. W. Kelsey, *Friends and the Indians,* p. 176.

102. ABHMS, *Annual Report, 1883,* p. 19.

103. BFMPCUSA, *Annual Report, 1871,* p. 23.

104. MMS, *Annual Report, 1880,* p. 194.

105. ABHMS, *Annual Report, 1880,* p. 35; *1881,* p. 41.

106. *RBIC, 1873,* pp. 195—96.

107. BMPEC, *Proceedings, 1874,* p. 185; see also Howe, pp. 94—108.

108. *RBIC, 1871,* p. 165; ABCFM, *Annual Report, 1872,* p. 80.

109. *RBIC, 1870,* pp. 246—47, 253; *1873,* pp. 174—75, 181—82, 187—90.

110. *RBIC, 1870,* pp. 213—14, 214—15; *1871,* pp. 165, 169, 170 to 171; *1873,* pp. 175, 187—90; *1879,* p. 98; AMA, *Annual Report, 1874,* p. 5.

111. *RBIC, 1871,* p. 169; *1873,* pp. 174—75.

112. AMA, *Annual Report, 1879,* p. 7; *1881,* p. 15; *American Missionary,* XXXII 11 (November 1879), 333; XXXV, 12 (December 1881), 403.

113. Howe, pp. 52, 229.

114. ABCFM, *Annual Report, 1881,* p. 88.

115. *Missionary Herald,* LXXV, 7 (July 1879), 248; *RBIC, 1873,* p. 174.

116. *RCIA, 1869,* pp. 119—20.

117. ABCFM, *Annual Report, 1877,* pp. xxxvii—xxxviii.

118. *RBIC, 1878,* pp. 127—28.

119. Whipple, pp. 510 ff.

120. *RBIC, 1881,* pp. 77—79.

121. Howe, p. 54.

122. ABCFM, *Annual Report, 1873,* p. 83.

A Note on the Attitude of the Churches in Later Years

The active partnership of the mission boards with the United States government in the administration of the agencies until 1882 and in education until the middle of the last decade of the century had stimulated the churches to far greater concern and action with respect to the Indians than had ever before been the case. After the dissolution of the partnership there was a very evident slump in interest in the Indians. A few of the major boards continued and enlarged their work, and a few additional churches began Indian missions; but neither the Indians nor the Indian missions were in the foreground of the churches' interest. During the early years of the 20th century the American Baptist Home Mission Society passed resolutions noting that the government was doing well in Indian education and expressing satisfaction. There were no critical notes on policy at the time. It was much the same in other churches. The mission boards no longer stimulated one another to interest and action. The discontinuance of the annual conference of the secretaries with the Board of Commissioners for Indian Affairs had removed a hitherto potent source of mutual sharing of information, consultation, and consensus. Some of the secretaries and workers attended the annual Lake Mohonk Conference on Indian Affairs, and it was a help to them, but it was not an agency or instrument of the missions.

There was a tendency for some years to rely on the Indian Rights Association to perform the functions of criticism of policy and quest for justice which the boards had jointly exercised.

The transfer of all Indian mission work from foreign mission boards to home mission agencies tended to reinforce individualism among the Indian missions also over against the recent tradition of concerted policy and action. The home mission boards were at the turn of the century still competitive and opportunistic. Then the usual course of retirements and deaths brought a change in personnel in the management, and the tradition of sharing in a common cause was to a considerable extent forgotten. Consequently, Indian missions became largely a housekeeping affair concerned mostly with the maintenance rather than expansion of existing operations. The old methods were followed with little change. Then after the founding of the Home Missions Council of North America, the 14 members' boards which carried on Indian mission work established the Committee on Indian Affairs in 1909. Its very name indicated that it intended to be concerned with more than the internal matters of mission work. It included in addition to the denominational boards such allied organizations as the American Bible Society, the YMCA, and the Indian Rights Association. Association in the common cause created a sense of unity among the people associated with the committee, and, through the fellowship and consultation which it provided, once again a consensus on most matters relating to missions and general Indian affairs was attained. The Council of Women for Home Missions also had an Indian Committee, and it produced an occasional study book on the Indians in the annual series which the Women's Council published. The first conference of Indian mission workers was held in 1919, and in 1935, under the auspices of the Home Missions Council, a professional society called the National Fellowship of Indian Workers, was organized, comprising missionaries, mission board members, and government employees. The cooperating denominations and their missionaries henceforth had ample means for consultation, study, speaking to the churches and the nation, and for action, should they so desire.

There appears to have been little fundamental change in attitudes and viewpoints during the first third of the 20th century. Instead of partnership there had developed close collaboration between the missions and the churches. Some government schools were actually staffed by Roman Catholic sisters. It was claimed that in many schools Protestant and Roman Catholic missionaries actually controlled the institution. One finds complaints that children were forced to take part in worship and take religious instruction and thus were denied religious liberty. At any rate there was fairly warm cooperation between mission workers and government employees on most of the reservations. Closer relations at headquarters in Washington were fostered by the appointment of H. B. F. MacFarland as legal counsel to the Committee on Indian Affairs (1912—1916). Congress in 1922 gave the missions title to the land which they were occupying on the reservations.

Despite the often close collaboration of the missionaries and government officers on the reservations, the churches were still committed to their position on separation of church and state which they had assumed during the last decade of the previous century. The ground of it appeared still to lie more in fear of and opposition to Roman Catholic aims and strategy than in fundamental theory. The earliest instances of concerted action by the churches after the creation of the Committee on Indian Affairs were directed toward Roman Catholics actions and practices. The Home Missions Council in 1911 vigorously opposed a government grant of 300,000 acres of land in New Mexico to a Roman Catholic training school. The council was consistent and at the same time opposed a grant of $20,000 to a Protestant society in California. The next year the council threw the weight of its support to Commissioner Valentine's effort to eliminate the wearing of religious garb by teachers in government schools.

About 1915 the organization joined forces with those who were fighting to protect the interests of the Mescalero Apache and Papago tribes of Arizona in their lands.

The churches were in general agreement with the government's policy of working toward the termination of wardship and the integration of the Indians into the general American society. This was in line with the position of the missions on Indian civilization and citizenship at the beginning of the century, but with the passage of time and the failure of segregation to produce the expected blessings the churches began to ask the abandonment of segregated schools. They also became concerned about the migration of the Indians from the reservations to the cities with all the consequent problems encountered by the transplanted people. A special Home Missions Congress in 1930 therefore asked vigorous efforts to combat the exploitation and commercialization of the Indian, disavowed a permanent policy of segregation, and recommended the gradual abandonment of segregated schools and the educating of Indian children in the public schools. The two councils voted jointly to provide directors of religious education in all government schools both on and off the reservations; and apparently there was no feeling that this measure might infringe upon the proper separation of church and state.

There was little conflict between the missions and the Indian Service over government policy toward the Indians until the appointment of John Collier as Commissioner of Indian Affairs by President Franklin D. Roosevelt. Up to that time the churches had usually approved the government policy in the main. Then the Indian Reorganization Act of 1934 encouraged return to tribal control and the limitation of giving of allotments of land to individuals because of the ease with which so many were then separated from their land. Collier also set out vigorously to rescue and foster the traditional tribal culture. The missions thought that the land and cultural policies of the Indian Service now meant a return to wardship and paternalism by the government, the making of the reservations into a kind of human zoo, and the end of official effort to integrate the Indians into society. They clashed with Collier over the Peyote cult and in general aligned themselves against him. The order of the commissioner, which prohibited any interference with Indian religious life or ceremonial expression, was resented. Collier was on firm ground when he sought to end compulsory attendance of Indian children at Christian classes of instruction and worship. He did offer continued use of school facilities for both worship and instruction of children whose parents approved and of youths over 18 who voluntarily consented. The council's pamphlet on "Indian Wardship" set forth the consensus of most of the churches and missions on wardship and citizenship. Its general tone is expressed in the words that halting the Indian's "modern adaptations and imprisoning him in his yesterday's culture is futility itself."

However, in the decade of the 1940s the churches began to awaken to the understanding that neither the government nor white voluntary agencies had the right to make unilateral decisions about the Indian's present and future but that his consent was needed. There came to be also a more realistic acknowledgement that speedy termination of wardship often made it easier for white men to exploit the Indian and deprive him of his possessions. And with both of these was joined the insight that much more was needed in inducing state and local governments to acknowledge concern for Indian welfare and to participate in the processes of adjustment. All of this was preparatory for a considerable shift of position in the decade of the 1950s. The Eisenhower administration reversed the principles on which the Indian Service had operated under Commissioner Collier and promoted a policy of rapid termination of federal responsibility for the Indians. The eagerness of business interests to deprive the Indians of their resources regardless of any questions of justice and some grave acts of injustice by governments, both national and state, alarmed the churches. Therefore the past decade or so has seen the churches increasingly insisting on the consent of the Indians to all legislation which affects them and a growth of tension between them and government on matters of fundamental policy. One can probably say with truth that in the decade of the 1950s the churches and their mission boards once more showed a range of concern about Indian affairs comparable to that of the 20 years following the end of the Civil War, but that neither the causes of Indian missions nor Indian rights drew a very large percentage of church members into passionate participation. The dissolution of the partnership of missions and government in Indian civilization and education was certainly required by the evolution of the interpretation of the doctrine of the separation of church and state. However, the American people have always been reluctant to face squarely their responsibility for and obligation to the Indians. The record of the churches is little better than that of the general populace, but so long as the partnership in civilization and evangelization endured there was more incentive for the churches to face and acknowledge their responsibility.

Bibliography

Adams, Nehemiah. *The Life of John Eliot*. Boston: Sabbath School Soc., 1847.

Addresses and Messages of the Presidents of the United States, Inaugural, Annual, and Special, from 1789 to 1846. . . . Comp. from official sources by Edwin Williams. 2 vols. New York: E. Walker, 1846.

American Archives. . . . Comp. and ed. by Peter Force. 6 series in 9 vols. Washington: published by an act of Congress, 1837—53.

Advance. Vols. 1—33, 1867—1900.

American Baptist Home Mission Society. *Annual Report, 1866—1900.*

American Baptist Missionary Union. *Annual Reports, 1846—1866.* Previous to 1846 named the General Missionary Convention of the Baptist Denomination in the United States.

American Board of Commissioners for Foreign Missions. *Annual Report, 1810—1882.*

American Missionary. Ser. 2, Vols. 1—20, 1857—76; New Ser., Vol. 1, 1877; Vols. 32—54, 1878—1900.

American Missionary Association. *Annual Report, 1873—1900.*

American State Papers. Documents, Legislative and Executive, of the Congress of the United States. 38 vols. Washington: Gales and Seaton, 1832—61.

American Unitarian Association. *Report of the Executive Committee, 1871—1878.*

Appleton, Nathaniel. *Gospel Ministers Must Be Fit for the Master's Use, . . . Illustrated in a Sermon Preached . . . at the Ordination of Mr. John Sargent,* . . . Boston: S. Kneeland and T. Green, 1735.
————. *A Sermon Preached October 9, Being a Day of Public Thanksgiving Occasioned by the Surrender of Montreal, and All Canada.* Boston: John Draper, 1760.

Baptist Denomination in the United States, General Missionary Convention of —, *Reports of the Triennial Conventions,* and *Annual Reports of the Board of Managers,* 1816—45; name then changes to American Baptist Missionary Union.

Baptist Home Mission Monthly. Vols. 1—22, 1878—1900.

Bacon, Francis. *The Works of Francis Bacon.* Coll. and ed. James Spedding et al. 7 vols. London: Longmans, 1857—59.

Bangs, Nathan. *A History of the Methodist Episcopal Church.* 4 vols. New York: Lane and Sandford, 1841.

Barclay, Wade C. *History of Methodist Missions.* 3 vols. (of 6 planned). New York: Board of Missions of the Methodist Church, 1949—.

Bass, Althea. *Cherokee Messenger.* Norman: University of Oklahoma Press, 1936.

Beaver, R. Pierce. "American Missionary Motivation Before the Revolution," *Church History,* XXXI, 2 (June 1962), 216—26.

————. *Pioneers in Mission. The Early Missionary Ordination Sermons, Charges, and Instructions.* Grand Rapids: Eerdmans, 1966.

Berkhofer, Robert F. *Salvation and the Savage: An Analysis of Protestant Missions and American Indian Response, 1787—1862.* Lexington: University of Kentucky Press, 1965. An excellent study published after this book was finished.

Beverley, Robert. *The History and Present State of Virginia,* ed. Louis B. Wright. Chapel Hill: University of North Carolina Press, 1947.

Biblical Repository and Quarterly Observer. Vols. 1—30, 1831—50.

Blodgett, Harold. *Samson Occum.* Hanover, N.H.: Dartmouth College, 1935.

Board of Indian Commissioners. *Annual Report, 1870—1907.*

Bradshaw, Harold C. *The Indians of Connecticut; the Effect of English Colonization and of Missionary Activity on Indian Life in Connecticut.* [Deep River, Conn.: New Era Press, 1935.]

Brown, Alexander, comp. and ed. *The Genesis of the United States; . . . a Series of Historical Manuscripts.* 2 vols. Boston: Houghton, Mifflin, 1897.

Buell, Augustus C. *Sir William Johnson.* New York: Appleton, 1903.

Butler, Nicholas M. *Education in the United States.* Albany, N.Y.: J. B. Lyon, 1900. "Education of the Indian." W. N. Hailmann, pp. 939—64.

The Catholic World. Vols. I—XXXV, 1865—1900.

Chalmers, Harvey. *Joseph Brant: Mohawk.* E. Lansing, Mich.: Michigan State University Press, 1955.

Charter of the Colony of Connecticut; 1662. Hartford: Case, Lockwood, and Brainard, 1900; same, New Haven: printed for the Tercentenary Commission by Yale University Press, 1933.

Cherokee Nation. *Constitution and Laws of the Cherokee Nation.* Saint Louis: R. and T. A. Ennis, 1875.

Christian Advocate and Journal and Zion's Herald. Vol. 1, 1832.

Collison, Richard, ed. *The Three Voyages of Martin Frobisher in Search of a Passage to Cathaia and India by the North-West, A.D. 1576—8.* London: published for the Hakluyt Society, 1868 (Hakluyt Soc. Pub. No. XXXVIII).

Connecticut Evangelical Magazine. Vols. 1—7, 1800—1807.

Dawson, William C., ed. *A Compilation of the Laws of the State of Georgia, Passed by the General Assembly since the Year 1819 to 1829, Inclusive.* Milledgeville, Ga., 1831.

Desmond, Humphrey A. *The A. P. A. Movement.* Washington: New Century Press, 1912.

Documents Relating to the Colonial History of the State of New York. 15 vols. Albany: Weed, Parsons, 1853—87.

Drury, Clifford M. *Presbyterian Panorama.* Philadelphia: Board of Christian Education, 1952.

Dyer, Edward O. *Gnadensee, the Lake of Grace; a Moravian Picture in a Connecticut Frame.* Boston: Pilgrim Press, ca. 1903.

Eckley, Joseph. *A Discourse before the Society for the Propagation of the Gospel among the Indians and Others in North America.* Boston: E. Lincoln, 1806.

Edwards, Jonathan. *The Works of Jonathan Edwards, A. M., with an Essay on His Genius and Writings* by Henry Rogers *and a Memoir* by Sereno E. Dwight. 2 vols., 10th ed. London: Henry C. Bohn, 1845.

Elsbree, Oliver W. *The Rise of the Missionary Spirit in America.* Williamsport, Pa.: Williamsport Printing and Binding Co., 1928.

Eells, Myron. *Father Eells; or, the Results of Fifty-Five Years of Missionary Labors in Washington and Oregon.* Boston: Congregational S. S. and Pub. Society, ca. 1894.

————. *Ten Years of Missionary Work at Skokomish, Washington Territory.* Boston: Congregational S. S. and Pub. Society, 1886.

Evans, Charles. *Friends in the Seventeenth Century.* Philadelphia: Friends Bookstore, 1875.

Finley, James B. *Autobiography of Rev. James B. Finley, or, Pioneer Life in the West.* Cincinnati: Methodist Book Concern, 1855.

————. *History of the Wyandot Mission at Upper Sandusky, Ohio, under the Direction of the Methodist Episcopal Church.* Cincinnati: Wright and Swormstedt, 1840.

————. *Life among the Indians, Personal Reminiscences.* Cincinnati: Curts and Jennings, 1855.

Firth, Charles H., and R. S. Rait, eds. *Acts and Ordinances of the Inter-Regnum, 1642—1660.* London: H. M. Stationery Office, 1911.

Flexner, James T. *Mohawk Baronet: Sir William Johnson of New York* New York: Harper, 1959.

Foreman, Grant. *Indian Removal.* Norman: University of Oklahoma Press, 1953.

Ford, John W., ed. *Some Correspondence between the Governors and Treasurers of the New England Company in London and the Commissioners of the United Colonies in America.* London: Spottiswoode, 1896.

Foxcroft, Thomas. *Observations Historical and Practical on the Rise and Primitive State of New England, . . .* Boston: S. Kneeland and T. Green, for S. Gerish, 1730.

Friends' Intelligencer. From Vol. 1, 1844.

Fritz, Henry Eugene. *The Humanitarian Background of Indian Reform,* a doctrinal dissertation of the University of Minnesota, 1956, available from University Microfilms, Ann Arbor, Mich. (Not available in time for use.)

Goodsell, Fred F. *You Shall Be My Witnesses.* Boston: American Board C. F. M., 1959.

Gray, Elma E. *Wilderness Christians, the Moravian Mission to the Delaware Indians.* Ithaca, N. Y.: Cornell University Press, 1956.

Hakluyt, Richard. See Taylor, E. G. R., ed.

Hamilton, John Taylor. *A History of the Church Known as the Moravian Church or Unitas Fratrum.* Bethlehem, Pa.: Times Pub. Co., 1900.

————. *The Recognition of the Unitas Fratrum as an Old Episcopal Church by the Parliament of Great Britain in 1749.* Bethlehem, Pa.: Times Pub. Co., 1925.

Hamilton, Kenneth G. *John Etwein and the Moravian Church.* Bethlehem, Pa.: Times Pub. Co., 1940.

Hare, Lloyd C. M. *Thomas Mayhew, Patriarch to the Indians (1593 to 1682).* New York: Appleton, 1932.

Hopkins, Samuel. *Historical Memoirs Relating to the Housatunnuk Indians.* Boston: S. Kneeland, 1753.

Holder, Charles F. *The Quakers in Great Britain and America.* New York: Neuner, 1913.

Howe, M. A. de W. *The Life and Labors of Bishop Hare, Apostle to the Sioux.* New York: Sturgis and Walton, ca. 1911.

Hunter, H. *A Brief History of the Society in Scotland for Propagating Christian Knowledge.* Edinburgh: 1795.

Hutchinson, Thomas. *The History of the Colony and Province of Massachusetts Bay,* ed. Lawrence S. Mayo. 3 vols. Cambridge: Harvard University Press, 1936.

Ibbotson, Joseph D. *Documentary History of Hamilton College.* Clinton, N. Y.: Hamilton College, 1922.

The Independent. Vols. 1—50, 1848—98; esp. 44, No. 2262 (April 1892), special issue on education of Indians and Negroes.

Indian Rights Association. *Annual Report, 1883—1900.*

Jackson, Helen M. Hunt. *A Century of Dishonor; a Sketch of the United States Government's Dealings with Some of the Indian Tribes.* New ed. Boston: Little, Brown, 1903.

Jones, Electa F. *Stockbridge Past and Present; or Records of an Old Indian Station.* Springfield, Mass.: Samuel Bowles, 1854.

Journals of the House of Commons. Vol. 1, 1547/1628 to present. London: 1742—; Vols. 2 and 5.

Kellaway, William. *The New England Company, 1649—1776.* New York: Barnes and Noble, 1962.

Kelsey, Rayner W. *Friends and the Indians, 1615—1917.* Philadelphia: Associated Executive Committee of Friends on Indian Affairs, 1917.

Klingberg, Frank J. *Anglican Humanitarianism in Colonial New York.* Philadelphia: Church Historical Society, 1940.

Latter Day Luminary. Vols. 1—6, 1818—25.

Lazell, J. Arthur. *Alaskan Apostle, the Life Story of Sheldon Jackson.* New York: Harper, 1960.

Lend a Hand. Vols. 1—18, 1886—97.

Lennox, Herbert J. "Samuel Kirkland's Mission to the Iroquois." Unpubl. diss., University of Chicago, 1932.

The Literary and Theological Review. Vols. 1—6, 1834—39.

Love, William de L. *Samson Occum and the Christian Indians of New England.* Boston: Pilgrim Press, 1899.

Lucas, Charles. *Religion, Colonizing, and Trade, the Driving Forces of the Old Empire.* London: S. P. C. K., 1930.

Lumpkin, Wilson. *The Removal of the Cherokee Indians from Georgia.* . . . 2 vols. New York: Dodd, Mead, 1907.

Lydekker, John W. *The Faithful Mohawks.* New York: Macmillan, 1938.

McClure, David. *Memoirs of the Rev. Eleazar Wheelock.* . . . Newburyport, Mass.: Edmund Little, 1811.

McCallum, J. D. *The Letters of Eleazar Wheelock's Indians.* Hanover, N. H.: Dartmouth College, 1932.

McCoy, Isaac. *History of Baptist Indian Missions.* Washington: William N. Morrison, 1840.

M'Ferrin, John B. *History of Methodism in Tennessee.* 3 vols. Nashville: Southern Methodist Pub. House, 1871—74.

Malone, Henry T. *Cherokees of the Old South, a People in Transition.* Athens: University of Georgia Press, 1958.

Manross, William M. *A History of the American Episcopal Church.* New York: Morehouse-Gorham, 1959.

Markham, Albert H., ed. *The Voyages and Works of John Davis, the Navigator.* London: published for the Hakluyt Society, 1880, also 1910 (Hakluyt Society Pub. No. LIX).

Markham, Clements R., ed. *The Hawkins Voyages during the Reigns of Henry VIII, Queen Elizabeth, and James I.* London: pub. for the Hakluyt Society, 1878 (Hakluyt Soc. Pub. No. LVII).

Mather, Cotton. *Magnalia Christi Americana.* 2 vols. Hartford: Andrus, Roberts, and Barr, 1820. First American ed. from the London ed. of 1702.

Methodist Episcopal Church. *Journal of the General Conference, Quadrennial Reports,* from 1796, various.

The Methodist Magazine, changing title to *Methodist Quarterly Review* and *Methodist Review.* Vols. 1—82, 1818—1900.

Methodist Missionary Society. *Annual Reports,* various.

Minutes of the Provincial Council of Pennsylvania. Philadelphia: published by the State, 1852.

Missionary Advocate. Vols. 1—32, 1845—76.

Missionary Herald, succeeding the *Panoplist* in 1821. Vols. 17—79, 1821 to 1883.

Moody, Marshall D. *A History of the Board of Indian Commissioners and Its Relationship to the Administration of Indian Affairs, 1869—1900;* thesis of the Catholic University of America, 1951. (Not available when this book was written.)

Morgan, Thomas J. *Indian Education.* (Data lacking.)

————. *Roman Catholics and Indian Education.* Boston: The American Citizen Co., ca. 1893.

Morse, Jedediah. *Report to the Secretary of War of the United States, on Indian Affairs, Comprising a Narrative of a Tour Performed in the Summer of 1820 . . . for the Purpose of Ascertaining . . . the Actual State of the Indian Tribes in Our Country.* New Haven and elsewhere: various publishers, incl. Davis and Force of Washington, 1822.

The National League for the Protection of American Institutions. *Documents Nos. 1—17.* New York: 1890—92.

New Plymouth Colony. *The Compact with the Charter and Laws of the Colony of New Plymouth.* Boston: Dutton and Wentworth, printers to the State, 1836.

New York Missionary Magazine. Vols. 1—4, 1800—1803.

New York Missionary Society. *Annual Report of Directors, 1799—1815.* Appendices to the several annual sermons.

Orcutt, Samuel. *The Indians of the Housatonic and Naugatuck Valleys.* Hartford: Case, Lockwood, and Brainard, 1882.

Panoplist. Vols. 1—3, 1805—1808. *Panoplist and Missionary Magazine.* Vols. 4—13, 1808—1817. *Panoplist and Missionary Herald.* Vols. 13—17, 1817—21; thereafter *Missionary Herald.*

Parks, George B. *Richard Hakluyt and the English Voyages,* ed. James A. Williamson. New York: American Geographical Society, 1928.

Pound, Arthur. *Johnson of the Mohawks.* New York: 1930.

Presbyterian Church in the U. S. A., Board of Foreign Missions. *Annual Reports, 1837—1893.*

Presbyterian Church in the U. S. A. *Minutes of the General Assembly.* New Ser., 1—18, 1870—1900.

Priest, Loring B. *Uncle Sam's Stepchildren, the Reformation of United States Indian Policy, 1865—1887.* New Brunswick: Rutgers University Press, 1942.

Princeton Review. Vols. 1—4, 1825—28; Ser. 2, Vols. 1—43, 1829—71.

Protestant Episcopal Church, Board of Missions of the Domestic and Foreign Missionary Society. *Proceedings of the Annual Meeting,* various.

Protestant Episcopal Church. *Journal of the General Convention, 1871, 1874, 1877, 1880, 1883, 1886.*

Public Records of the Colony of Connecticut, 1636—1776. 15 vols. Hartford: Case, Lockwood, and Brainard, 1850—90.

Public Statutes at Large of the United States, from the Organization of the Government in 1789 to March 3, 1845. 5 vols. Boston: Little, Brown, 1848.

Quarterly Christian Spectator. Vols. 1—8, 1819—26; New Ser., Vols. 1—2, 1827—28; Ser. 3, Vols. 1—10, 1829—38.

Rahill, Peter J. *Catholic Indian Missions and Grant's Peace Policy, 1870 to 1884.* Washington: Catholic University of America Press, 1953.

Raleigh, Walter. *The English Voyages of the Sixteenth Century.* Glasgow: MacLehose, 1906.

The Record of the Presbyterian Church in the United States of America, changes title to *The Monthly Record.* Vols. 1—37, 1850—86.

Records of the Governor and Company of Massachusetts Bay in New England, ed. Nathaniel Shurtleff. Boston: William White, 1853; Vols. 1 to 4.

Records of the Virginia Company of London, ed. Susan M. Kingsbury. Washington: Govt. Printing Office, 1906—35. Vol. 1.

Reformed Church in America, Board of Foreign Missions. *Annual Report,* various.

Richardson, James D., ed. *A Compilation of the Messages and Papers of the Presidents, 1789—1897.* 10 vols. Washington: Govt. Printing Office, 1896—99.

Richardson, Leon B. *An Indian Preacher in England.* Hanover, N.H.: Dartmouth College, 1933.

Riggs, Stephen R. *Mary and I. Forty Years with the Sioux.* Boston: Congregational S.S. and Pub. Society, ca. 1880.

————. *Táh-Koo Wah Kán or the Gospel Among the Dakotas.* Boston: Congregational S.S. and Pub. Society, 1869.

Robbins, H., ed. *Handbook of the Church's Mission to the Indians.* Hartford: Church Mission Publishing Co., 1913.

Rundle, Thomas. *A Sermon Preached at St. George's Church, Hanover Square, on Sunday, February 17, 1733/4, to Recommend the Charity for Establishing the New Colony of Georgia.* London: Printed for T. Woodward and J. Brindley, 1739.

Rushmore, Elsie M. *The Indian Policy during Grant's Administration.* Jamaica, N.Y.: Marion Press, 1914.

Schmeckebier, Laurence F. *The Office of Indian Affairs, Its History, Activities, and Organization.* Baltimore: Johns Hopkins Press, 1927.

Schwarze, Edmund. *Moravian Missions among the Southern Indian Tribes.* Bethlehem, Pa.: Times Pub. Co., 1923.

Sewall, Joseph. *Christ Victorious Over the Power of Darkness, by the Light of His Preached Gospel.* Boston: Kneeland and Green, 1733.

Slattery, Charles L. *Felix Reville Brunot, 1820—1898.* New York: Longmans, Green, 1901.

Smith, de Cost. *Martyrs of the Oblong and Little Nine.* Caldwell, Idaho: Caxton Printers, 1948.

Society for the Propagation of the Gospel among the Indians and Others in North America. *Annual Reports,* from 1787, usually appended to the annual sermons.

Society of Friends, Indiana Yearly Meeting. *Address to the People of the United States and to the Members of Congress in Particular.* Cincinnati: A. Pugh, 1838.

[Society of Friends.] *Appeal to the Christian Community.* New York: 1841.

[Society of Friends.] *The Case of the Seneca Indians in the State of New York.* Philadelphia: Merrihew and Thompson, 1840.

Society of the United Brethren for Propagating the Gospel among the Heathen. *Proceedings, Sesquicentennial Number, 1937.*

Spedding, James. *The Letters and Life of Francis Bacon.* 7 vols. London: Longmans, Green, 1868—90.

Spirit of Missions. Vols. 1—64, 1836—1900.

Starkey, Marion L. *The Cherokee Nation.* New York: Knopf, 1946.

Stoddard, Solomon. *Question Whether God Is Not Angry with the Country for Doing So Little Towards the Conversion of the Indians.* Boston: B. Green, 1722.

Stokes, Anson Phelps. *Church and State in the United States.* 3 vols. New York: Harper, 1950.

Strong, William E. *The Story of the American Board.* Boston: Pilgrim Press, 1910.

Taylor, E. G. R., ed. *The Original Writings and Correspondence of the Two Richard Hakluyts.* Pub. for the Hakluyt Society, 1935 (Hakluyt Soc. Pub. Nos. LXXVI—LXXVII), London.

Thompson, H. P. *Into All Lands: The History of the Society for the Propagation of the Gospel in Foreign Parts, 1701—1950.* London: S. P. C. K., 1951.

Torbet, Robert G. *Venture of Faith: The Story of the American Baptist Foreign Mission Society and the Woman's American Baptist Foreign Mission Society, 1814—1954.* Philadelphia: Judson Press, 1955.

Tracy, E. C. *Memoir of the Life of Jeremiah Evarts, Esq.* Boston: Crocker and Brewster, 1840.

Tracy, Joseph, ed. *History of American Missions to the Heathen, from Their Commencement to the Present Time.* Worcester, Mass.: Spooner and Howland, 1840. Contents: A. B. C. F. M., by Joseph Trace; Baptist General Convention, by Enoch Mudge; Protestant Episcopal, by William Cutler; Free Will Baptist Miss. Society, by Enoch Mack; Presbyterian Church in the U. S. A., by Joseph Tracy.

Trumbull, Benjamin. *A Complete History of Connecticut, Civil and Ecclesiastical.* 2 vols. New London, Conn.: Utley, 1898.

Trumbull, James H. *Origin and Early Progress of Indian Missions in New England, with a List of Books in the Indian Language Printed at Cambridge and Boston, 1653—1721.* Worcester, Mass.: for private distribution, 1874.

[Tuttle, Sarah.] *Letters and Conversations on the Cherokee Mission.* Boston: Mass. S. S. Union, 1830.

United Foreign Missionary Society. *Annual Report, 1818—1826.*

Walker, Francis A. *The Indian Question.* Boston: J. R. Osgood, 1874.

Walker, Robert S. *Torchlights to the Cherokees, the Brainerd Mission.* New York: Macmillan, 1931.

Weis, F. L. *The Society for the Propagation of the Gospel among Indians and Others in North America.* Dublin, N. H.: privately printed.

Wheelock, Eleazar. *A Plain and Faithful Narrative of the Original Design,*

Rise, Progress, and Present State of the Indian Charity-School at Lebanon, in Connecticut. Boston: Richard and Samuel Draper, 1763: *A Continuation of the Narrative . . . from Nov. 27th, 1762, to Sept. 3d, 1765.* Boston: Draper, 1765.

Whipple, Henry B. *Lights and Shadows of a Long Episcopate.* New York: Macmillan, 1899.

Whitner, Robert L. *The Methodist Episcopal Church and Grant's Peace Policy: A Study of the Methodist Agencies, 1870—1882.* University of Minnesota dissertation, 1959; now available from University Microfilms, Ann Arbor, Mich. Not available at writing of this book.

Williamson, James A. *A Short History of British Expansion,* 2d ed. New York: Macmillan, 1931.

Wilson, Thomas. *The Knowledge and Practice of Christianity Made Easy to the Meanest Capacities, or An Essay towards an Instruction for the Indians.* 9th ed. London: D. Dodd, bookseller to the S. P. C. K., 1759.

Winship, George P. *The Cambridge Press, 1638—1692.* Philadelphia: 1945.

————. *The New England Company of 1649 and John Eliot.* Boston: Prince Society, 1920.

Winslow, Miron. *A Sketch of Missions; or a History of the Principal Attempts to Propagate Christianity among the Heathen.* Andover, Mass.: Flagg and Gould, 1819.

Woodford, Frank. *Lewis Cass, the Last Jeffersonian.* New Brunswick, N. J.: Rutgers University Press, 1950.

Wright, Louis B. *Religion and Empire: The Alliance between Piety and Commerce in British Exploration, 1538—1625.* Chapel Hill: University of North Carolina Press, 1943.

Index